W9-CAU-395

Smart Guide to Personal Computers

Stephen L. Nelson

The company and product names used in this book are the trademarks or registered trademarks of their respective owners.

Special editions of this title are available for premium or corporate sale. For information, contact: Corporate Sales Department, Barnes & Noble, 1400 Old Country Road, Westbury, NY 11590-5130

Copyright © 1999 by Stephen L. Nelson, Inc.

This edition published by Barnes & Noble, Inc.,
by arrangement with Stephen L. Nelson, Inc.

All rights reserved. No part of this book may be used or reproduced in any manner whatsoever without the written permission of the Publisher.

1999 Barnes & Noble Books

ISBN: 0-7607-1236-0

Printed and bound in the United States of America

99 00 01 02 M 9 8 7 6 5 4 3 2 1

FG

Smart Guide to
Personal Computers

Contents

INTRODUCTION

Before you jump in and begin reading Chapter 1, you should know a couple of things. First, you should know a little about this book so you can make the best use of it. Second, you should know what assumptions this book makes about you and your computer system and skills.

Notes *Although this book discusses a variety of general computing terms and activities, the specific steps outlined in this book describe how to accomplish tasks on computers running Microsoft Windows 95 or Windows 98.*

About This Book

Let's start by describing the purpose of this book. Then we can talk about the book's organization and the conventions I've used while writing the book.

The Purpose of This Book

You might want to know why I decided to write this book and what my intentions for this book are before you take the time to read it, so I thought I'd tell you up front. I have two goals in mind for this book.

My first goal is to make computer purchases less daunting. After reading the latest computer advertisements, I realized that I didn't even know what some of the abbreviations in them meant, and I've been using computers and writing computer books for years. So I can imagine how confusing the choices must be for people who have little or no computer experience. With this book, I want to help you make informed decisions about which computer equipment to invest in.

My second goal is to open doors to personal computing by making it more fun and less anxiety-producing. Low computer prices have made computers available to people who haven't been able to afford them before, and I hope to make using the computer easier and within reach of those people who might have little previous experience with computers. As the computer becomes an increasingly important tool in everyday life, computer skills and confidence working with the computer become increasingly important in many realms of society. For some people, computer skills are key to staying competitive in the workforce. For others, learning how to use the computer means being able to keep in touch with future generations. With this book, I want to make computer mastery an achievable goal for all.

How This Book Is Organized

The *Smart Guide to Personal Computers* has ten chapters and a glossary. The chapters are arranged according to the order in which I assume most people need to know how to do things. For example, I assume that you need to first buy and unpack your personal computer (PC) before you can turn it on and begin using it. If this isn't the case (say, because you're getting the feel for computers by using someone else's before you buy one of your own), this order might not make much sense to you. So you might want to read the chapters in a different order.

Here are some brief descriptions of the chapters in this book:

- Chapter 1, "PC Basics," defines the term *PC* and talks about what makes up a PC. It also walks you through a PC advertisement, helping you make sense of the acronyms and numbers commonly seen in computer advertisements.
- Chapter 2, "Meet Your PC," discusses taking the computer parts out of their boxes and getting them all plugged in. It talks about turning on and off your computer and familiarizes you with what you first see when your computer is up and running. Chapter 2 also introduces you to communicating with your computer so you can tell it to do something.
- Chapter 3, "The Windows that Make Up Microsoft Windows," tells you how to use the windows (after which Microsoft Windows was named) to make your work at the computer most efficient.

- Chapter 4, "Organizing the Information on Your PC," discusses how to use Windows Explorer as a kind of microscope to view and work with the insides of your computer. It talks about the filing system used on a computer and shows you how to move, copy, rename, delete, and find files and folders. Chapter 4 also introduces the idea of connecting two or more computers together so you can share information between them.
- Chapter 5, "Getting Your PC Just the Way You Like It," talks about how to customize your computer so it fits your style. This chapter includes customization options that are purely aesthetic in nature, as well as those that are more functional. With these options, you can make working at your computer easier and more enjoyable.
- Chapter 6, "Common Program Tasks," describes how to accomplish basic tasks common to most programs.
- Chapter 7, "Exploring the Internet," introduces the Internet and tells you how to get connected to it. It then shows you how to use free programs for the Internet that might already be on your computer.
- Chapter 8, "Corresponding Over the Internet," talks about ways to use the Internet to correspond electronically. This chapter gives you directions for using free software (which might already be installed on your computer) to accomplish the most common e-mailing tasks.
- Chapter 9, "Using Popular Programs," introduces the most popular types of programs available and describes in general terms how to use each type of program.
- Chapter 10, "Upgrading and Maintaining Your PC," reviews some basic PC care tips and ways to troubleshoot common problems yourself. It also lists other resources you can turn to for help.
- "Glossary," defines key computing terms.

One other thing you should know is why this book covers the topics it does. Personal computing is a large subject. Someone could write volumes on it. (In fact, people have written volumes on it.) So in a small book about personal computers, it's impossible to cover everything. In choosing what to cover and what not to cover, I used a couple of criteria. First, I thought about what I believe all people should know how to do on the computer. For example, I talk about how to set up the computer. But I avoid the more difficult and esoteric tasks that people can either inexpensively pay to have done or that they don't need to mess around with in the first place. So I don't talk about opening up and fiddling about with the insides of your computer, nor do I talk about changing various advanced settings that could get you into trouble. The other criteria I used for deciding what to include is interest level. The Internet is hot right now among computer users, so I devote two chapters to Internet topics. But I don't discuss some of the less popular programs that might have come with your computer.

How to Read This Book

If you're brand new to computers and haven't yet purchased one, it probably makes most sense for you to read this book from start to finish. But reading the book from start to finish isn't required. If, for example, you've worked with computers a little in the past and you've already purchased the main portion of the computer equipment you want, you might want to skip around. You might not need to read Chapters 1, 2, and 4, for example. Instead, you might want to start with Chapter 3 and then continue on with Chapter 5. Or you can use this book as a reference whenever you get stuck or are considering purchasing some new piece of equipment for your computer. Just turn to the Contents or to the Index to look up a topic you're confused about or one that's causing you trouble. Then you can dip right in, read a few paragraphs to answer your questions, and get back to work. I wrote this book in a way that allows you to read it using all of these techniques.

Conventions Used Here

This book uses a handful of simple conventions for presenting information. So let me explain before you dive in.

Sometimes I want to share with you a tidbit of information that is relative to the topic at hand, but it interrupts the flow of discussion. When this happens, I'll set that information apart with a nifty little icon in the margin.

A Note provides backup or additional information that applies to what I'm discussing, but it isn't critical to your understanding. A Note is also used to make exceptions for special situations.

A Tip offers advice or presents information that can save you time and trouble.

A Warning alerts you to potential dangers or mistakes easily made.

Finally, from here on out, whenever you see a **boldface** term, it means that the term is defined in the glossary. I'll boldface glossary terms the first time I use them in a chapter. For example, if I use the term **operating system**, and you don't know what an operating system is, you can flip back to the glossary and look it up.

Assumptions About You

Inevitably, I had to make a few assumptions about you as a reader as I wrote this book. I tried to make as few as possible so this book applies to the widest range of people and experiences. But the fact remains that different people have vastly different computer systems and a wide variety of tasks that they need to accomplish using the computer. Not only that, but people also possess a wide range of knowledge about computers. In a little book such as this one, there's just not room to describe all of the different ways of accomplishing tasks to address every single person and every single computer setup.

Your Computer Skills

This book assumes you're either a beginning or an intermediate user of computers. Although this book introduces some rather complicated terminology and steps you through some difficult tasks, this book is intended to be user-friendly so people who have never before worked on a computer can understand it and follow right along. You don't need to have any special computer knowledge to read this book. The *Smart Guide to Personal Computers* can work rather nicely for beginners—people who are brand new to computers and to **Windows** 95 or Windows 98. If you've already worked with **PCs**, or have worked on the **Macintosh** or on previous versions of Windows, you can also use this book to expand or refresh your computer skills. So the *Smart Guide to Personal Computers* can also work well for intermediate computer users who just want to brush up their knowledge in certain areas.

Your Computer

This book assumes only that you're interested in buying a PC or that you already have one. The first few chapters cover the PC purchasing decision, so you don't need to own a PC before you can begin using this book.

Notes

This book applies to almost all current brands, shapes, and sizes of PCs. (Except for the Macintosh and palmtop computers.)

In terms of all of the stuff that you can connect to your computer, this book assumes very little. I'm assuming you have or will purchase a **monitor,** a **keyboard**, a **mouse,** and a **CD-ROM** drive. (New PCs all come with a keyboard and a mouse, so you almost never need to purchase these items separately.) To accomplish other tasks described in this book, however, you'll need other items. I'll tell you when your computer needs to be equipped with another item in order to do something. For example, if you want to print what you type on the computer, as described in Chapter 9, I'll tell you that you need to have a **printer**.

This book also assumes that the computer you have or will soon purchase runs Windows 95 or Windows 98. In order to follow the steps described in this book, you'll need to have Windows 95 or Windows 98 installed on your computer. When there are differences between the way Windows 95 works and the way Windows 98 works, I'll let you know. This book doesn't include specific information on how to accomplish tasks on the Macintosh or with Windows 3.x.

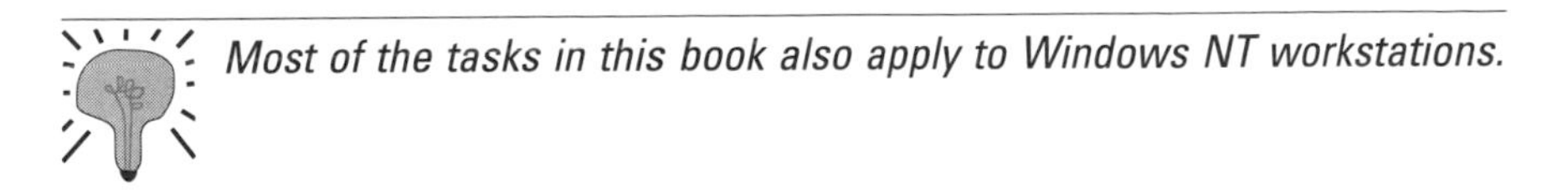

Most of the tasks in this book also apply to Windows NT workstations.

CHAPTER 1

PC Basics

Because you're reading this book, I assume you either own or are thinking of purchasing a **PC**. So you probably already have some notion of what a PC is and what you hope to accomplish with a PC. This chapter begins by defining some important terms. Then it takes you through the PC purchasing process. This chapter covers the following topics:

- What is a PC?
- PC **hardware**
- PC **software**
- The different types of PCs
- How to read a PC advertisement
- Buying a PC

What Is a PC?

The term *PC* stands for *personal computer*. But what exactly does that mean? To understand what a personal computer is, we need to break down the term into its parts and define each one.

As you might guess, the *personal* part of *personal computer* means that manufacturers originally designed these computers primarily for individual use. While this for the most part still holds true, it isn't always the case. PCs have become so much more powerful that today many function in a different role, being used by several people instead of just one.

Now we move on to the trickier task—defining the word *computer*. What exactly qualifies as a computer? The answer to this question isn't as clear as you might think.

In the word computer, *you can see the word* compute. *This is because the first computers were primarily fancy adding machines. But personal computers today are much more than that.*

Basically, a computer is any machine that does the following three things:

1. It accepts input from you.
2. It does something with the input you give it according to a set of rules that you (or someone else) have provided.
3. It returns the results.

The results can come in many forms—not just in numbers or letters. Take the following example:

1. You put a bag of popcorn in your microwave, and push a couple of buttons: Popcorn and Start, for example. This is the input.
2. The microwave follows the orders connected with those buttons. (It cooks on high for 4 minutes and beeps when it's done.) This is the microwave processing the input according to a set of rules.
3. The microwave returns a cooked bag of popcorn to you. This is the result.

If you think about this a little bit, you quickly realize that computers are all around you. They're everywhere. And even if you haven't recognized it, you've probably used computers dozens of times before. Have you ever used a calculator? That's just a simple computer. You can find computers in many objects of modern life: telephones, radios, VCRs, kids' toys, watches, electronic games, cash machines and cash registers, and even cars. So there's no need to be anxious about working with a personal computer—you've undoubtedly worked with computers numerous times before.

"But wait a second," you might be thinking to yourself, "If something like a calculator is a computer designed for personal use, is it a personal computer?" Well, no, we usually don't think of it as one. In general, you can use a PC to accomplish a variety of tasks, many of which I'll talk about later in this chapter and throughout this book. For example, you can use your PC to make calculations, sure enough, but you can also use your PC to listen to music, write letters, and even videotape yourself. Other computers, for instance, your calculator, can do only a limited range of specific tasks. You probably can't do much with your calculator except crunch numbers.

That much said, I should add that as computer technology begins to evolve, more and more household items begin to work and look like PCs. This makes the distinction between PCs and other computers less clear. Newer televisions often include, or are capable of including, PC functionality. And take the calculator, for example—a person certainly wouldn't call your normal pocket calculator a computer. But newer, fancy calculators can perform a wider range of tasks.

The most important thing to know about all computers, PCs included, is that they're dumb. They possess no intelligence on their own. They can't solve a problem unless a person instructs them how to solve it. Computers are only as smart as people make them, and they can do only the things people tell them to do. Take, for example, the computer in your car radio. By programming its buttons for the stations you listen to most, you play the part of the computer programmer. If your car battery dies, the program is lost and the computer in your radio forgets what you told it to do. Without you telling it what to do, it's helpless. Computers can do fascinating things, but it's not the computers that are smart, it's the people.

PC Hardware

Two elements make up all computers: hardware and software. Hardware doesn't mean the tools you find in a hardware store. In computer language, hardware means all of the gadgets that in one way or another plug into your computer. This includes stuff outside your computer that connects via cables (shown in Figure 1-1) as well as the various parts and pieces neatly aligned and plugged in on the inside of your computer. The following paragraphs describe the primary hardware devices of most PCs.

FIGURE 1-1

Basic components of a personal computer.

A Monitor

Every PC needs a **monitor.** A monitor is the big television-like object that sits on your desk, as shown in Figure 1-2. You use a monitor to see the goings-on of your PC. Unlike a typewriter, where what you type shows up immediately on paper, with a PC you need a monitor to see what you're typing. Monitors are called *output devices* because PCs use them to display the results of what you do on the PC.

FIGURE 1-2

A monitor.

A Keyboard

All PCs come with a **keyboard.** A PC keyboard looks and works much like the rows of keys on a typewriter, as you can see in Figure 1-3. It includes the regular letters and numbers you're familiar with. You can use these keys to type just as you would on a typewriter. A keyboard also includes a few other special keys that you use to give instructions to your PC. Keyboards are called *input devices* because you use them to tell your PC what to do.

FIGURE 1-3

A standard keyboard.

A Mouse

Although you don't need a **mouse** to work with your PC, most PCs come with one and using a mouse makes many tasks quicker and easier. A mouse is a little tool that you rest your hand on and roll around on your desktop. Figure 1-4 shows a top view of a mouse on a desk. Like a keyboard, a mouse is an input device. You use it to tell your computer what to do.

FIGURE 1-4

The mouse you use at the computer gets its name from its real-life counterpart.

Memory

Inside of the main box of a PC (this box is called a **system unit**), you can find at least one board about the size of a stick of gum. Attached to this board are little pieces of circuitry. Despite the board's small size, it plays an important role in the workings of the PC—it's the PC's **memory.** All computers come with memory. Memory is a relatively small amount of space set aside for the PC to use to quickly move information around. A PC uses this space to temporarily hold the information you're working with. So every time you tell the PC to do something, it needs to use its memory. You can think of the memory in a PC as its short-term memory. A PC needs short-term memory to remember what you just did and to prepare for what you'll do next so it can respond quickly to your next instruction.

Storage Space

All computers also come with at least a couple of storage devices. Computers use storage space to hold information for extended periods of time. You can think of storage space in a PC as its long-term memory. A PC can potentially store the information in its storage space indefinitely. Unlike short-term memory, the information stored on a PC storage device isn't lost once you turn off the PC.

Most PCs have at least three places set up for storing. The first, and biggest, is called a **hard disk.** The hard disk is a stack of hard, round platters inside of the main box (or system unit) of the PC. A PC uses its hard disk for storing most of the information it needs to run. Most PCs have only one hard disk, but some have more than one.

The other storage devices on PCs work a little differently. Unlike with a hard disk, which remains inside the system unit at all times, these other devices allow you to insert and remove different disks. Somewhere on most PCs, you'll find a couple of slots. These slots are not coffee-cup holders or change machines. These slots hold different types of **disks** used for storing information. The two most common such disks are called **floppy disks** and **CD-ROM** discs (shown in Figure 1-5). Floppy disks (sometimes called floppies) are small disks protected by a 3½-inch-square hard plastic cover. People use floppy disks to share information with other PC users because floppy disks are inexpensive, small, lightweight, and usable on most PCs. CD-ROM

discs are the round shiny discs that look like the compact discs (CDs) you see in music stores and can play on a CD player. But instead of storing just music, CD-ROMs also store other types of information.

You can use floppy disks to both store information and retrieve previously stored information. With normal CD-ROMs, however, you can't store information yourself. You can only retrieve information. You need a special type of drive to be able to record information on CDs.

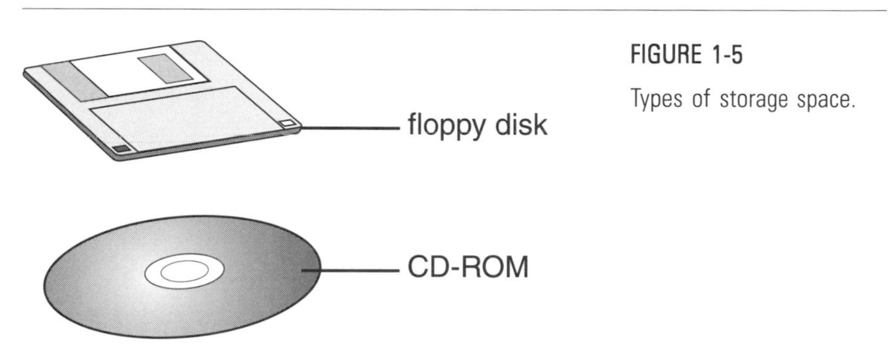

FIGURE 1-5

Types of storage space.

A Microprocessor

A **microprocessor** is a tiny box of circuitry attached on the inside of all computers. This package of circuitry executes the instructions you give to the computer. All PCs have at least one microprocessor. The main microprocessor, which does almost all of the work of the PC, is called the central processing unit, or **CPU.** The CPU is like the powerhouse of the whole computer.

PC Software

The second element of all PCs is software. Software provides the instructions that tell your computer what to do. Earlier in the chapter, I said that your car radio needs you to program it so it knows what to do when you click its buttons. Likewise, your PC needs software (which is just complicated programming created by engineers) so it knows what to do when you type something on the keyboard or move the mouse. PC software comes in two varieties: **operating system** software and **program** software. The following sections define and describe the two types of PC software.

Programs

A program is a set of instructions that belongs to a group of similar tasks. For example, you might have a program on your computer that lets you write letters. The program software you purchase has all sorts of instructions that relate to letter-writing tasks. If you have a program on your computer that lets you create greeting cards, that program software has all sorts of instructions that tell your computer what it's supposed to do to help you create greeting cards.

Operating Systems

An operating system isn't just another program. An operating system is more than that. An operating system controls your hardware. It keeps track of where your PC stores data and where you've plugged devices (such as a **printer**) into your PC. Programs use the operating system's rules to communicate with the hardware.

When you purchase software programs, you need to make sure they were written for the operating system you have.

This book assumes that you have (or will purchase) either **Microsoft Windows** 95 or Windows 98 (the two most popular operating systems for home PC users). But other operating systems exist that you might be familiar with. For example, you might have heard of or worked with one of the previous versions of Windows, such as Windows 3.0, 3.1, or 3.11. Or maybe you've heard of Microsoft's **MS-DOS**, IBM's OS/2, or one of the UNIX operating systems, such as Linux. The Apple **Macintosh** (or just Mac for short) uses a different operating system as well, called Mac OS.

You might hear some people refer to an operating system as a platform. This usage isn't quite correct. You should use the term operating system.

1

Some people consider the Mac a PC. Other people don't. According to most definitions, a Mac surely qualifies as a personal computer, or PC. However, the term PC *is frequently reserved to describe only IBM PC-compatible personal computers. (By IBM PC-compatible, I mean any one of the number of computer brands using an x86-compatible microprocessor—basically any brand except the Apple Macintosh. IBM PC-compatible computers also conform to a standard for the hardware that they can accept.) Because Macs almost always use a different operating system, they require different programs. Macs also usually require different hardware. But whether or not you consider a Mac to be a PC, for this book I'm assuming your computer runs or will soon run Windows 95 or Windows 98, and so your computer fits the definition of a PC in any case.*

The Different Types of PCs

PCs come in many shapes and sizes. A computer's appearance doesn't determine whether it qualifies as a PC.

Desktop PCs

A desktop PC is the most common type of PC, the kind you probably picture when you think of a PC. (If you flip back to Figure 1-1, you'll see a picture of a desktop PC.) The desktop PC got its name because it generally sits on top of a desk. And it usually stays there because it's much too heavy and awkward to lug around.

Some desktop computers rest horizontally on desktops. Other computers stand vertically on or underneath desks. The ones that stand are called tower systems.

Laptop PCs

Another common type of PC is a laptop, or notebook computer. As the name implies, laptop computers are lightweight enough to sit on people's laps as they work. You couldn't do this with a desktop computer because it would be too heavy and bulky. Laptops usually fold in half like a notebook, with the screen on one side and the keyboard and system unit on the other. For this reason, some people refer to laptops as notebooks. (Figure 1-6 shows a laptop PC.) Laptops fit neatly into briefcases, so they can be carried around. You'll often see people using them at the library, on an airplane, in a café, or on the bus.

FIGURE 1-6

A laptop PC.

Palmtops

Another new type of computer is the palmtop. Palmtop computers, as the name suggests, are small enough to rest in the palm of your hand. Palmtop PCs usually use AA batteries and don't generally have disk drives like laptops and desktops. This makes it more difficult to add new software to palmtops.

Notes *Palmtop computers run a special operating system, such as Windows CE, which includes miniature versions of several programs.*

How to Read a PC Advertisement

Computer advertising carries a lot of information that you need to understand in order to make a wise and informed PC purchase. Unfortunately, PC ads also contain a lot of technical terms and numbers that you might find daunting at first sight. This section takes you through the process of deciphering a PC ad. The sample ad shown in Figure 1-7 lists several of the common items you see in PC ads. I'll explain what each line of the ad means and tell you what you want to look for when purchasing a computer.

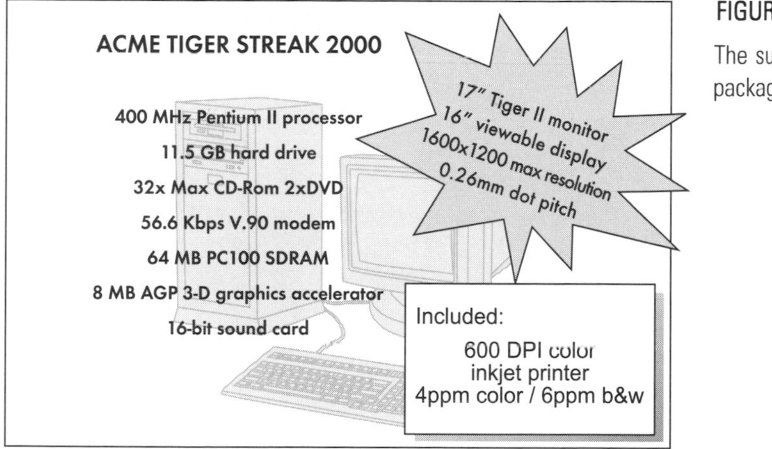

FIGURE 1-7

The super PC package.

The Make and Model

The first line of the ad names the computer: the Acme Tiger Streak 2000. Acme is the name of the computer maker and Tiger Streak 2000 is the name of the model. Many computer manufacturers give their PCs long, complicated names. Don't let the name of the computer distract you from closely reviewing its specifications. The computer's name and large model number say nothing about the computer's capabilities, regardless of how powerful they sound.

Many companies make computers. Some companies are large, national companies with long histories in the computer business. Others are lesser-known local companies. Different people have different ideas about which companies make the highest quality computers. I can't say that one is better than another. I've purchased computers from several different companies, some large, some small, and have had good luck with all.

The CPU

The second line of the ad tells you about the brand, model, and speed of the PC's CPU, its main microprocessor. A microprocessor is a little piece of circuitry that carries out the actual work of a task you do on the computer. The CPU, or central processing unit, is the main microprocessor because it functions like the brain of the computer. It performs and controls all the computer's goings-on. The CPU is so important that a PC is often referred to solely by its CPU. In the example, the Acme Tiger Streak has a Pentium II processor, so you could call this PC a "Pentium II machine."

Several companies make the microprocessors used as CPUs. **Intel's** Pentium processors are probably the most well known. But **AMD** and Cyrix make processors of comparable quality for most users and these processors often sell for less.

You can think of processor speed as your computer's horsepower. Processor speed is described in megahertz, or MHz. The greater the number (in this case 400), the faster the processor. Although processor speed (sometimes called **clock speed**) doesn't always directly correspond with the maximum speed at which your PC can work, it greatly affects it.

If you plan to use your computer for games, or to do a lot of work with graphics, you need to make sure that the brand of processor you purchase works well with games. Intel's processors (such as the Pentium II) have in the past usually worked well for games. Other processors have features that improve their game performance as well. However, you might need to make sure that the games you want to play support these features. If you have a question about which processor works best for you, ask a salesperson.

Hard Disk Space

The next line of the ad describes the size of the PC's internal storage space, its hard disk. This space is usually described in gigabytes, which are equal to 1 billion **bytes.** The larger the number of gigabytes, the more space you have on your computer for storing information—you can install more programs and save more files that you create.

Notes

Computers store information in a code somewhat similar to Morse code. Like Morse code, computer code uses only two symbols, 0 and 1, to describe all information. When you string the 0s and 1s together, they represent numbers, letters, and other characters. A string of eight 0s and 1s equals 1 byte. So a hard disk that stores 8 billion bytes, as in the example ad, can hold a lot of information.

To put hard disk space into perspective, Table 1-1 shows how many bytes some common types of information take up.

Information	**Space It Takes Up**
The Windows operating system	Around 200 megabytes (MB), which is equal to about 200 million bytes.
A program like Microsoft Word	Around 40 or 50 MB (about 40 or 50 million bytes).
A letter you write at the computer	Around 30 kilobytes (KB), which is equal to about 30 thousand bytes.

TABLE 1-1: How much space information takes up on a PC.

Other Information Storage Devices

The fourth line of the ad describes the other storage devices included on the PC. In this case, the PC comes with a CD-ROM **drive** and a **DVD** drive. You use a CD-ROM drive to play music and install programs. You use a DVD drive to play videos and install programs. The numbers in front of the description of each drive tell you the maximum speed of the drive. Virtually every PC also comes with a floppy disk drive, which is why the ad doesn't even mention a floppy disk drive.

A Modem

The fifth line of the ad describes the **modem** included with the PC. You probably want to have a modem for your PC so you can access the **Internet.** It's easiest to purchase a PC with a modem already in it, but if the PC doesn't come with a modem, you can purchase a modem separately later. The 56.6 Kbps is the maximum transfer speed of the modem. The larger the number, the faster you can move around on the Internet and share information with other people. Kbps stands for kilobits per second. One kilobit is equal to a little over 1,000 bits. With a 56.6 Kbps modem, you can move about 56 thousand bits of information in one second. This equates to almost 7 KB. If you look at Table 1-1, and do a little math in your head, you can see that it would take only about 4 seconds to send a letter you wrote on the computer. In one minute, you can move about 400 KB of information and it takes about two and a half minutes to move a MB. The V.90 part of the modem description says that the modem conforms to the V.90 standard, the most compatible standard. Make sure you buy a modem with this standard so you can exploit the modem's full potential. Note that some modems include other capabilities you may or may not be interested in. Most modems allow you to use your computer as a fax machine. Some modems also include an advanced answering machine-type functionality, called voice mail, so you can have your computer answer the phone and record messages.

Memory

The sixth line of the ad describes how much memory the computer has. The amount and type of memory allow you to perform more tasks simultaneously, including tasks that require more work on the part of the computer. Like storage space, people measure the amount of memory in bytes. But because PCs have only a fraction of the amount of memory that they have storage space, memory is expressed in megabytes, symbolized by the letters MB. The Tiger Streak 2000 has 64 MB of memory. The PC100 means that the memory is capable of working at a high speed along with the processor, sending data to the CPU at a frequency of 100 MHz.

Graphics and Sound

The seventh and eighth lines of the ad describe the hardware that helps your PC work with graphics and play sounds. A graphics **accelerator** is just a device that increases the speed at which your computer can display graphics. A **sound card** is required in order for your computer to play sounds.

One thing to keep in mind about graphics accelerators is this: The more memory your graphics accelerator supplies, the higher the image quality you can display on your monitor.

A Monitor

Every PC needs a monitor. However, PC retailers often advertise and sell PCs without monitors because they expect that you'll want to purchase your monitor separately. As you comparison shop for a PC, always check whether the price includes a monitor. This example includes a monitor so you can understand the terminology used in ads to describe monitors.

This ad, like most, states the most important piece of information about the monitor first: its size. In this case, the Tiger Streak 2000 comes with a 17-inch monitor. This means that the display glass of the monitor measures 17 inches diagonally. The ad also includes another piece of information about the size of the monitor. The second line of the ad for the monitor tells you the size of the actual screen. This is good to know, because a bigger monitor won't help you see any better if the extra amount of display glass is covered by the plastic frame of the monitor.

The third line of the monitor ad relates some information about the maximum fineness of detail the monitor can display, called **resolution.** Resolution defines how many squares of light your monitor can display horizontally and vertically (in this case 1600 across and 1200 down). Monitors work by displaying thousand of tiny squares of light, called **pixels.** When the pixels are small and close enough together, it looks to the eye like a solid picture. The more pixels your monitor can display, the more detail you can see in the images on your screen.

The last line of the monitor ad relates some information about the crispness of the monitor display. The smaller the dot pitch (or dp) number, the clearer the display. Dot pitch is a measurement of the space between each row of pixels.

This monitor ad is typical of many monitor ads: it lacks some information. It doesn't provide a refresh rate. Nor does it provide a maximum resolution at a common frequency. Before you purchase a monitor, you should check out these two specifications. Here's why: Your screen works something like a movie projector. Although the screen looks static, your PC actually refreshes the screen at a rate of at least 60 times per second. This number of times per second is called a refresh rate. The higher the refresh rate, the less the screen appears to flicker. It's also useful to know the maximum resolution your monitor can display at a given refresh rate. Although the monitor can refresh 1600 by 1200 pixels at a slow rate, it can probably only refresh 1280 by 1024 pixels at a normal rate.

When buying a monitor, the biggest you can get isn't always best. Keep in mind that larger monitors take up more desk space. And always check out the size of a large monitor's actual display area.

A Printer

Most PCs don't come with printers. This package includes one so you can see how computer retailers describe printers in advertisements. You probably want to buy a printer sooner or later to use with your PC. This example ad comes with a 600 **DPI** color **inkjet** printer. The 600 DPI part of the description refers to the printer's maximum resolution. DPI stands for dots per inch. Like an image you see on your screen (or a picture in a newspaper, or a Seurat painting), the images and text that printers print aren't actually made up of full blocks of color. Instead, printers print little dots of ink. The more dots they can print per inch, the higher the quality of the image. While printer resolution doesn't matter so much for text, a high resolution can drastically improve the quality of images that you print.

The ad also describes the printer as a color inkjet printer. Color means that the printer is capable of printing in color and not just shades of black. Inkjet refers to the technology the printer uses to get the ink on the paper. The printers for sale today are usually **bubble-jet**, inkjet, or **laser**. Bubble-jet and inkjet printers both shoot ink from nozzles onto the paper. They just have different ways of preparing the ink. Laser printers work more like copy machines. They shine a laser onto a special drum to create an electric charge. The ink then sticks to the drum and is transferred to the paper using heat. Laser printers tend to be faster (but also more expensive) than bubble-jet or inkjet printers.

Notes

Another type of printer is an impact printer (such as a dot-matrix printer). Impact printers work more like typewriters—they have an inked ribbon that they mechanically hit against the paper to transfer the ink to the paper. Impact printers are usually louder and slower than non-impact printers, but they work well for carbon copy forms.

The last line of the printer ad reveals a little information about the speed of the printer. The acronym ppm stands for pages per minute. The 4ppm color/6ppm b&w means that the printer can print four pages per minute for pages with colored items or six pages per minute in black and white.

Notes

*If you plan to use your printer for **desktop publishing** (for instance, printing newsletters or brochures), you might want to invest in a **PostScript** printer. With a PostScript printer, when you resize (or scale) PostScript fonts in a document, the fonts print the same way they look on screen. PostScript is also necessary for compatibility with high-end output devices such as image setters.*

Buying a PC

Now that you have been introduced to much of the terminology included in PC ads, you're ready to begin shopping for a PC. This process involves three steps. First, you need to decide what you want to do with a PC. Then, based on what you want to accomplish, you need to determine which features your PC should include. Last, you need to find the PC that best meets your needs. The following section takes you through these steps.

Deciding What You Want to Do with a PC

You probably have some notion of what you expect to do with a PC. Maybe you want a PC to help your children or grandchildren do their homework. Or maybe you want a PC because you're starting a small business and you want to keep records and create signs and brochures. Perhaps you're buying a PC to keep in touch with someone far away. Or perhaps you're buying a PC just for fun—you want to play games on it and use it for home shopping. The number of ways you can use a PC goes on and on. To help you come to a decision, write a list of all the things you expect to do with the computer. If this is the first time you're buying a PC, you probably won't know all the ways you'll end up using it, so just write as many ways as you can think of.

Notes

If one of the ways you hope to use the computer includes taking it with you to work or when you travel, you're looking at buying a laptop computer. Laptop computers have a few extra features you need to take into consideration when you purchase them. These features are described later in this chapter.

Determining Which Features Your PC Needs

Once you've decided what you want or think you might want to do with a computer, you can figure out the hardware and software you need.

To determine the minimum hardware requirements your PC needs in order to perform the tasks you want to accomplish, follow these steps:

1. Take the list of activities you want to do with a computer to a computer software store. Bring a pen and notepad as well.
2. Find software programs you might want to use for these activities. (You might need to ask a salesperson for help. Just tell the salesperson what you want to do and follow his or her recommendations.) For example, if you want to use your PC to help you with your taxes, look at some tax software programs. If you want to use your PC to write letters, look at some word processing programs. If you want to use your PC to play games, look at some games.
3. As you browse the software boxes, look for the list of system requirements for each program. Figure 1-8 shows an example.

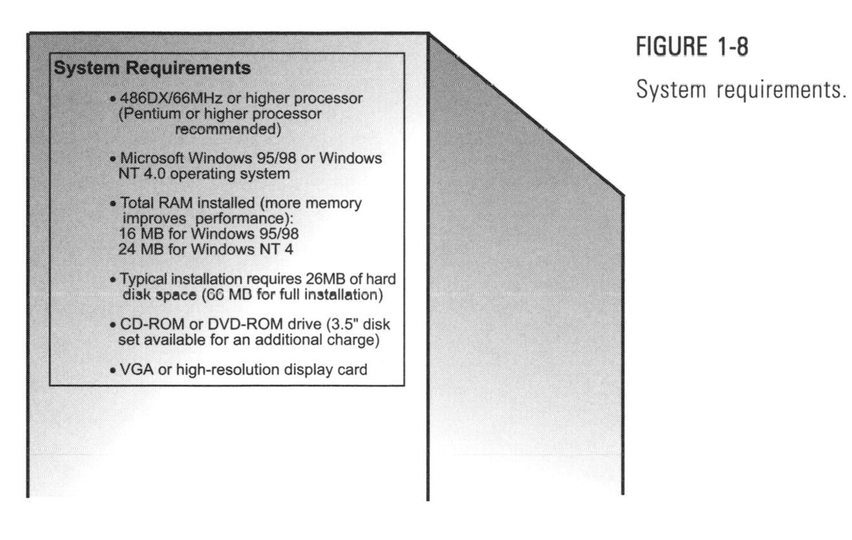

FIGURE 1-8

System requirements.

4 Compile a list of minimum hardware requirements for the programs you might want to run.

Note that this list is the absolute minimum you need. As a general rule, you want to purchase the fastest system you can afford with as much storage space and memory as you can afford. You'll want to do this for two reasons. First, even though most programs don't require powerful systems, they run faster with more powerful systems. Second, future versions of programs will undoubtedly have higher requirements. Although you can continue using the programs you buy for as long as you want, you'll probably want to someday buy newer versions of these programs. Newer versions often include improved features. Purchasing newer versions of programs also lets you more easily share information with other people you know who use these programs.

Some activities you might want to do using the computer require extra hardware I haven't yet discussed in this chapter. Because it's often easiest to order or purchase a PC with this hardware preinstalled, Table 1-2 on the next page lists the most common extra devices and what you can do with each one.

Device	What It Does
Scanner	With a **scanner**, you can take a relatively flat object, such as a photograph or a drawing, and create a picture of that object on your computer. You can then work with the image you create. For example, you can edit it and include it in something you print, such as a letter. If you think you might want to send copies of photographs to people, either over the Internet or on printouts such as greeting cards, you might want to purchase a scanner.
Speakers	Speakers allow you to listen to music on your computer. You can use speakers to play music from CDs or from radio stations on the Internet.
Microphone	A microphone lets you record yourself using your computer. You can also use the microphone like a speakerphone on a telephone and converse with people across the world—for much less than an international phone call.
Video camera	With a camera connected to your computer, you can videotape yourself. If you also have a microphone, you can use the Internet to hold meetings with people from far away. The other people can then also see you as you speak.
Digital camera	Using a digital camera, you can take pictures as you would with a regular camera. But instead of using film, digital cameras create electronic versions of the pictures you take. You can transfer these electronic versions to your computer to view, work with, or print.
TV tuner	With a TV tuner card, you can watch TV on your computer.
Joystick	A **joystick** is another input device that people often use for games. Joysticks come in various sizes and shapes designed for different types of games. If you plan to play games, you probably need a joystick. See what type of joystick the game recommends.

Device	What It Does
Zip/Tape drive	Many computers come with extra storage devices, such as Iomega Zip drives or tape backup drives. **Zip** drives and other such devices allow you to quickly make portable copies of the information you have stored on your hard disk. This way, you can have a safe copy of your information in case anything should happen to your hard disk. The Zip disks that go in Zip drives work better for this purpose than floppy disks because they can hold much more information. Such disks allow you to easily share large amounts of information with other people because you can fit the information on a single disk instead of on a stack of floppies.

TABLE 1-2: A list of devices commonly used as PC accessories.

Choosing a Brand and Deciding Where to Buy

Once you know your requirements for a PC, you're almost ready to make the purchase. You have only a couple of decisions left to make. First you need to decide when to buy a PC. Second you need to decide which brand of PC to buy and possibly also where to buy it. This section provides some tips for these last few decisions.

When do you want to buy a PC—now or later? If you take a look at a few computer advertisements and find that you can't afford the PC that meets the requirements or recommendations for what you want to do, you might have to wait a few months and see whether computer prices drop. As a general rule, computer prices do drop so you can get more for your money all the time. Unfortunately, however, program requirements tend to increase at almost the same rate. This means that although you might be able to wait and get more for your money, by that time, you might need even more than you planned on buying.

The second factor to take into consideration relates to the timing of new technologies. You probably don't want to buy a PC right before the release of some large new development in the technology. You probably also don't want to buy a computer with a fancy new expensive device. Chances are, the cost of the device will rapidly decline after its initial introduction.

So how do you find information to help you time your purchase? PC magazines are a good source. For example, you might discover that the laptop computer you think you want to buy is supposed to drop in price in a couple of months. In this case, it might make sense to wait.

Before you buy a PC, check with the computer manufacturer or retailer to see whether they have a rebate plan if the PC's price drops within, say, 30 days from when you buy it.

Once you've decided that the time is right to buy a PC, you need to decide on a brand. Here are some ideas on how to choose a brand:

1 Ask around. Find out whether your friends have had trouble with a brand or were especially pleased with a brand. They might be able to recommend a local or small company that offers good deals. They might also share experiences about the quality of customer service and technical support they received from a company.

2 Check out reviews and advertisements in magazines. Many PC and consumer magazines rate national-brand PCs regularly throughout the year. See whether any PCs are on sale or will soon go on sale. And check out advertisements for PCs available only through mail-order.

3 Take a peek at your local computer store. Get a feel for the different keyboards, check out the monitors, see whether one brand looks more well-built. Compare prices. Think about where you want to put the PC (Chapter 2 offers some tips), and see whether one style fits your space requirements better than another.

Notes

If you're purchasing a laptop PC, you have a few extra hardware choices to make:

1 *Laptop PCs come with built-in monitors. This means that picking a laptop with a good monitor is critical because you can't just replace a monitor you don't like with a new one. Carefully check out the quality of the display (for example, by looking at the screen from different angles) and the size of the display area.*

2 *To use your laptop without plugging it in, your laptop needs battery power. Compare the batteries that come with various laptops. Some types of batteries work better as rechargeable batteries than others,*

and some last longer. If you're planning on working on your laptop over long international flights, make sure that the laptop has enough battery power to last several hours.

3 *Laptop computers come with different types of pointing devices, instead of the conventional mouse used with a desktop computer. Different people have different preferences for these devices. Some devices tend to get dirtier than others. Some you might find too sensitive; others might stick. Test them out at a computer store to see which one you feel most comfortable with.*

4 *Laptops come in different shapes and sizes. You need to compare the general comfort of the laptop. How heavy is it? Keep in mind that with the convenience of a smaller laptop, you also sacrifice the comfort of the keyboard. Depending on the size of your hands, you might want to choose a larger laptop.*

5 *For fun, compare the cost of a laptop to the cost of a comparable desktop. Almost always, laptops are more expensive for the speed and storage space you get. You might come to the conclusion that the portability isn't worth the money. Laptops are also more expensive to repair and upgrade.*

After you decide what brand and model of PC to purchase, you might still need to decide where to buy the PC. Some companies only sell PCs directly to the public (such as Gateway and most local companies). Others sell at computer stores, at mail-order businesses, and directly. If you have a choice of where to buy the PC, see which benefits each choice offers. For example, one choice might offer extended warranty plans. One choice might offer lower prices. Another might provide easier access to support.

You might also want to consider buying a used computer either from a computer store or from an individual. Because many people need (or at least feel that they need) to stay on the leading edge of technology, they often trade in computers that are only a few months old. If you decide to buy a used computer, take as many precautions as possible. See whether the computer is still covered under warranty or have a computer technician check out the computer for problems before you buy it. Also make sure to get all the documentation and licenses that come with the hardware and software included on the computer.

CHAPTER 2

Meet Your PC

This chapter gets you up and running on the **PC**. It familiarizes you with your PC the very first time you turn it on and provides a quick course in the different ways you can communicate with your PC to tell it what to do. This chapter covers the following topics:

- Setting up your PC
- Turning on your PC
- Introducing the Windows computing environment
- Using the **mouse**
- Using the **keyboard**
- Turning off your PC

Setting Up Your PC

The process of setting up your PC includes four steps: choosing a location for your PC, unpacking your PC, connecting all the pieces of your PC, and creating a comfortable workplace. This first section offers advice and describes how to carry out all four steps.

Choosing a Location for Your PC

After you purchase a PC, you first need to decide where you want to locate it before you begin unpacking all the parts and pieces.

Notes

If you purchased a laptop PC, you don't need to decide on a semipermanent location for the PC because you can easily move it.

Here are some tips to keep in mind when choosing the right location for your PC:

- You need a desk that is large and sturdy enough to hold at least the **monitor**, the keyboard, and the mouse. The desk should allow enough room for your legs to clear when you sit in your desk chair, but it shouldn't be much taller than your lap. If the desk is much taller than your lap, you should look into buying a keyboard tray and a footrest, which you can find at most computer and office supply stores.
- A desktop PC needs power—which means you need to plug it into an electrical outlet. (To be specific, you need to plug it into a grounded socket.) Position your PC close to an outlet so you don't have to use an extension cord. Also make sure that the circuit you choose to plug your PC into doesn't already have a bunch of energy-hungry appliances running on it. You don't want to trip a circuit breaker and lose your work every time you or someone else turns on the oven or plugs in a hairdryer.
- If you plan on using your PC for work that requires concentration, you probably want to locate it in a room or corner that is quiet or can be closed off.
- PCs don't like moisture, dust, or grime. If you want to work by an open window, make sure your PC won't get wet if it rains. Don't put your PC next to a coffeemaker, a workbench, a sink, or any other source of spills or messes.
- If you have animals or young children who like to play with cords or chew on things, find a location where you can keep all of the PC parts out of their reach.
- Choose a location that has enough light, but don't plan on setting up the computer so the monitor faces a window. Light hitting the screen causes glare and can quickly tire your eyes.
- PCs don't like heat, so don't locate your PC in direct sunlight (which also yellows the plastic). Also, don't plan on placing the PC next to a heater or backing it up to a wall so it doesn't have any ventilation. And when you set up your PC, don't block the ventilation areas with other objects.

Unpacking Your PC

Once you've come up with a good location for your new PC, you're ready to unpack it. This can sometimes be a little tricky because the different parts might fit rather snuggly in their boxes. Here are a few guidelines to follow as you unpack your PC:

- If you need to cut packing tape or staples, be careful with your use of tools. You don't want to accidentally gouge your PC.
- Handle the boxes carefully; try not to shake or drop them. The electronic components in your PC are sensitive.
- Follow the instructions on the PC boxes. You can sometimes use gravity to your advantage by opening the box on the bottom and lifting the box up off of your PC rather than trying to lift a heavy PC part out of the box.
- Unpacking a PC is often much easier with two people. See if someone can help you lift the heavy parts or squeeze the items out of their boxes.
- Take a brief inventory to make sure that the boxes include everything that the packing slips say they do.
- Keep all the **floppy disks** and **CD-ROMs** that come with your PC. You're likely to need them later.

It's a good idea to hold on to the boxes and packing material for a while. If you find that some part of your PC is defective or damaged in shipping, you can return it in the original packaging. Also, don't throw away any of the manuals or warranties that come with your PC. You might need to refer to the manuals and you probably want to keep the warranty information to register your computer.

Put all of the manuals and warranty information for your PC together in a file folder and label it with the computer model and the purchase date so you can easily find this information.

*Write down the computer's serial number from the back of the **system unit** and store this number in a safe place so you can report it if your PC is ever stolen.*

Connecting Your PC

After you've chosen a location and unpacked your PC, you're ready to begin setting it up and plugging everything in. To do this, follow these steps:

This set of steps applies to desktop PCs. If you purchased a laptop PC, you probably only need to insert and charge the batteries according to the manufacturer's instructions, and follow steps 8 and 10.

1. Set the system unit (the big box) where you want it to go. You can set it on your desk, but if it lies horizontally, don't plan on putting the monitor on top of it. This will almost surely make the monitor too high. If possible, set the system unit on the floor.

If you decide to keep the system unit on the floor, it's a good idea to set it on a small shelf (or even on a short stack of books) to keep dust and insects out of the computer.

2. If necessary, attach the stand that came with the monitor to the bottom of the monitor.
3. Set the monitor on the desk.
4. Sit in the chair you plan to use at the desk. Your monitor should be about 18 to 24 inches away from your face and about 15 degrees lower than your eyes (so you look slightly down at the monitor). Adjust the monitor's position if you need to.

In general, monitors don't need any special stands—they are already at about the right height for most people. If your monitor sits too low, you can buy a stand or make your own stand. (I use an old telephone book.)

5. Set the keyboard in front of the monitor.

Even though your keyboard most likely has a couple of small legs that fold out on the underside to prop up the keyboard, you probably don't want to use these legs. They put the keyboard too high and at the wrong angle for most people.

6 Set the mouse beside the keyboard with the cord pointing away from you.

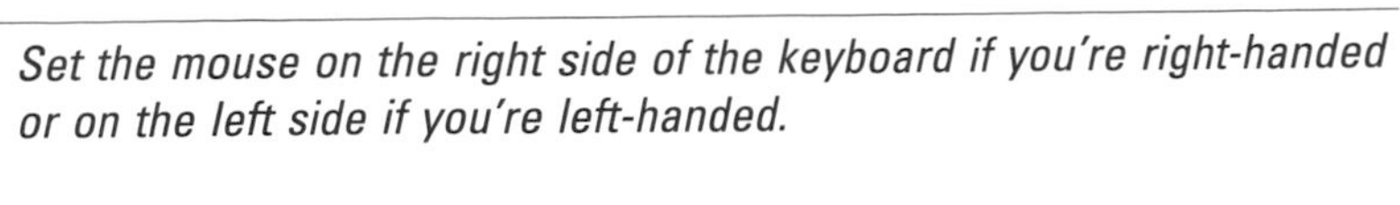

Set the mouse on the right side of the keyboard if you're right-handed or on the left side if you're left-handed.

7 Plug the keyboard and the mouse into the back of the system unit. Many computer companies label the sockets on the back of the computer or color-code them so you can easily tell what goes where. If the sockets aren't labeled, look closely at the connectors on the ends of the cables. (Figure 2-1 shows some common types of connectors used with computer cables.) Count the pins or holes, and see how they are arranged. Then, find the matching socket on the back of the system unit, and plug in the cable.

Don't force a connector into a socket. If a cable doesn't plug in easily, it either doesn't fit or is turned at the wrong angle. Forcing a connector can bend the pins and ruin the cable.

The plugs on the back of your PC are called sockets. Your PC gives each one of these sockets a name, called a ***port****. PC ports come in a few varieties, but you should know some of them. Parallel ports, which your PC often labels LPT1 and LPT2, have the widest sockets and work with 25-pin connectors.* ***Printer****s frequently plug into parallel ports. Serial ports, which your PC often labels Com1 and Com2, look like parallel ports except they usually have smaller sockets and work with 9-hole connectors. Mice often plug into serial ports. Keyboards and mice also often use round connectors. The largest of these connectors is called a keyboard connector and has 5 pins. The smaller is called a PS/2 connector and has 6 pins. New computers come with another type of port called a* ***USB*** *port. A USB port works with very small connectors that are about ½ inch wide and ⅛ inch thick. If your PC has a USB port, you can use that port for all sorts of different* ***hardware*** *devices.*

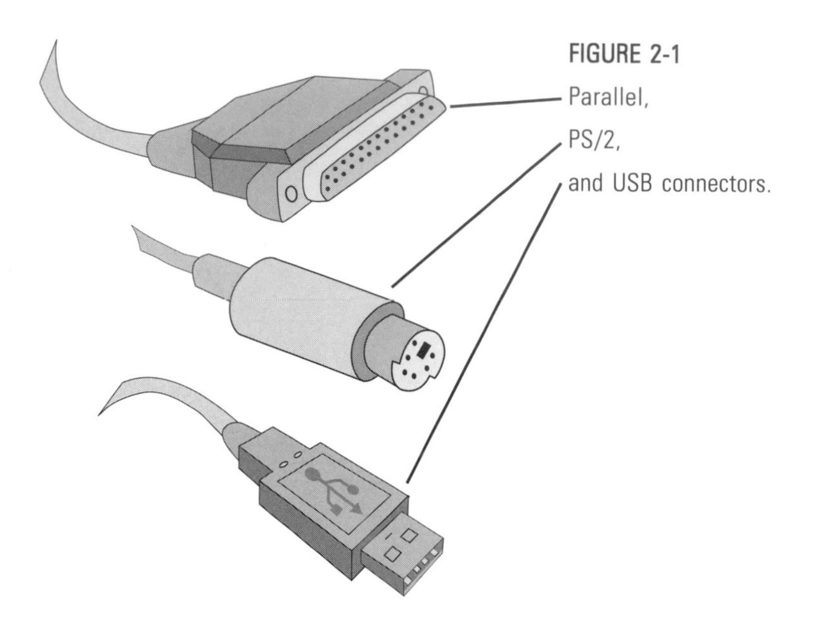

FIGURE 2-1 Parallel, PS/2, and USB connectors.

8 Plug the monitor into the system unit. As with the keyboard and mouse, the socket for the monitor might be color-coded or otherwise marked so you can tell where it plugs in on the back of the system unit. If not, look closely at the end of the cable. Count the pins, and see how they are arranged. Then find the matching socket on the back of the system unit, and firmly plug in the cable. If the other end of the cable is not already connected to the monitor, plug in this end as well.

Often the cable that connects the monitor to the system unit is permanently attached to the back of the monitor. If this is not the case, you might need to first determine which cable to use for plugging the monitor into the system unit. A monitor comes with two cables. One cable connects the monitor to an outlet, the other connects the monitor to the system unit. You can identify the cable that connects the monitor to the system unit because the connectors on the ends of this cable don't look like the ends of an extension cord.

9 Attach any other hardware devices to the system unit. If you purchased speakers, a printer, a microphone, an external modem, or any other device for your new PC, now is a good time to plug in these devices. As with the keyboard, mouse, and monitor, look closely at the connectors and gently, but firmly, plug them into their respective sockets.

If you purchased a laptop PC, it probably came with a special kind of port called a ***PCMCIA*** *port. You can plug PCMCIA devices into this port by opening the door to the port and sliding the PCMCIA card on the device's cord into an open slot.*

10 Attach the power cables to the back of the monitor, the system unit, and any other devices that require power.

11 Plug in the power cables.

Buy a surge protector for your PC. A surge protector protects your computer from spikes of electricity and usually provides you with several outlets for plugging in all of your PC's hardware devices. If you're worried about losing data in a power outage, invest in a temporary battery backup for your PC called an uninterruptible power supply, or UPS. With a UPS, when the power goes out, the UPS kicks in so you have a few minutes to save your work and properly shut down your PC.

Don't place anything sharp, heavy, or hot on power cords. Damage to a power cord can start an electrical fire or cause shock.

Ergonomic Tips

Before you begin to work extensively with your new PC, set up your workspace in a way that minimizes the risk of injury.

You might be wondering how a person could injure him- or herself while sitting and working at the computer. Actually, sitting long hours at the computer frequently results in injury. Most of these injuries are repetitive stress injuries—ones that arise from not supporting the body well while repeating the same tasks, such as typing. Other injuries include those caused by attempting to lift, pull, or push something heavy from an awkward position. For example, twisting your torso to reach and open a filing cabinet drawer rather than moving over to face the cabinet and then pulling the drawer toward you can result in a back injury.

Here are some tips to make your workspace safer and more comfortable:

- If you plan to use your PC for typing documents, buy a copy-holder that sits on your desk or hangs on the side of your monitor. Use this holder to rest papers on as you type.
- Don't use bright lights in the room when you're working at the computer. Overhead lighting often produces screen glare. Consider using a torchiere to light your entire workspace and a desk lamp to light any papers you're working on. Just make sure that the desk lamp doesn't reflect against your monitor.
- If you wear glasses or contact lenses, tell your eye doctor that you work at a computer. He or she might prescribe special glasses for computer use.
- Put the items you use most within easy reach so you don't have to bend or twist to get them.
- Position the monitor so it is directly in front of you when you sit at the desk. If you think you'll most often use the computer for typing text instead of entering numbers, center the alphabet part of the keyboard directly in front of the monitor. Keep the mouse as close to the keyboard as possible so you don't have to extend your arm much to use it.
- Buy a good chair that supports your lower back. A good desk chair allows you to adjust the height of the chair and the backrest, and maybe even the angle of the base of the chair and the backrest. If possible, buy a chair with armrests that allow your elbows to rest close to your sides and your forearms to be parallel to the floor.
- If you find that your wrists begin to hurt after working at the computer, buy a wrist rest for your keyboard and your mouse.
- Adjust the height of your chair so your lap is flat or angled down slightly toward your knees. Your feet should rest flat on the floor or on a footrest.

Figure 2-2 shows what an optimized workspace looks like and how you should sit at the computer.

FIGURE 2-2

Creating a workstation that fits.

When working at your computer, sit up straight and try not to cross your legs. If you work at your computer for long hours at a time, be sure to get up for a few minutes each hour to stretch and readjust your positioning in your desk chair.

Turning on Your PC

After you unpack and set up your PC, you're ready to turn it on. Turning on your PC works much like turning on any other household appliance, but you might have to flip a few more switches. To turn on your PC, follow these steps:

1 Make sure the surge protector is turned on. Usually, when the surge protector is on, it displays a light. If your surge protector doesn't display any lights, you might need to flip a switch or press a button.

2. Make sure there is no floppy disk (or a piece of cardboard left over from shipping) in the floppy disk drive. If there is, remove it.

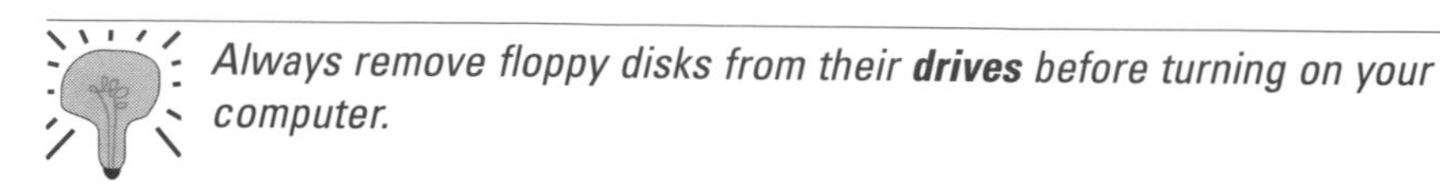

*Always remove floppy disks from their **drives** before turning on your computer.*

3. Turn on the power for the system unit. How you do this varies by computer. Sometimes it means pressing a button labeled POWER. Other times the button might have a picture of a circle with a vertical line in the center or at the top. Some computers have switches marked ON and OFF or with a 1 for on and a 0 for off. And some PCs have power buttons that aren't even labeled at all—but all of the other buttons are. You might need to figure out which one turns on the power by referring to your user's manual or through the process of elimination.
4. Turn on the power for the monitor. How you turn on the monitor differs among the various brands of monitors, just as it differs among the various brands of PCs. (Look for a button on the front of the monitor.)

Notes

The display for a laptop PC turns on when you turn on the PC. You don't need to turn on the monitor separately.

After you first turn on your computer, it goes through a few steps that are known as **booting.** When your computer boots, this is what you might see:

1. A black screen with a few lines of text. Your PC is testing its hardware and reporting on what it finds. It adds lines of information and might run through numbers as it checks the various hardware devices. When your PC tests its **disk** drives, their lights go on and they make a few whirring noises.
2. The **Microsoft Windows** welcome screen. This says Windows across the middle and has a sky blue background with some clouds.
3. If this is the first time your computer has been turned on, you'll see a screen or two that asks you for some information, such as your name and the name of your company (if your

company purchased the copy of Windows you're using). You'll probably also see a screen that asks you for the product key that came with your copy of Windows. If you have Windows 95, you can find this on the Certificate of Authenticity on your Windows manual. If you have Windows 98, you can find this on a sticker on the CD case. Type the information these screens request by using the keyboard. You can move from one entry blank to the next by pressing the Tab key. When you've filled in the information on a screen, press the Enter key.

4 Possibly, a **logon** screen. This is just a box that asks for your name and the **password** you want to use to identify yourself. If you're the only person who will use the PC, leave the name and password boxes blank and press the Enter key. If more than one person will use the PC, you probably want to tell Windows who you are. By identifying yourself, you can create your own personal settings for working in Windows. Type a name in the User Name box, and press the Tab key on your keyboard. Then make up a password, and type it in the Password box. (When you type the letters or numbers of your password, they show up as asterisks on the screen. This is so no one can see your password as you type it.) Press the Enter key. From now on, when you customize a feature on your PC, Windows associates the customization with you. So when you log on in the future (by entering the same username and password you just specified), Windows remembers exactly how you like your PC to look and work.

Notes

*If you're working in an office on a **network,** ask the person in charge of the network for your username and password.*

Any other people who will work at the PC need to enter their own usernames and passwords.

Introducing the Windows Computing Environment

After you turn on your PC and go through the booting process, you'll probably hear a chiming noise and then your screen will look much like the one shown in Figure 2-3. Windows has started and is all ready to go. The screen you see is called the Windows **desktop.** It gets its name from the fact that, like a desktop, it holds many of the tools you use when you work at your desk. The Windows desktop is an important part of Windows—it's the springboard you use while working at your PC. So you need to get to know it well. The following paragraphs introduce you to the various elements on the desktop.

FIGURE 2-3

The Windows desktop.

Shortcut Icons

Lined up along the left side of your screen are a series of pictures called **icons.** These icons are shortcuts to **programs, folders,** and **files.** If you move your mouse so the mouse pointer rests on one of these icons and then quickly press and release the left mouse buttom two times, Windows starts the program or opens the file to which the shortcut leads.

If you've never used a mouse or are having trouble using it, you might want to skip ahead and read the "Using the Mouse" section that comes later in this chapter.

You might not have all the same icons shown in Figure 2-3. You might have a few more or a few less.

Many programs automatically add icons to the desktop when you install them. But you can also create your own icons to make shortcuts to the programs, files, or folders you use most. Chapter 5 describes how to make shortcuts.

Although desktop icons differ among PCs, the following list describes some of the standard icons common to many PCs:

- The My Computer icon starts a program that allows you to see and organize the information stored on your PC. Although you can use the My Computer program, I recommend using **Windows Explorer.** Chapter 4 describes how to use Windows Explorer.
- The Internet Explorer icon starts a program that allows you to browse the **Internet.** Chapter 7 describes how to use Internet Explorer.
- The My Documents icon displays a folder on your PC that stores most of the files you create on your PC. Chapter 4 describes files and folders.
- The Network Neighborhood icon opens a **window** that allows you to see and work with other computers on your **network.** Chapter 4 describes how to use the Network Neighborhood.
- The Outlook Express icon starts a program that allows you to send and receive messages using **e-mail** and **newsgroups.** Chapter 8 describes how to use Outlook Express.
- The Online Services icon opens a folder that you can use to sign up for and set up an account with a company that provides connection to the Internet. To learn about setting up an Internet connection, see Chapter 7.
- The **Recycle Bin** icon opens a window that stores information you've deleted. It works like a kitchen trash bin, holding information (in case you need to sort through the trash to find something you inadvertently threw away) until you take out the trash. Chapter 10 describes how to empty the Recycle Bin.

The Taskbar

A gray bar runs along the bottom of the desktop, as shown in Figure 2-4. This bar is called the **Taskbar**, and it facilitates **multitasking**, or the ability to work on more than one task with more than one program at a time. The Taskbar helps you keep track of the programs you're currently using. With the Taskbar, you can easily switch between programs when you have more than one program open at the same time.

FIGURE 2-4
The Windows Taskbar.

On the far left of the Taskbar is the word Start, as shown in Figure 2-5. This is the **Start button**, a useful feature that allows you to start programs, open files, and access the control panel tools that let you customize Windows. The Start button and the Start menu are discussed later in this chapter.

FIGURE 2-5
The Start button.

Next to the Start button, you might see a series of icons. The icons usually include a blue letter "e," an envelope, a pencil and piece of paper on a desktop, and a satellite dish, as shown in Figure 2-6. These icons are actually buttons that quickly take you different places. This group of buttons is called the Quick Launch toolbar. If you move the mouse so the mouse pointer rests over one of the buttons, and then press and release the left mouse button, Windows performs the task associated with the button.

FIGURE 2-6
The Quick Launch toolbar.

The Quick Launch toolbar buttons are described in the following list:

- The blue letter "e" button starts Internet Explorer, a program that lets you browse the Internet.
- The button with the picture of an envelope (and sometimes a small blue letter "e") starts Outlook Express, a program that lets you correspond with people over the Internet.
- The button with the pencil and paper on a desktop returns you to the desktop—the screen you see in front of you right now.

- The satellite dish button starts Internet Explorer and displays a list of **channels.** Chapter 7 describes channels and how to use them.

Notes

If your computer is running Windows 95 and doesn't have Internet Explorer 4 or higher installed, you won't have the Quick Launch toolbar buttons.

You can tell what many buttons in Windows do by looking at their icons. But sometimes, the icons are a bit difficult to decipher. If you're ever confused as to what a button does, just ask Windows for a hint. Move the mouse so the mouse pointer rests over the button. Windows pops open a small yellow box that displays the button's name, as shown in Figure 2-7.

FIGURE 2-7

This button's name tells you what it does.

On the right side of the Taskbar, you probably have a few more icons as well as a clock, as shown in Figure 2-8.

10:47 AM

FIGURE 2-8

The row of icons on the right side of the Taskbar.

As with the other elements of the desktop, which icons you have depends on which programs came installed on your PC and how Windows was set up. The two most common icons are as follows:

- An icon that looks like a white box with a calendar in the upper-left corner and a red clock in the lower-right corner. If you move the mouse so the mouse pointer rests over this picture, and then quickly press and release the left mouse button twice, Windows opens a window that lists maintenance tasks Windows has scheduled to run on your PC.
- An icon that looks like a yellow loudspeaker. If you move the mouse so the mouse pointer rests over this picture, and then press and release the left mouse button, Windows opens a Volume Control box where you change your PC's volume.

And last, on the far right side of the Windows Taskbar is the clock. The clock displays the current time (at least according to your computer). To see the current date, move your mouse so the mouse pointer rests over the time. Windows pops open a small yellow box that displays the day and date, as shown in Figure 2-9.

FIGURE 2-9

The day and date.

The Start Button and Start Menu

The Start button (shown in Figure 2-10) opens a menu, called the Start menu, which contains many avenues for working on the PC. This section describes some of the features of the Start menu.

FIGURE 2-10

The Start button.

To open the Start menu, move the mouse so the mouse pointer rests over the word Start. Then press and release the upper-left corner of the mouse. This opens a menu that looks similar to the one shown in Figure 2-11.

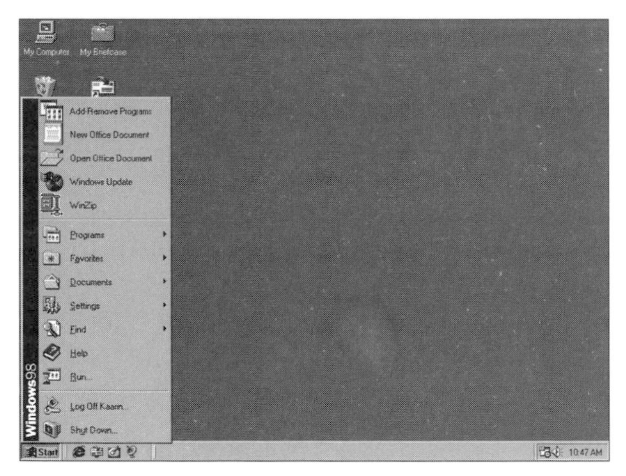

FIGURE 2-11

The Start menu.

Your Start menu might look a little different than the one shown here. Which items you see on the Start menu depend on whether you're running Windows 95 or Windows 98 and which programs you have installed.

Move the mouse toward you and away from you to highlight the different items, called commands, on the Start menu.

The following are some of the most common commands on the Start menu:

- Windows Update
- Programs
- Favorites
- Documents
- Settings
- Find
- Help
- Run
- Log Off
- Shut Down

Let's go over each of these items.

The Windows Update command opens Internet Explorer and connects you to the Internet. It then compares your copy of Windows 98 to the latest Windows 98 **software.** If the Windows Update Wizard finds newer Windows software, it allows you to install the newer elements. This tool comes in handy because it keeps your copy of Windows up-to-date and running smoothly.

The Windows Update command appears on your Start menu only if you're running Windows 98. It doesn't appear if you're running Windows 95.

Chapter 10 describes how to use the Windows Update feature.

The Programs command opens a menu listing the programs, or groups of programs, installed on your computer, as shown in Figure 2-12. By selecting a program from this menu, you start the program.

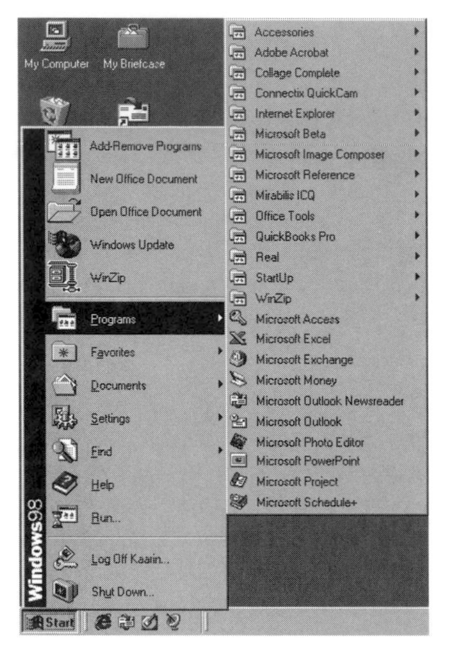

FIGURE 2-12

The Programs menu.

The Favorites command opens a menu of the folders, files, or **web pages** that you have selected as favorites. You can use this menu to quickly access the items you view or work with most.

The Documents command opens a menu that contains up to 15 of the files you worked with most recently, as shown in Figure 2-13. Select a file from this menu to start the program associated with that file and open the file. You can then continue working on the file.

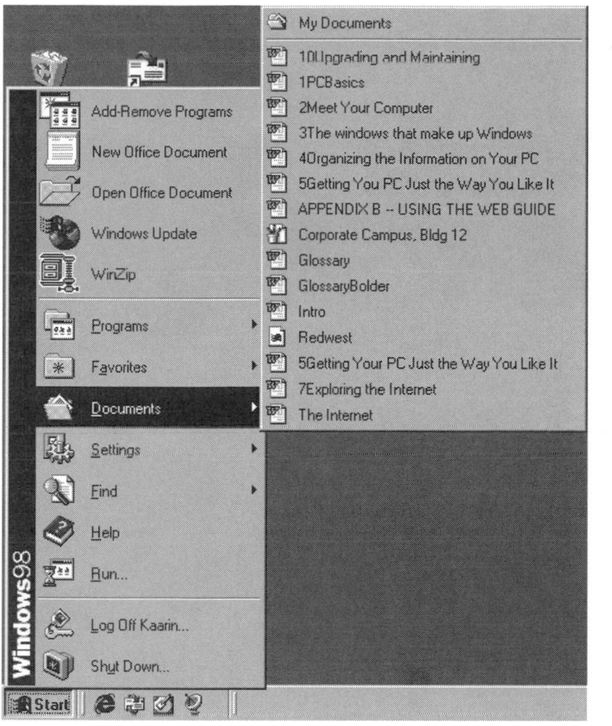

FIGURE 2-13

The Documents menu.

Notes

The Documents menu provides one way of opening files. Chapters 4 and 6 describe two other ways to open files.

The Settings command opens a menu (shown in Figure 2-14) containing options you can use for changing Windows settings. The **Control Panel** command on the Settings menu opens a window you can use to customize several different aspects of Windows. The Printers command opens a window that allows you to see which printers you have installed and the status of your printing. The Taskbar and Start Menu command allows you to customize the Taskbar and Start menu. The Folder Options command allows you to customize the way folders, icons, and other elements look and work. The Active Desktop command has a menu of commands you can use for adding pieces of Internet content to your desktop.

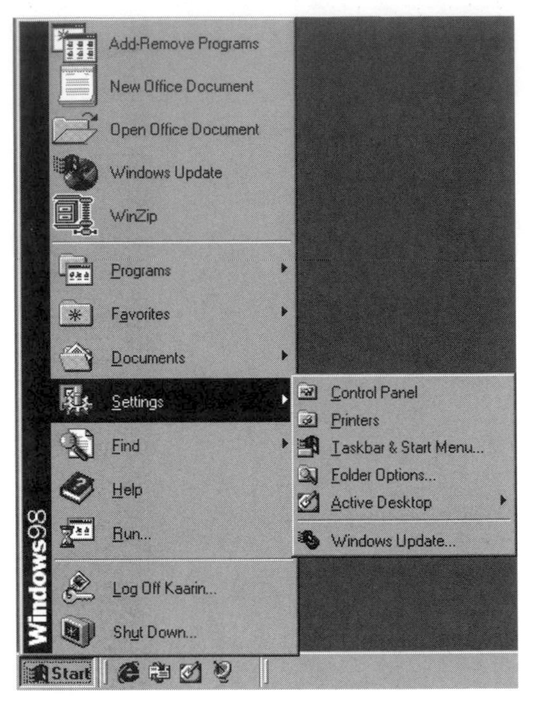

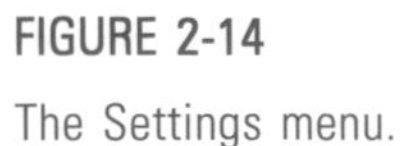

FIGURE 2-14

The Settings menu.

The Find command opens a menu of options you can use to find a variety of items using your computer. You can use the Find menu's Files Or Folders command to find lost information on your computer. (Chapter 4 describes how to do this.) The Find menu's Computer command allows you to find another computer on the local network. The Find menu's On The Internet command starts Internet Explorer and displays a web page you can use to find a resource on the Internet. (Chapter 7 describes how to use this search tool to find information on the Internet.) And the Find menu's People command helps you find the e-mail addresses of long lost friends, acquaintances, and family members.

The Help command opens a window you can use to find help in Windows. Chapter 10 describes how to use this tool.

The Run command tells Windows that you want to run a program. (You might never use the Run command because Windows offers so many other, faster and easier ways to start programs.)

The Logoff command lets you log off the computer so someone else can then log on.

The Shut Down command shuts down or restarts your computer. Always use the Shut Down command and wait for Windows to shut down before you turn off the power to your computer. I describe how to shut down the computer at the end of this chapter. Chapter 10 describes what to do when the Shut Down command doesn't work.

Using the Mouse

The previous section introduced you to the desktop. Because using the mouse is an integral part of working with the desktop (and the rest of Windows), you already had to jump in and use the mouse. This section provides a little more assistance for maneuvering the mouse and defines some mouse procedures.

Always keep the cord of the mouse pointing away from you when you use the mouse.

Moving the Mouse

Rest your hand on the mouse. Now gently slide the mouse to the left and then to the right. Do you see the mouse pointer on your screen move to the left and to the right? Good. To move the mouse pointer toward the top of your screen, gently push the mouse away from you, keeping the mouse on your desk. To move the mouse pointer in a downward direction on your screen, gently pull the mouse toward you.

Notes

A pointing device on a laptop doesn't usually work like a desktop mouse as described here. Refer to the manual that came with your laptop computer for instructions on how to operate your type of pointing device.

Practice moving the mouse pointer on the desktop. Try making the outline of a square. Then try making a circle. Move the mouse so the mouse pointer rests on a shortcut icon. Then move the mouse so the mouse pointer rests on a Quick Launch toolbar button. Do you see how Windows outlines the button and pops up a little box displaying the button's name?

Mice vary in their sensitivity to movement. Some require that you move them very little before the mouse pointer moves to the very edge of the screen. If you find making such slight movements difficult, you can change your mouse's sensitivity. Chapter 5 describes how to do this.

Clicking

Clicking is a two-step process that works like this:

1. Move the mouse pointer to the object you want to click.
2. Press and release the upper-left corner of the mouse.

The pressable upper-left corner of the mouse is called the left mouse button.

To try this out, let's practice a couple of times. First, move the mouse pointer to the loudspeaker icon on the right side of the Taskbar. Now click it. Do you see a Volume Control as shown in Figure 2-15? To close the Volume Control, click a blank area of the desktop.

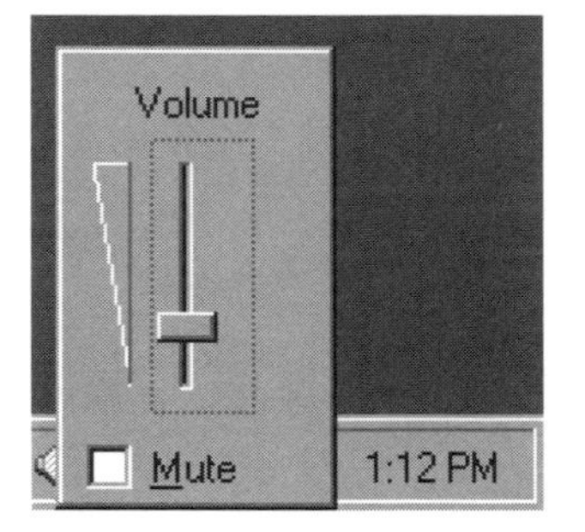

FIGURE 2-15

Click the loudspeaker icon to open the Volume Control.

Now click the Start button to open the Start menu. To close the Start menu, click a blank area of the desktop.

Double-Clicking

Double-clicking is a two-step process that works like this:

1. Move the mouse pointer to the object you want to double-click.

2 Quickly press and release the left mouse button two times, one right after another.

To try this out, let's practice a couple of times. Double-click the My Computer icon on the desktop to open a window similar to the one shown in Figure 2-16. Now double-click the icon for your **hard disk.** (This icon looks like a PC system unit and probably says something like "Drive_c (C:).") To close the windows you just opened, move the mouse pointer to the upper-right corner of each window and click the button with an X on it.

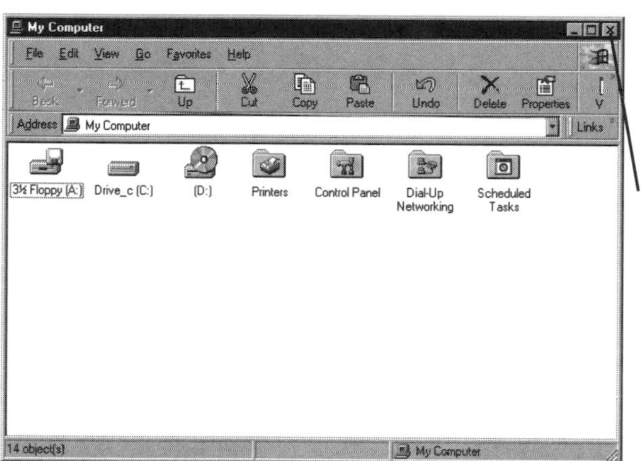

FIGURE 2-16

Double-clicking the My Computer icon opens this window.

Click here to close the window.

Right-Clicking

Right-clicking works much like regular clicking, except that you press the upper-right corner of the mouse. Here's how to right-click:

1 Move the mouse pointer to the object you want to right-click.

2 Quickly press and release the upper-right corner of the mouse.

The pressable upper-right corner of the mouse is called the right mouse button.

Let's practice this a couple of times. First, right-click a blank area of your desktop. This opens a menu, called a shortcut menu, as shown in Figure 2-17.

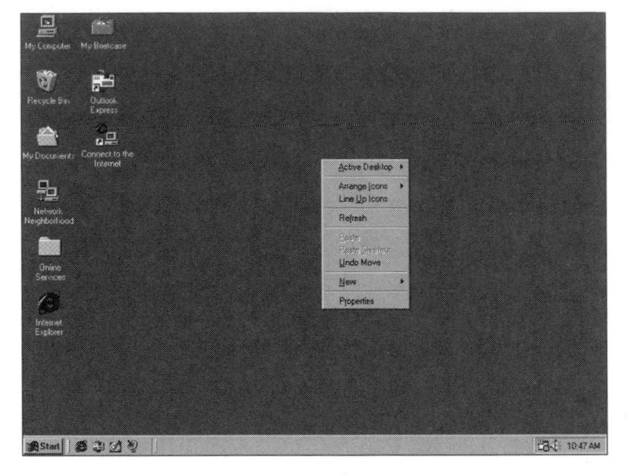

FIGURE 2-17

Right-clicking the desktop opens this shortcut menu.

To close the menu, click a blank area of the desktop. Now, to open a different shortcut menu, right-click the My Computer icon. To close this shortcut menu, click a blank area of the desktop.

If you are left-handed, you can customize your mouse so you can use it more easily. Windows can reverse the functions of the left and right mouse buttons so you click with the right mouse button and "right-click" with the left mouse button. (This allows left-handed people to use their index fingers for clicking.) Chapter 5 describes how to customize the mouse for left-handed users.

Dragging

You **drag** the mouse to select items or to move items on your PC. Let's practice by dragging the knob to increase your PC's volume. To display the Volume Control, click the loudspeaker icon on the right side of the Taskbar. Then follow these steps to drag the volume knob:

1. Move the mouse so the mouse pointer rests over the volume knob.
2. Press the left mouse button, and hold it down.
3. Move the mouse forward to push the volume knob up.
4. Release your finger from the left mouse button. Windows beeps at the new, higher volume.

To decrease the volume, just drag the volume knob back down in the same way.

A great way to practice dragging (and the rest of your mouse skills) is by starting and playing the card game Solitaire, which comes with Windows. To start Solitaire, follow these steps:

1. Click the Start button.
2. Point to Programs. Windows opens the Programs menu.
3. Point to Accessories. Windows opens the Accessories menu.
4. Point to Games. Windows opens the Games menu.
5. Click Solitaire. This starts the Solitaire program, as shown in Figure 2-18.

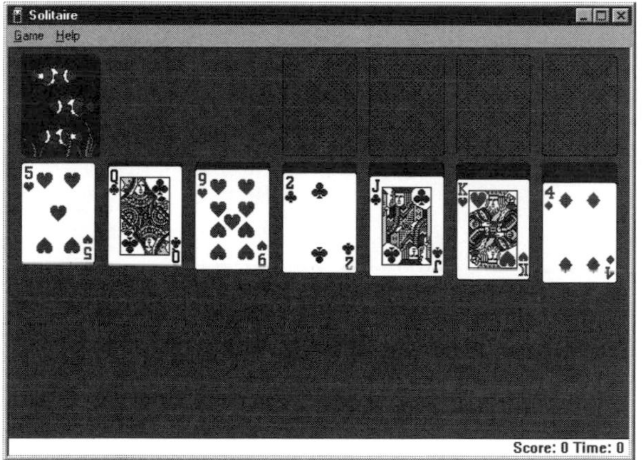

FIGURE 2-18

The Solitaire program.

To move a card from one stack to another, you drag the card. Here's how to drag using the mouse:

1. Move the mouse so the mouse pointer rests over the card you want to move.
2. Press the left mouse button, and hold it down.
3. Move the mouse so the mouse pointer rests over the stack on which you want to place the card you're moving. Note how the card moves with you as you move the mouse.
4. Release the left mouse button to drop the card on top of the stack.

Solitaire won't let you move any card anywhere you want. There are several rules defining the allowable moves. Here's a brief summary: King is high and Ace is low. For the stacks running across the bottom, you can only move a card (or stack) onto a stack where the bottom card is one card higher and of the other color. The four empty spaces in the upper right are for stacking cards of the same suit in order from low to high, beginning with the Ace. If you run out of moves, click the overturned deck in the upper-left corner and use the cards it turns over by dragging them. Once the deck runs out, click the circle in the upper-left corner to go through the deck again.

Practice playing Solitaire for a while to get the feel of the mouse and to work on your clicking and dragging. When you've had your fun, click the small button with an X in the upper-right corner of your screen.

Using Special Mouse Features

Many mice come with a third button or a wheel in between the left and right mouse buttons. You can usually customize the way the button or wheel works. For example, you can program the third button to open Windows Explorer when you click it. The wheel is usually used for scrolling, which is described in Chapter 3. Chapter 5 describes how to customize the mouse.

Using the Keyboard

If you've ever worked on a typewriter, you'll find the PC's other input device, the keyboard, much more familiar and easy to work with than the mouse. And if you're a fast typist, you might also find the keyboard a quicker way of accomplishing tasks that most people perform with the mouse.

Notes

Although most computer books and manuals describe how to perform tasks using the mouse, almost all mouse tasks have keyboard equivalents.

To practice the keyboard tasks described in the following paragraphs, you need to open WordPad, a **word processor** that comes with Windows. WordPad lets you type letters and other **documents.**

While this discussion of using the keyboard talks in terms of the WordPad program, note that you can use the keyboard in the same manner to work with Windows and most other programs.

To open WordPad, follow these steps:

1. Click the Start button.
2. Point to Programs and then to Accessories.
3. Click WordPad. WordPad displays a blank sheet of paper for you to type on, as shown in Figure 2-19.

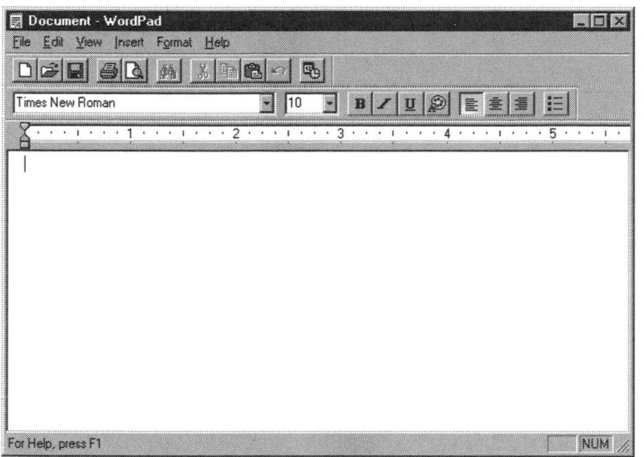

FIGURE 2-19

Immediately after WordPad starts, it's ready for you to begin typing. Notice that the mouse pointer has become an I-beam shape called a **cursor.**

Practice typing some text, just as you would on a typewriter. Figure 2-20 shows a screen with some text.

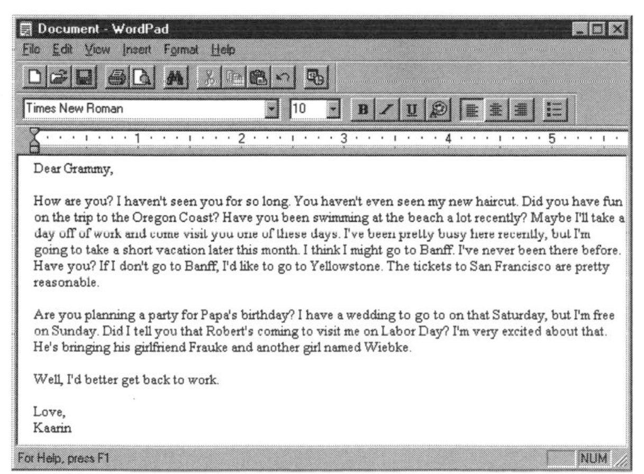

FIGURE 2-20

A letter in WordPad.

When you get to the end of a line, you don't need to add a carriage return. WordPad automatically continues on the next line. At the end of a paragraph, press the Enter key.

In case you've forgotten from typing class, hold down the Shift key to make the next letter you type uppercase. (Or if you press one of the number keys above the letters on your keyboard, the symbol printed on that number's key is entered.) The Caps Lock key makes all your text uppercase. And the Num Lock key allows you to use the numeric keypad on the right side of the keyboard for entering numbers. (To turn on the Caps Lock or Num Lock function, simply press the key once. To turn off the function, press the key again.)

Moving by Using the Keyboard

After you've typed some text, you might find that you want to move to another place in your text to make a change. Unlike with a typewriter, this is easy to do with a word processor. To move back a space, press the left arrow key on your keyboard. To continue moving backward, hold down the arrow key and watch the **cursor** move. To move forward a space, press the right arrow key on your keyboard. To continue moving to the right, hold down the arrow key and watch the cursor move.

To move up a line, press the Up arrow key on your keyboard. Hold down the Up arrow key to continue moving up line by line. To move down a line, press the Down arrow key on your keyboard. Hold down the Down arrow key to continue moving down line by line.

To move to the beginning of a line, press the Home key. To move to the end of a line, press the End key. To move up a page, press the Page Up key. To move down a page, press the Page Down key.

If you can't move up or down a page (because you're already at the beginning or end of your text), Windows beeps when you press the Page Up or Page Down key.

If Num Lock isn't on, you can use several of the numbers on the numeric keypad to move around. You can tell what each number does because it's written right on the key. For example, the 8 key has an up arrow on it, so it works just like the Up arrow key. The 9 key says Pg Up on it, so it works like the Page Up key.

Selecting Information with the Keyboard

Selecting a range of text allows you to apply a change to the whole range of text all at once rather than applying it letter by letter. To select text using the keyboard, click to place the cursor where you want the text selection to begin. Then hold down the Shift key and use the End, Page Down, or arrow keys to place the cursor where you want the selection to end.

To select a word with the mouse, click the word twice. To select a paragraph with the mouse, click the paragraph three times. You can also select text with the mouse by dragging the mouse from the beginning of the selection to the end of the selection.

Deleting with the Keyboard

Figure 2-21 shows how to delete (or "erase") text using the keyboard. To delete the character to the left of the cursor, press the Backspace key. Hold down the Backspace key to continue deleting text. To delete the character to the right of the cursor, press the Delete key. Hold down the Delete key to continue deleting text.

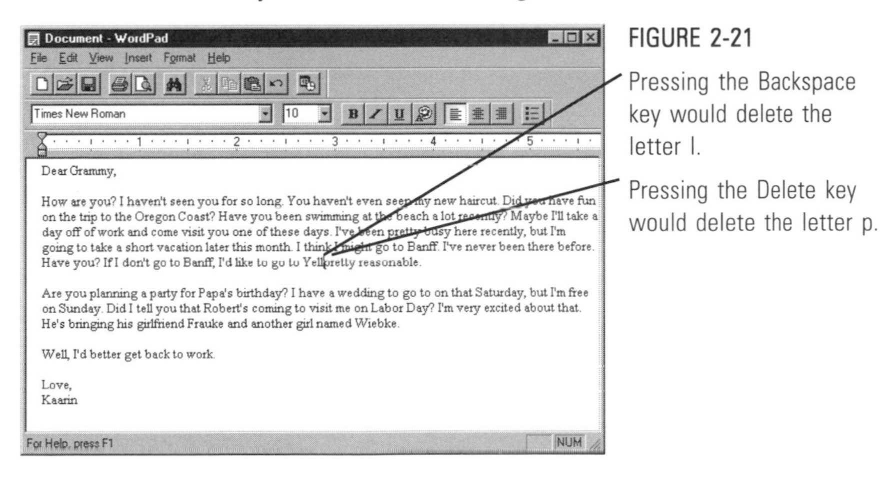

Dear Grammy,

How are you? I haven't seen you for so long. You haven't even seen my new haircut. Did you have fun on the trip to the Oregon Coast? Have you been swimming at the beach a lot recently? Maybe I'll take a day off of work and come visit you one of these days. I've been pretty busy here recently, but I'm going to take a short vacation later this month. I think I might go to Banff. I've never been there before. Have you? If I don't go to Banff, I'd like to go to Yellpretty reasonable.

Are you planning a party for Papa's birthday? I have a wedding to go to on that Saturday, but I'm free on Sunday. Did I tell you that Robert's coming to visit me on Labor Day? I'm very excited about that. He's bringing his girlfriend Frauke and another girl named Wiebke.

Well, I'd better get back to work.

Love,
Kaarin

FIGURE 2-21

Pressing the Backspace key would delete the letter l.

Pressing the Delete key would delete the letter p.

If you have text selected when you press the Delete or Backspace key, pressing the Delete key deletes the entire selection.

Special Keyboard Keys

A PC keyboard includes several keys that you won't recognize from a typewriter. You might not use many of these keys; however, there are a few keys you should know about.

Flanking the Spacebar at the bottom of the keyboard are the Alt keys. These keys are used in combination with a letter of the alphabet to open menus. (Menus are found in the row at the top of the WordPad window. Menus provide the commands that you use to work in a program.) For example, if you hold down the Alt key in WordPad and then press the F key, WordPad's File menu opens, as shown in Figure 2-22. This key combination, known as a keyboard shortcut, is frequently abbreviated as Alt+F.

FIGURE 2-22

Pressing Alt+F opens the File menu in WordPad.

You can tell which letter to press in combination with the Alt key to open a menu because that letter is underlined in the menu's name. For example, to open the Edit menu, hold down the Alt key and press the letter E.

Flanking the Alt keys on the keyboard are the Ctrl keys. These keys provide another shortcut for issuing commands in programs. If you open the File menu in WordPad, you see key combinations next to many of the items on the menu. For example, next to the New command is the combination Ctrl+N. If you hold down the Ctrl key and then press the N key, WordPad creates a new document.

Chapter 5 describes how to customize your keyboard for different languages or for people with disabilities.

Turning Off Your PC

If you've been reading along and following the instructions in this chapter, you're probably ready to call it a day. After you finish working with your PC, you need to shut it down before you turn it off. Shutting down the PC properly gives it a chance to quickly tie up any loose ends of its computing and protect itself against shakes and rattles when it's turned off.

Before you shut down, save any work that you want to keep (how you do this is described in Chapter 6) and close the programs you were working in. (You can close a program by clicking the button with an X in the upper right corner of the screen.) Then follow these steps:

1. Click the Start button.
2. Point to Shut Down. Windows displays a box similar to the one shown in Figure 2-23.

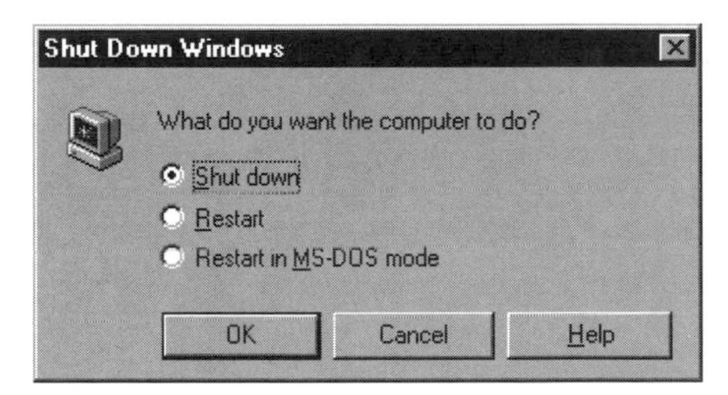

FIGURE 2-23

The Shut Down box.

3. Click the Shut Down button if it is not already marked.
4. Click OK.
5. Wait until Windows shuts down and tells you Windows is closed and it is safe to turn off your computer.
6. Turn off the power on the monitor, your PC's other hardware devices, and the system unit.

CHAPTER 3

The Windows that Make Up Microsoft Windows

This chapter talks about the foundation of **Microsoft Windows'** appearance—**windows.** It describes windows and their elements and introduces how to perform a variety of tasks in the following sections:

- What is a window?
- Common window elements
- Working with windows

What Is a Window?

A window is a rectangle that Windows uses to display the information you see on your screen. These rectangles vary in size and shape, but all true windows have one important characteristic that distinguishes them from other windows: they can be moved to the background and hidden so you can work with another window. To facilitate this, a true window has a row of three buttons in the upper-right corner, as shown in Figure 3-1. When you see a window with these buttons, you know you are looking at a true window.

While a row of three buttons in the upper-right corner provides a good criterion for identifying true windows, it is not a foolproof method. Sometimes, especially in newer programs, these buttons are hidden or look a little different.

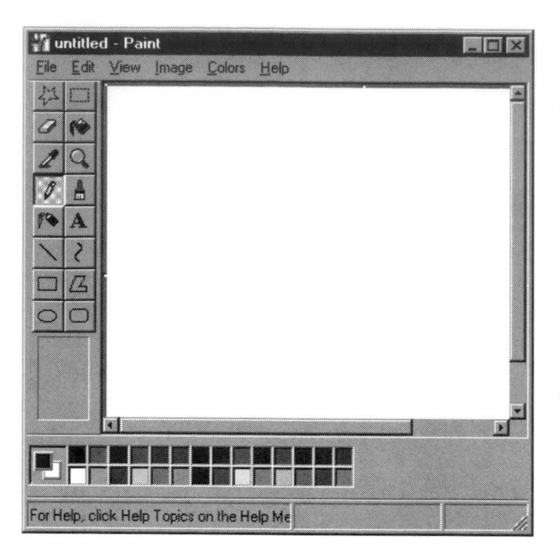

FIGURE 3-1

A true window has three buttons located in the upper-right corner.

These three buttons allow you to shrink the window into a button, change the size of the window, or close the window. The right-most button with the X on it is called the Close button. It allows you to close the window, as described later in this chapter. The middle and the left-most buttons change their names and appearance depending on the size of the window, but all true windows include some combination of the following three buttons:

Minimize.

 Restore.

Maximize.

Program Windows versus Document Windows

True windows come in two types: **program** windows and **document** windows. A program window names the program and contains the controls for working with **files** in the program. A document window names the file and allows you to move and resize the area for displaying the file. Only programs that allow you to work with more than one file at a time have document windows. Figure 3-2 shows two document windows inside the Microsoft Word program window.

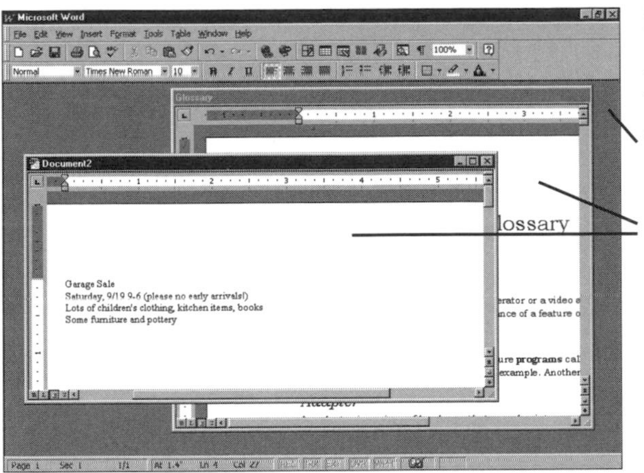

FIGURE 3-2

A program window and two document windows.

The Microsoft Word program window.

Document windows.

Dialog Boxes

Another type of window, called a **dialog box** or just dialog, doesn't have all three of the buttons a true window does, as shown in Figure 3-3. This is because you can't hide or resize a dialog box to work in another window. Unlike true windows, dialog boxes require you to close them—either by executing a command or by canceling the command—before you can work with another window or dialog box.

Notes *If you have a dialog box displayed and click somewhere outside the dialog box, your **PC** might beep at you.*

FIGURE 3-3

You can't resize or hide a dialog box, so it doesn't have the same three buttons as a true window.

Most dialog boxes have two buttons in the upper-right corner. Like other windows, they have the Close button. Unlike most other windows, dialog boxes also usually have a button with a question mark on it, called the Help button. **Click** this button to learn about any dialog box element that you don't understand. After you click the button, the **mouse** pointer turns into a question mark. Now click the element you don't understand. Windows displays a yellow box with a description of the element you clicked, as shown in Figure 3-4.

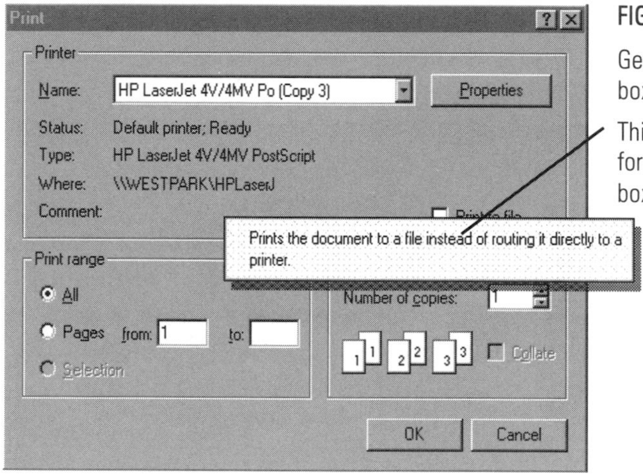

FIGURE 3-4

Getting help in a dialog box.

This is a help description for the Print To File check box.

Message Boxes

You will occasionally encounter a third type of window, called a message box. A message box is usually smaller than a dialog box. It doesn't have room for you to enter any information, as a dialog box does. Instead, a message box usually includes only a couple of buttons, as shown in Figure 3-5.

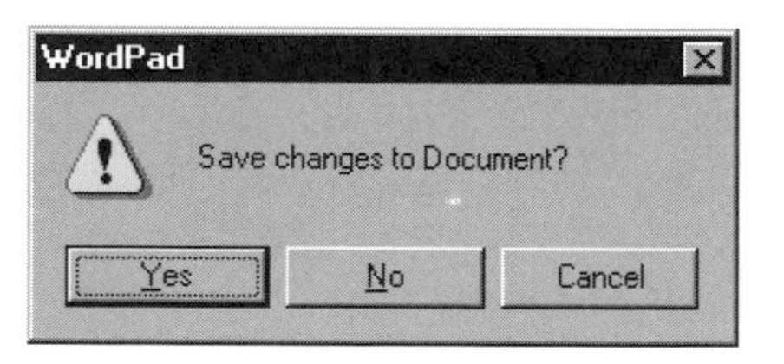

FIGURE 3-5

A message box.

Common Window Elements

Windows and dialog boxes contain several standard elements you use to tell your PC what to do. The following sections describe some of these elements.

Title Bars

Almost every window and dialog box has a title bar. The title bar runs across the top of the window or dialog box. A program window title bar usually displays the program and often the document's filename if the document window is maximized. A document window title bar usually displays the document's filename. A dialog box's title bar names the dialog box, which usually has something to do with the task at hand. For example, if you use the dialog box for printing, the program probably labels the dialog box "Print."

Menus

Almost all program windows include a menu bar listing the names of several **menus.** Figure 3-6 shows the WordPad menu bar. Each of the words on the menu bar opens a list containing several tasks related to that word. For example, the File menu contains several commands for working with files. The Edit menu contains commands for editing files, and so forth. To open a menu, click the menu's name on the menu bar. To choose a command from a menu, click that command.

FIGURE 3-6

The WordPad menu bar.

Click a menu name to see the list of commands on that menu.

Toolbars

Most programs also include some type of **toolbar** you can use to quickly access the most commonly used menu commands. For example, if you want to underline some text you've selected in WordPad, you must go through a long and much less obvious process using menu commands: First, you click the Format menu. Then, you click the Text command. Then, you use the **Font** dialog box to specify underlining. However, the toolbar turns underlining into a one-step process. To underline the selected text, just click the Underline toolbar button, shown in Figure 3-7. The icons on most toolbar buttons suggest the button's purpose, but if you're ever unclear, rest the mouse pointer over the button to display the button's name in a small yellow box.

Notes *Sometimes you might see the buttons on a toolbar referred to as tools. In this book, however, I refer to them as buttons.*

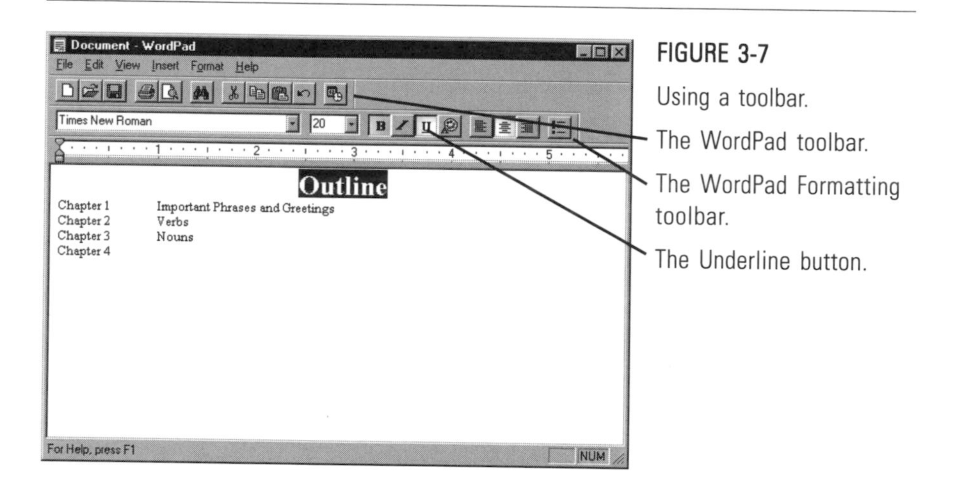

FIGURE 3-7

Using a toolbar.

The WordPad toolbar.

The WordPad Formatting toolbar.

The Underline button.

Notes *Many programs have several toolbars, each containing a set of buttons related to a certain task. For example, Microsoft Word contains an extra toolbar especially for creating pictures, another toolbar solely for working with tables, and so on.*

Scrollbars

When the information in a window won't completely fit in the window, Windows adds **scrollbars** to the window, as shown in Figure 3-8. Using the scrollbars, you can move back and forth or up and down to see the sides of the window that don't fit. To use a scrollbar, click the arrows on either end to move by small increments or drag the scrollbar's slider. You can also click the area on either side of the slider to move up or down a screenful of text at a time.

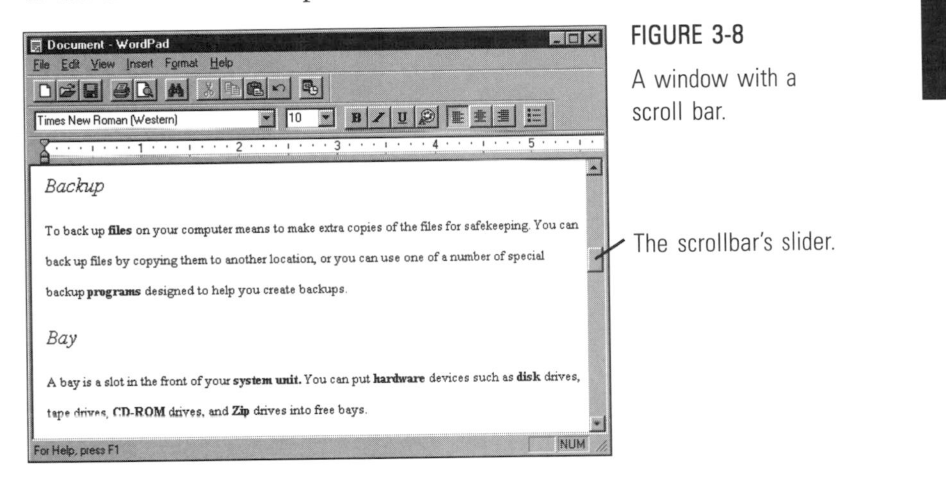

FIGURE 3-8

A window with a scroll bar.

Notes: *List boxes and drop-down list boxes also usually include scrollbars.*

List Boxes

Windows and dialog boxes use list boxes to allow you to select an item from a list of choices. List boxes come in two varieties, the standard list box and the drop-down list box. A standard list box looks similar to the one shown in Figure 3-9.

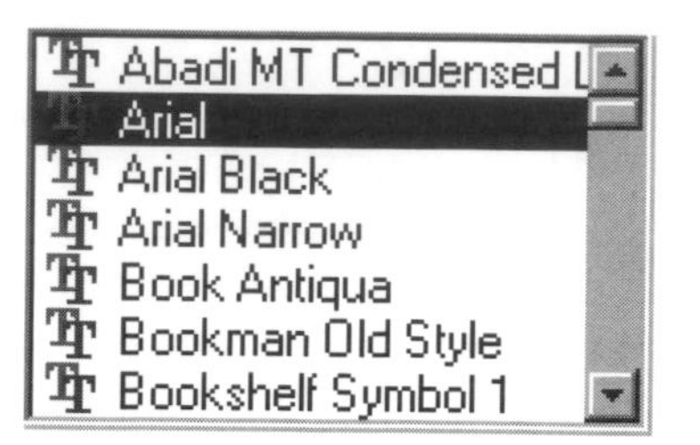

FIGURE 3-9

A list box.

To select an entry from a list box, scroll down the list box until you see the entry you want and then click it.

Drop-down list boxes look similar to the one shown in Figure 3-10.

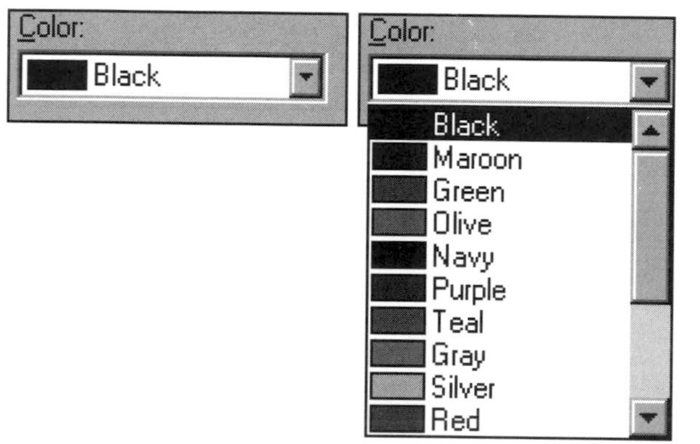

FIGURE 3-10

A drop-down list box before and after displaying the list.

To select an entry from a drop-down list box, click the down arrow in the list box. This displays the list. Then, scroll down the list until you see the entry you want, and click it.

Text Boxes

A text box is an area of a window or dialog box in which you can type text. Text boxes vary widely in size. Some allow you to type only a few characters. Others allow you to type sentences or even paragraphs. Figure 3-11 shows a text box.

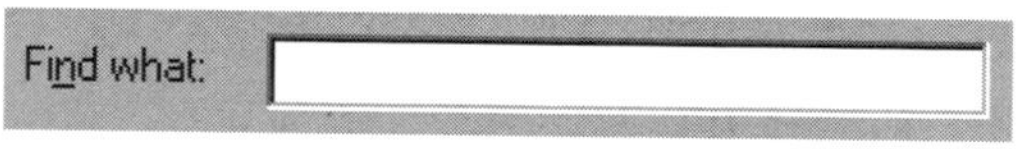

Find what:

FIGURE 3-11

A text box.

Notes

Boxes that allow you to either type your own text or select an entry are sometimes referred to as combo boxes because they combine the features of a text box and a drop-down list box.

Command Buttons

All dialog boxes and message boxes include at least one, and usually two, command buttons. To issue a command, click a command button. The New dialog box in Figure 3-12 includes two common command buttons: OK and Cancel. The OK button executes the command; the Cancel button cancels it. Almost all dialog boxes include a Cancel or No command button. The button they include to issue the command might change depending on the command. For example, the button that issues the command in the Open dialog box might be called Open. The button that issues the command in the Save As dialog box might be called Save. And in several dialog boxes and message boxes, the button that issues the command is called Yes instead of OK.

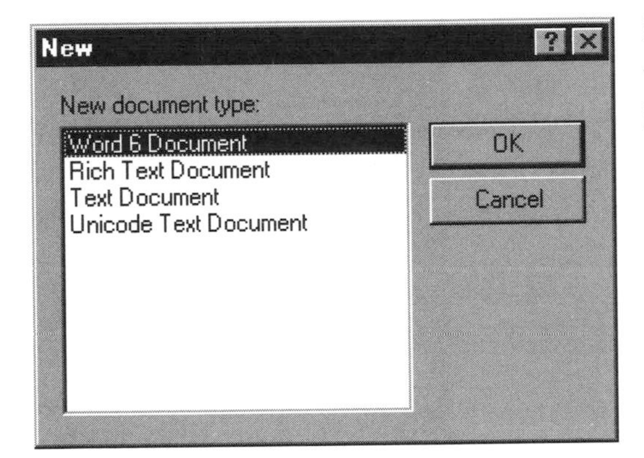

FIGURE 3-12

The New dialog box in WordPad includes two command buttons.

Option Buttons

Option buttons, sometimes called radio buttons, look like bubbles you darken on computer-read forms. Dialog boxes use sets of option buttons to present a small group of mutually exclusive choices. For example, in the Print dialog box shown in Figure 3-13, WordPad offers you the choice of printing the entire document, printing only the text you've selected, or printing only the pages you specify. To select an option, just click the small round button beside the option. To change your selection, click another option. Windows clears your first selection when it adds the new mark.

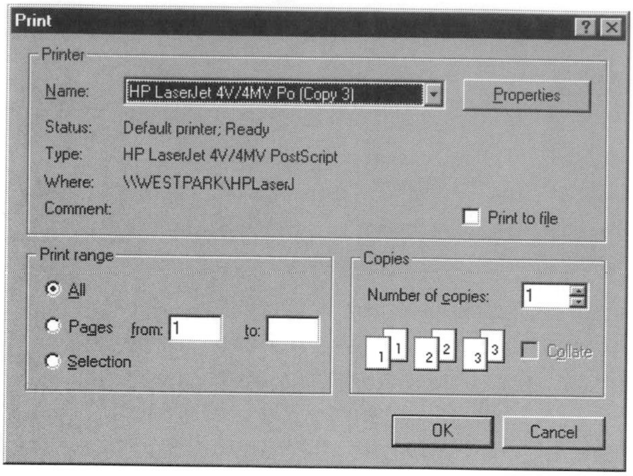

FIGURE 3-13

The option buttons in this Print dialog box allow you to specify what you want to print.

Check Boxes

Dialog boxes use check boxes to allow you to turn features on or off. Unlike option buttons, check boxes don't come in mutually exclusive sets. Sometimes they appear in groups, but usually you can select as many check boxes as you need. When a check box is selected, a check mark is in it. To select an empty check box, click the box. To remove a check mark from a box, click the box again. Figure 3-13 includes one check box, called the Print To File check box.

Tabs

When a dialog box needs to contain more information than it can fit in a relatively small box, it uses tabs to hold the information, as shown in Figure 3-14. To display the dialog box shown in Figure 3-14, choose the View menu's Options command in WordPad.

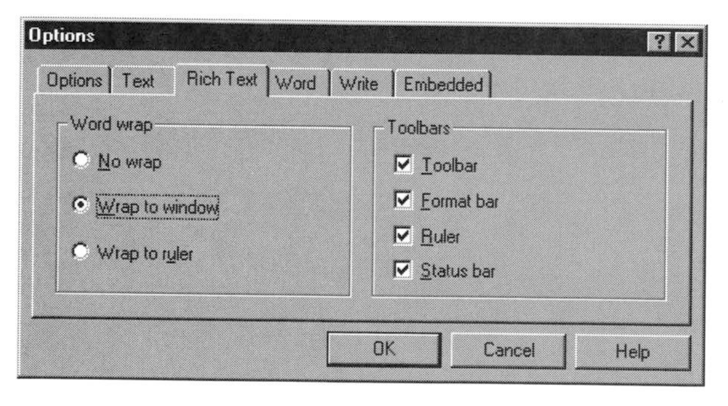

FIGURE 3-14

The Options dialog box contains six tabs: Options, Text, Rich Text, Word, Write, and Embedded.

To display the information on a different tab, just click that tab's heading.

Working with Windows

Windows are a handy invention because they allow you to work efficiently at the PC. You can resize and move windows so you see just what you want to see, but you can quickly access other information when you need it.

Sizing a Window

Before you can change a window's size, you first need to make sure that the window isn't set to take up the maximum space it's allowed. In the case of program windows, this means covering the entire screen; in the case of document windows, it usually means filling the entire area within the program window. If the window you want to resize takes up this maximum-allotted space, click the Restore button. (The Restore button looks like two small overlapping boxes, as shown in Figure 3-15 and on page 58.)

FIGURE 3-15

Click the Restore button to make a window resizable.

This Restore button makes the program window resizable.

This Restore button makes the document window resizable.

Now you can resize the window in one of three ways:

- To increase or decrease a window's width, move the mouse to the window's left or right side. When the mouse pointer becomes a double-sided arrow, **drag** the side of the window in or out to make the window narrower or wider.

- To increase or decrease a window's height, move the mouse to the top or bottom of the window. When the mouse pointer becomes an up-and-down pointing arrow, drag the edge of the window up or down to make the window taller or shorter.
- To change a window's height and width at the same time, move the mouse to the lower-right corner of the window (shown in Figure 3-16). This corner is called the resizing box. When the mouse pointer becomes a diagonally pointing arrow, drag the corner inward or outward to resize the entire window.

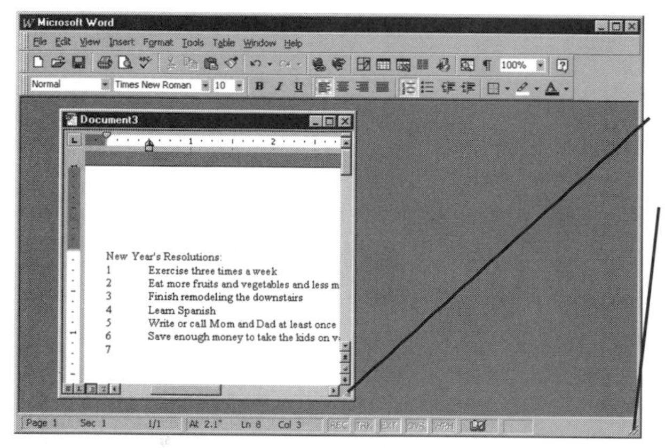

FIGURE 3-16

Resizing a window.

Drag this corner to resize the document window.

Drag this corner to resize the program window

If a window takes up less than the entire allowable space, you can tell Windows to increase the size of the window so you can see the largest possible area. This is called maximizing the window. To maximize a window, click the Maximize button. (This button looks like a box with a dark band at the top, as shown in Figure 3-17.)

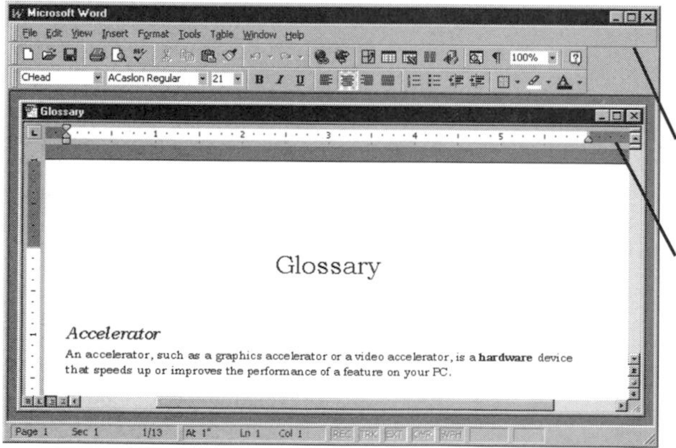

FIGURE 3-17

Maximizing a window.

Click this button to maximize the program window.

Click this button to maximize the document window.

Moving a Window

As long as a window isn't maximized, you can move the window to the area of your screen where you want it, as shown in Figure 3-18. To reposition a window on your screen, drag the title bar at the top of the window.

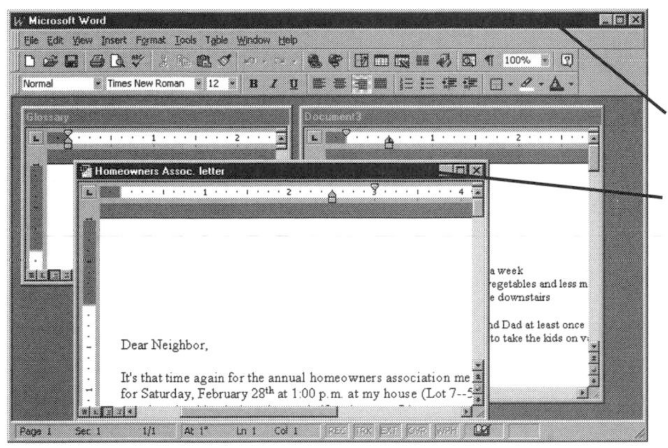

FIGURE 3-18

Moving windows.

Drag the title bar to move the program window.

Drag the title bar to move the document window.

Hiding and Displaying Windows

You can shrink windows into buttons when you're not using them so they don't take up much room on your screen, but are still readily available when you need them again. Shrinking a window into a button is called minimizing the window. When you minimize a program window, the window shows up as a button on the Taskbar. When you minimize a document window, the window shows up as a button in the lower-left corner of the program window. To minimize a window, click the Minimize button shown in Figure 3-19. (This button has a short dark line on the bottom.)

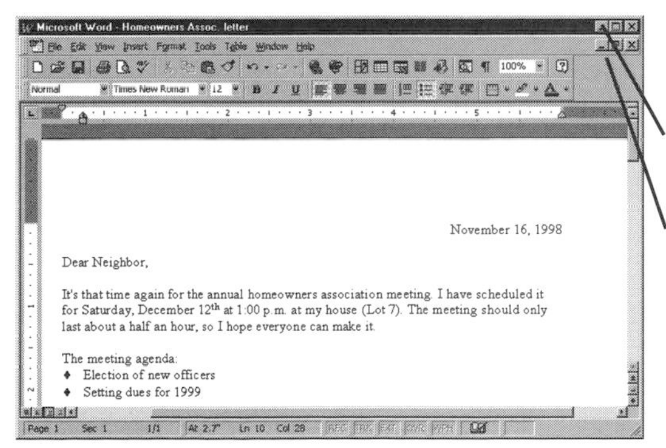

FIGURE 3-19

Minimizing windows.

Click this button to minimize the program window.

Click this button to minimize the document window.

After you minimize a window, you can easily redisplay the window. To redisplay a document window, click either the Restore or Maximize button, as shown in Figure 3-20. (The Restore button turns the minimized document window into a resizable window; the Maximize button maximizes the size of the document window.) To redisplay a minimized program window, click the program window's button on the Taskbar.

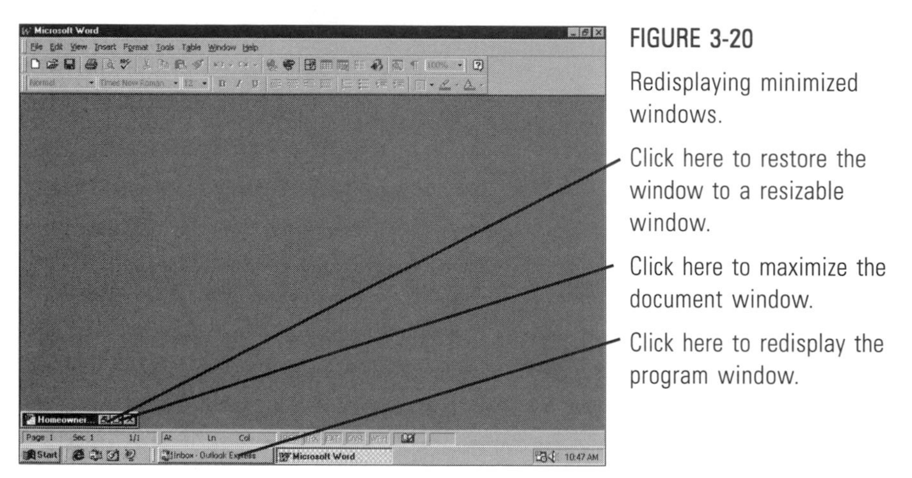

FIGURE 3-20

Redisplaying minimized windows.

Click here to restore the window to a resizable window.

Click here to maximize the document window.

Click here to redisplay the program window.

Notes

When you choose to redisplay a minimized program window, Windows displays the window the way you last viewed it. If you last viewed it as a resizable window, that's how Windows redisplays it. Or if you last viewed it as a maximized window, that's how Windows redisplays it.

Closing a Window

To close a program window, document window, or dialog box, click its Close button, as shown in Figure 3-21. If you attempt to close a document window without saving your changes, the program will prompt you to first save your work. If you attempt to close a program window containing one or more files with unsaved changes, the program will also prompt you to save your work in each of these files. If you close a dialog box without clicking a command button, the program does not execute a command.

FIGURE 3-21

Closing windows and dialog boxes.

Click here to exit the program.

Click here to close the file.

Click here to close the dialog box if you decide not to print.

CHAPTER 4

Organizing the Information on Your PC

Regardless of how you use your **PC**, one of its most important functions is to store information. And the more work you do on your computer, the more information it needs to store. One of the reasons computers are so popular is because they can store huge amounts of information relative to the amount of space they take up. But in order for your computer to be a practical tool for holding information, it needs to be well organized. Making use of your computer's organizational structure when you work can make your time spent at the computer more efficient. This chapter discusses the following topics on organization:

- Defining PC storage terms
- Understanding your PC's organization
- Working with **Windows Explorer**
- Working with **files** and **folders**
- Sharing information among PCs

Defining PC Storage Terms

Before you can understand how you collect and store information on your computer, you need to understand four key terms: file, folder, **disk**, and **drive.**

Disks and Drives

A disk is a thin, flat, round plate made of plastic or metal that stores information: **floppy disks**, **hard disks**, and **CD-ROMs** are all types of disks. A drive (or disk drive) is the hardware that holds the disk and writes information on it or reads information from it.

Sometimes you'll see the word disk *spelled* disc *(as in compact disc). This spelling means that the drive uses* ***lasers*** *to read from or write to the disk.*

Your PC probably has a couple of drives. It surely has a hard disk drive, where the hard disk is located, for example. That's just a stack of metal platters inside the system unit. Your computer probably also has a CD-ROM drive, which you use to install **programs**, listen to music, and read information on CD-ROM. Almost all computers have at least one floppy disk drive as well. Some computers even have additional types of storage drives, such as tape drives or Zip drives.

Because your hard disk always resides in your hard disk drive, people use the terms hard disk and hard drive interchangeably.

Files

All the information stored on your PC is stored in what are called files. A file is just a document. If you type a letter to your mother, for example, **Microsoft Windows** stores this letter, or **document**, as a file. If you use your PC to draw a picture that you want to include with your letter, Windows stores the picture, or document, as a file as well. Some files you create yourself; some files you receive from other sources. For example, if you purchase a program such as Microsoft Word or Corel WordPerfect to write that letter to your mother, the program comes with files that also get stored in your computer.

Technically speaking, your PC stores two types of files: document files and program files. The files that you create—the letter, for example—are called document files. The files that you don't create are program files. Program files store the instructions that a program (like your ***word processor****) uses to function.*

Folders

Windows uses folders to segregate, or organize, the files you've stored on a disk. You can also use folders-within-folders, called **subfolders**, to further organize the files in a folder.

In the case of a disk and its folders, you use folders to group files. For example, you might use one folder to hold all your letters. And you might use another folder to hold all your pictures. Other folders might even be empty.

Now that you know what files, folders, disks, and drives are, let me make one last point. Practically speaking, you get to name your folders and files—and you can name them whatever you want. Okay, in truth, some rules do apply, but they are very loose. If you unintentionally break a rule, nothing bad happens. Windows just says, "Oh, you can't use that name because it violates this rule. . ." Windows, however, names its drives using the letters of the alphabet. Your floppy disk drive is probably named A. Your hard disk drive is probably named C. And your CD-ROM drive is probably named D. If your computer has other drives, Windows uses other letters—E, F, G, and so on—for their names.

Understanding Your PC's Organization

To make the best use of your PC's organization, you need to understand how that organization works. Specifically, you need to understand two concepts: the folder tree structure and the pathname convention for describing that structure.

The Folder Tree Structure

This whole topic of folders and subfolders can get kind of complicated, so let's clear up the confusion from the start. Windows uses a concept called a folder tree to organize your files. The folder tree is a hierarchical way of classifying files and folders that helps you group files and folders that belong together. It works sort of like the organization of a grocery store. A Granny Smith apple belongs in a group with other apples, which belongs in a larger group with other types of fruit, which belongs in an even larger group called produce. If grocery stores didn't follow this organization, you would never know what section to look in to find the apple. It could be in the bakery section or in the dairy case.

Let me give you an example of how this works with computer files. Say you're writing a letter to your mother. In that letter, you include two pictures that you have in electronic form on your computer. When you're ready to send or print the letter, you want to know where all the parts of the letter are: the text and the two pictures. You don't want to have to look all over your computer to find the letter and the pictures in some arbitrary locations. To make it easy to find what you're looking for on your computer, you use folders. In this case, you could create a folder (as described later in this chapter) and call it Valentine's Day Letter to Mom. Then you could store the letter and the pictures in that folder. Figure 4-1 shows what this would look like on your computer.

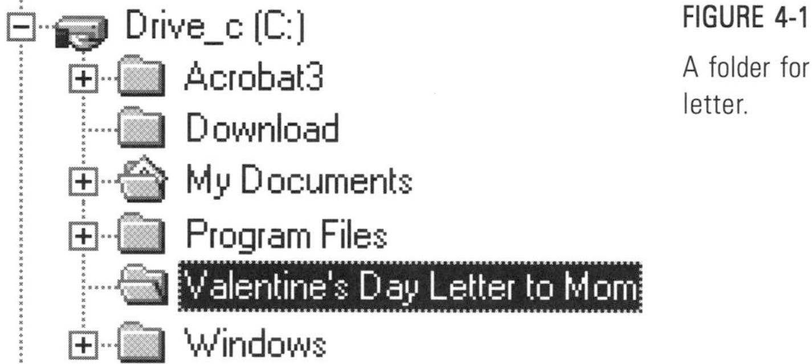

FIGURE 4-1

A folder for storing a letter.

Now let's say your mother's birthday rolls around. And Mother's Day too. Each time you write another letter to your mother and include a couple of new pictures. Pretty soon, you have a whole bunch of folders storing letters and pictures to your mother. To keep your computer from becoming cluttered, you could create a folder called Letters to Mom. Then you could move all the folders storing individual letters into this folder. (Moving folders is described later in this chapter.) The folders containing the letters and pictures become what are called subfolders. Figure 4-2 illustrates what your folder tree might look like after a year or so.

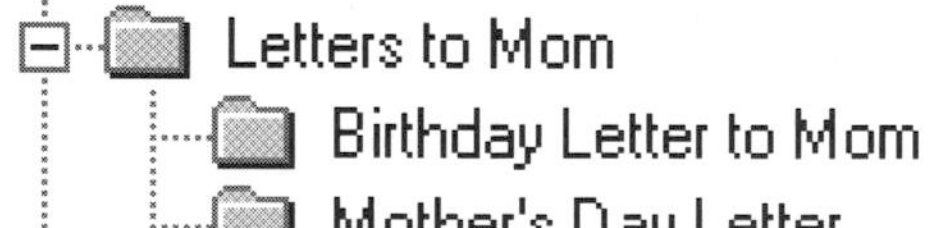

FIGURE 4-2

Several subfolders for storing letters to Mom.

If you're an avid letter writer and correspond with several people, you could make the Letters to Mom folder a subfolder of a larger Letters folder, as shown in Figure 4-3.

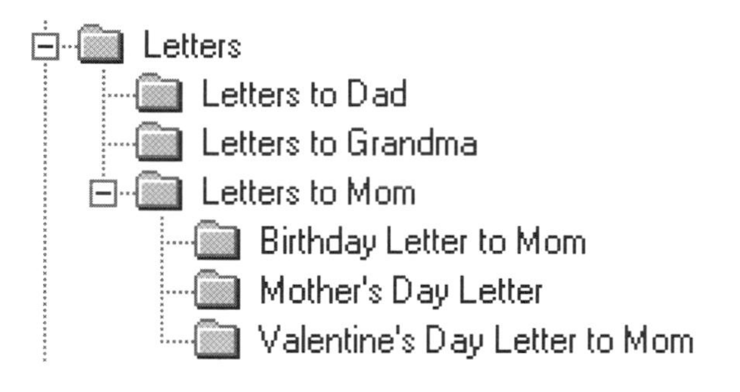

FIGURE 4-3

A Letters folder and its subfolders.

Pathnames

To describe the location of a file on your computer in a clear and concise way, a convention called a **pathname** is used. A pathname works like this: If someone from far away asks where you live, you might say that you live in the United States. If the person asks where you live in the United States, you might answer with the name of the state in which you live, for example, Washington State. If the person then asks where you live in that state, you might answer with the name of your city, for instance, Seattle. If the person asks for still more information, you might respond with the name of the street or the part of the city where you live.

In computer language, you would write the pathname that describes your location as follows:

Earth:\United States\Washington\Seattle\Fremont

On your PC, it works like this: Say, for example, you have a file called New Year's Letter to Mom, which you stored in the Letters to Mom subfolder of your Letters folder on your C drive. For a quick and easy way to describe this location, start at the top level. In this case, it's your C drive. Type the "C drive" part like this:

C:\

The next level of the folder tree is the Letters folder. Add Letters\ to the pathname so it now looks like this:

C:\Letters\

The next level of the folder tree is the Letters to Mom subfolder. Add this to the pathname so it looks like this:

C:\Letters\Letters to Mom\

Now you need to specify the file, New Year's Letter to Mom. If you wrote the file using Microsoft Word, the **file extension** is probably .doc. This is the complete pathname:

C:\Letters\Letters to Mom\New Year's Letter to Mom.doc

The main area of a disk is called a root directory. Folders and files that aren't inside other folders, but show up directly when you display the contents of a disk, are referred to as being in the root directory.

Working with Windows Explorer

Once you understand how your computer organizes the files on a disk using folders and subfolders, you're ready to begin working with these items. You can work with them in a variety of ways, but the best way to get the inside picture of your computer is by using Windows Explorer.

Starting Windows Explorer

To start Windows Explorer, follow these steps:

1. **Click** the **Start button**
2. Point to Programs.
3. Click Windows Explorer, as shown in Figure 4-4.

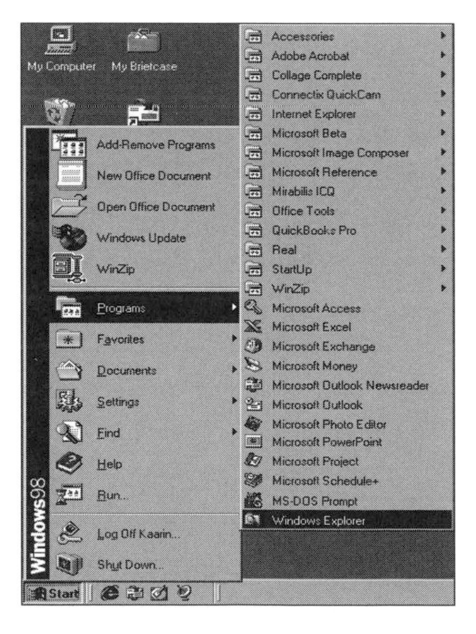

FIGURE 4-4

Opening Windows Explorer from the Start menu.

Here's a trick for quickly opening Windows Explorer like a pro: right-click the Start button, and choose Explore from the shortcut menu.

Introducing the Windows Explorer Window

The Windows Explorer **window** has two sides, called panes. The left pane, called the folder pane, shows **icons** representing the drives on your computer (see Figure 4-5). If you click one of these drives, the right pane, called the file pane, of the Windows Explorer window lists the folders and files on the disk in that drive. If you **double-click** a drive, the right pane still shows the folders and files on the disk, but the left pane also lists the folders on the disk.

To see which files are stored in a particular folder, click the folder once if it's listed in the folder pane or double-click it if it's listed in the file pane. If there are folders inside a folder—these are also called subfolders—follow the same steps to see their contents.

To move back to the disk that holds a folder or the folder that holds a subfolder, click the Up toolbar button.

FIGURE 4-5

The Windows Explorer window showing the folders on the C disk.

The Up toolbar button.

This is a folder.

This is a drive.

This is a file.

Click the plus or minus sign next to a drive or folder in the left pane to expand or hide the folder tree in the left pane while keeping the contents of the right pane the same.

Windows places an icon in front of a filename to identify the type of file. In Figure 4-5, for example, notice there's a file named Letter to Tom toward the bottom of the list of files and folders (in the file pane). In front of the filename is an icon with a "W." That "W" is the icon for Microsoft Word, and it identifies the file as a Microsoft Word document. Do you see the file named New Year's budget almost at the bottom of the list of files and folders? The "X" in front of that file's name identifies the document as a Microsoft Excel document.

Notes

*Microsoft Excel is a **spreadsheet** program. You use spreadsheet programs to develop budgets and financial forecasts. Microsoft Word is a word processor program. You use word processors to create text documents.*

Changing the Windows Explorer Display

Let me mention one last point about the Windows Explorer window. If your window doesn't look quite like the one shown in Figure 4-5, never fear. You can change the way the Windows Explorer window looks. Just click the down arrow next to the Views toolbar button, and choose one of the Views menu's commands: As Web Page, Large Icons, Small Icons, List, or Details (see Figure 4-6).

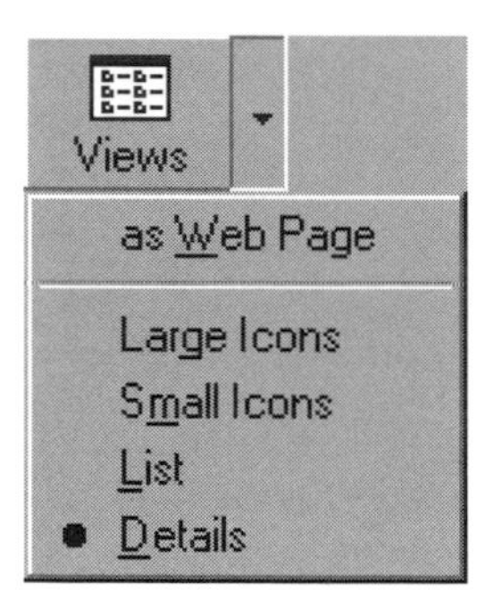

FIGURE 4-6

The Views menu lets you change the way information appears in the Windows Explorer window.

The As Web Page command is a toggle switch that's used in combination with any of the other views. If you choose this command, Windows displays either information about, or a small picture of, the file you select in the file pane of the Windows Explorer window (see Figure 4-7). When you turn on the As Web Page view, Windows places a check mark next to the menu command on the Views menu to indicate that the As Web Page view is on.

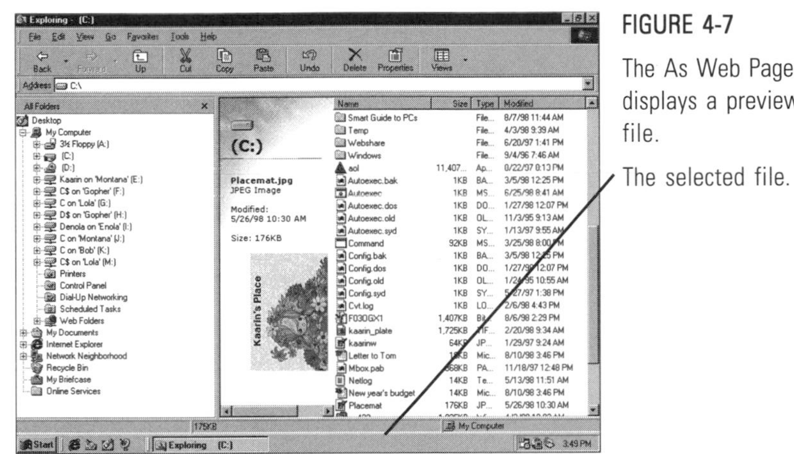

FIGURE 4-7

The As Web Page view displays a preview of the file.

The selected file.

If you choose any of the other Views menu's commands, Windows provides more or less information or changes the size of the icons. If you choose the Large Icons command, for example, Windows uses big icons to represent files and folders. If you choose the Small Icons command, Windows uses tiny icons. If you click List, Windows uses even smaller icons and also lists some information about files and folders. If you choose Details, Windows lists more information about files and folders. If you have questions about the different views, just experiment with them.

Notes

If you click the Views toolbar button—not the down arrow next to the Views toolbar button but the actual button—Windows cycles through the different views. For example, if you click the Views toolbar button four times in a row, you'll see the Large Icons view, the Small Icons view, the List view, and the Details view.

Working with Files and Folders

The first sections of this chapter define some key terms and describe your PC's organization. This section describes how to perform tasks using Windows Explorer.

Opening Files

If you see a file in the Windows Explorer window that you want to open, you can open it directly from Windows Explorer. Windows will then determine which program it needs to use to work with the file, start that program, and then tell that program to grab the file and display it.

To open a file in Windows Explorer, open Windows Explorer and then follow these steps:

1 Double-click the disk that contains the file.

2 Double-click the folder that contains the file in the file pane of Windows Explorer. (Figure 4-8 shows the contents of the My Documents folder.) If necessary, double-click the subfolder that contains the file.

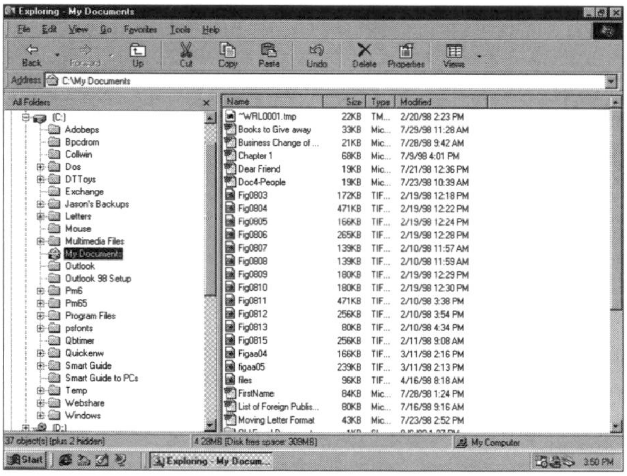

FIGURE 4-8

Windows Explorer showing the My Documents folder contents.

3 Double-click the file to open it.

Windows typically creates a special folder called My Documents and assumes that you'll use this folder to store the documents you create.

There are actually three ways of opening files. The previous steps described one of the ways. None of the methods is better than the other; which one works faster depends on what you're currently doing on your computer when you want to open a file. Chapter 2 describes how to open files using the Start menu's Documents menu. Chapter 6 describes how to open files from within programs.

Renaming Files and Folders

You can easily rename a file or folder. Just follow these steps:

1. Open Windows Explorer, and find the file or folder you want to rename.
2. Click the file to select it.
3. Pause, and then click the file's name. Windows adds a black box around the file's name (see Figure 4-9).
4. Type the new name.

FIGURE 4-9

The Windows Explorer window showing a renaming text box.

Don't rename program files, only rename document files. If you rename program files, your programs might not start correctly.

Creating New Folders

You can create new folders to better organize your documents. For example, if you know you'll be creating many documents and you want to segregate your documents into three categories—letters, reports, and memos—you would create three separate folders. To create a new folder, follow these steps:

1. Display the list of disks or folders into which you want to place the new folder. For example, if you want to create a new folder for your C disk, display the contents—this will be its files and folders—of the C disk using Windows Explorer. And if you want to create a new subfolder inside the My Documents folder, display the contents of the My Documents folder in Windows Explorer.
2. Choose the File **menu's** New command to display the New submenu, and then choose the Folder command (see Figure 4-10). Windows creates a new folder or subfolder for the disk.

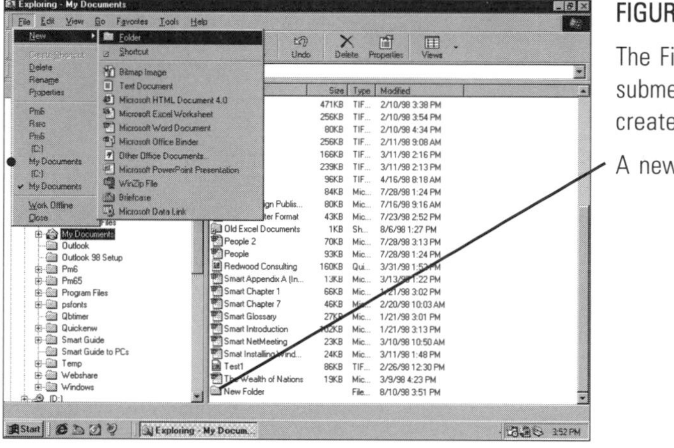

FIGURE 4-10

The File menu's New submenu and a newly created folder.

3. Enter a name for the folder.

After you create a new folder, you'll want to move or copy files to it. The later chapter sections "Moving Files and Folders" and "Copying Files and Folders" describe how you do this.

Deleting Files and Folders

You can delete any file or folder by selecting the file or folder and then clicking the Delete **toolbar** button.

*Never delete program files. If you want to remove a program, use the **Control Panel's** Add/Remove programs tool, which is described in Chapter 10.*

When you delete a file, Windows doesn't actually remove it from your disk. Instead, Windows moves the file to a special folder named the **Recycle Bin.** Periodically—and usually only when the Recycle Bin gets full—Windows removes a file from this folder.

*If you delete a file from any disk other than your hard disk (such as from a floppy disk or a disk on a **network** drive), the file is immediately deleted. You cannot restore it later from the Recycle Bin.*

Chapter 10 describes the Recycle Bin and how to empty it.

Undoing a Command

Most of the time, you can reverse the effect of your last, or most recent, file or folder command. For example, if you've just renamed a file or folder, you can undo the renaming. If you've just moved or copied a file, you can put everything back into its original place or condition. If you've just deleted a file or folder, you can undo this operation. To undo your last file or folder command, click the Undo toolbar button.

Undeleting Files and Folders

You can typically undelete, or restore, a file or folder you've previously deleted. To do this, follow these steps:

1. Double-click the Recycle Bin shortcut icon, which appears on the Windows **desktop.** Windows displays the contents of the Recycle Bin folder, as shown in Figure 4-11.
2. Right-click the file or folder you want to undelete.
3. Choose the shortcut menu's Restore command.

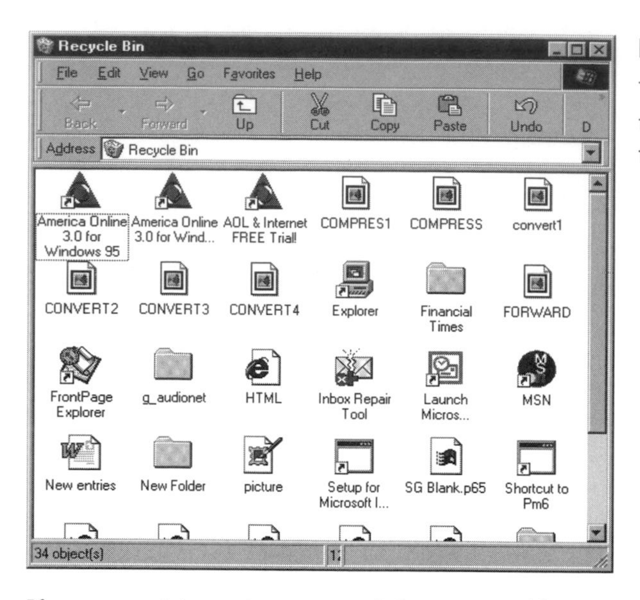

FIGURE 4-11

The Recycle Bin folder temporarily stores the files you've deleted.

If you want to restore several document files at once, simply select all the files, right-click one of the selected files, and choose the Restore command. To select multiple files, hold down the Ctrl key and then click each file you want to select. Or draw a box around the documents you want to restore by **dragging** the **mouse** between the opposite corners of an imaginary box that contains all the documents you want to restore.

Moving Files and Folders

You can move a document from one disk to another disk and from one folder to another folder. To do this, follow these steps:

1. Open Windows Explorer, and double-click the disk that contains the file or folder you want to move.
2. Double-click the folder that contains the file or folder you want to move. Figure 4-12 shows the contents of the My Documents folder.

FIGURE 4-12

Windows Explorer showing the My Documents folder.

The Paste toolbar button.

The Cut toolbar button.

3 Click the file or folder to select it.

4 Click the Cut toolbar button.

5 Double-click the disk to which you want to move the file or folder.

6 Click the folder to which you want to move the file or folder.

7 Click the Paste toolbar button. Windows moves the file or folder from the original location to the new location.

Note that you can easily move several document files at once. To do so, select all the files before clicking the Cut toolbar button. To select multiple files, hold down the Ctrl key and then click each file you want to select. To select a contiguous group of files, select the first file you want to be in the group, hold down the Shift key, and select the last file you want to include in the group. To select all the files in the folder, choose the Edit menu's Select All command or press Ctrl+A.

Copying Files and Folders

You can also copy a file or folder from one disk to another disk and from one folder to another folder. When you copy a file or folder, the original file or folder stays in its original location. The duplicate copy moves to another disk or folder. To copy a file or folder, follow these steps:

1 Open Windows Explorer, and double-click the disk that contains the file or folder you want to copy.

2 Double-click the folder that contains the file or subfolder you want to copy. Figure 4-13 shows the My Documents folder open.

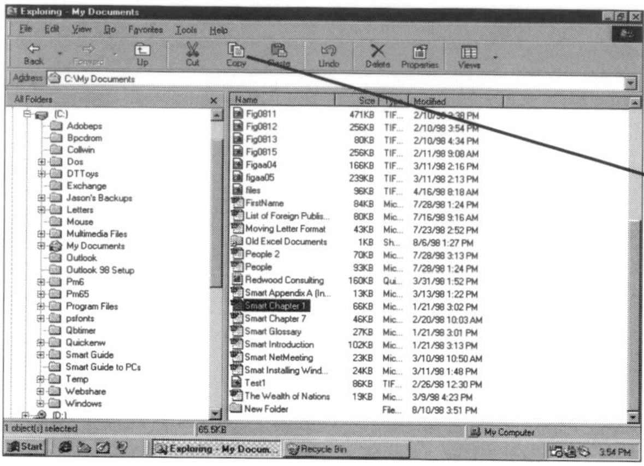

FIGURE 4-13

Windows Explorer showing the My Documents folder.

The Copy toolbar button.

3 Click the file or folder you want to copy to select it.

4 Click the Copy toolbar button.

5 Double-click the disk to which you want to move the duplicate file or folder.

6 Click the folder to which you want to move the duplicate file or folder.

7 Click the Paste toolbar button. Windows moves a copy of the file or folder from the source disk and folder to the destination disk and folder.

To copy several files or folders at once, select all the files or folders and then click the Copy button. As noted earlier, to select multiple files, hold down the Ctrl key and then click each file you want to select. To select a contiguous group of files, select the first file you want to be in the group, hold down the Shift key, and select the last file you want to include in the group. To select all the files in the folder, choose the Edit menu's Select All command or press Ctrl+A.

Finding Lost Files and Folders

Regardless of how carefully you organize and keep track of your files, sooner or later, you're bound to have difficulty locating that one file or folder you need. Luckily, Windows comes with a handy tool for locating lost files and folders. To find a lost file or folder, follow these steps:

1 Open Windows Explorer, and choose the Tools menu's Find command and the Find submenu's Files And Folders command. This opens the window shown in Figure 4-14.

FIGURE 4-14

The Find: All Files window in Windows 98.

You can also open the Find: All Files window from the Start menu by clicking the Start button, pointing to Find, and then clicking Files Or Folder.

2 Enter the name of the file or folder in the Named box. You don't need to enter the whole name if you aren't sure of it. Enter only the part you know. You can represent the character or characters you don't know using an asterisk as a **wildcard**. For example, let's say you have a picture of your pet bird Sam on your computer, but you don't remember if you named the file Sam or Sammy or Sam-bird. You can enter sam*. This reveals a list of all files that start with the letters sam.

The Named box is not case sensitive, so it doesn't matter if you type the name in uppercase or lowercase. If you want to make the Named box case sensitive, choose the Options menu's Case Sensitive command.

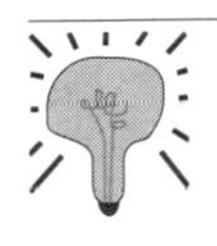

If you don't remember the name of the file you're looking for, click the Date tab to search for the file based on the date you created it, last saved it, or last worked on it. To search for a file based on file type or size, click the Advanced tab.

3 In the Look In drop-down list box, specify in which drive you want to search for the missing file or folder. (If you want to search only a specific folder in that drive, click Browse.)

4 Click Find Now. Windows begins searching the location you specified for a file or folder that meets your criteria. It displays any matches it finds in the list box at the bottom of the window, as shown in Figure 4-15.

FIGURE 4-15

Windows displays the results of a search.

5 If you see the file or folder you're looking for, click the Stop button to tell Windows to stop searching.

6 To open a file or folder, double-click it in the list.

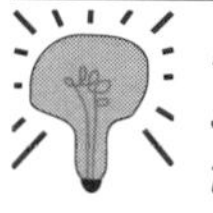

If you want to know where Windows found the file or folder, but can't see the complete pathname in the Find window, drag the bar between the In Folder and Size column headings at the top of the list box to the right.

Notes

To clear your search criteria and begin a new search, click New Search.

Sharing Information Among PCs

The earlier discussions in this chapter implicitly assume you're working with Windows on a stand-alone desktop or laptop PC. But I want to point out that all of the tasks discussed in this chapter apply to working on a **network** as well. A network is two or more computers that have been connected in a way that lets the people who use the computers share files, folders, drives, **printers**, and sometimes other hardware devices.

Using a Direct Cable Connection

A direct cable connection is the simplest type of network. Windows comes with an **accessory**, called Direct Cable Connection, that you can use to connect two computers, for instance, a laptop computer and a desktop computer. All you need is a cable to connect the two computers and a little time and patience. With the Direct Cable Connection accessory, you can quickly move or copy files between these two computers. A direct cable connection can be a little tricky to set up, however, so refer to online help in Windows or a good book on Windows for help.

Notes

If you find setting up or using the Direct Cable Connection that comes with Windows cumbersome, you might want to invest in another, more advanced and easier to set up program, such as LapLink, for connecting two computers.

Peer Networks

With a peer-to-peer network, you can connect several computers together and share several resources, such as drives and printers. If you want to regularly share information among several computers, you might want to set up a peer-to-peer network. A peer-to-peer network is handier than a direct cable connection because all computers can use programs such as Windows Explorer to easily work with the resources on the other computers. A peer-to-peer network isn't difficult to set up. All you need is some network cable and a piece of **hardware** called a network **adapter** that goes in each computer you want to connect. You can set up a peer-to-peer network for around $100 per computer. Figure 4-16 depicts how a peer-to-peer network might look.

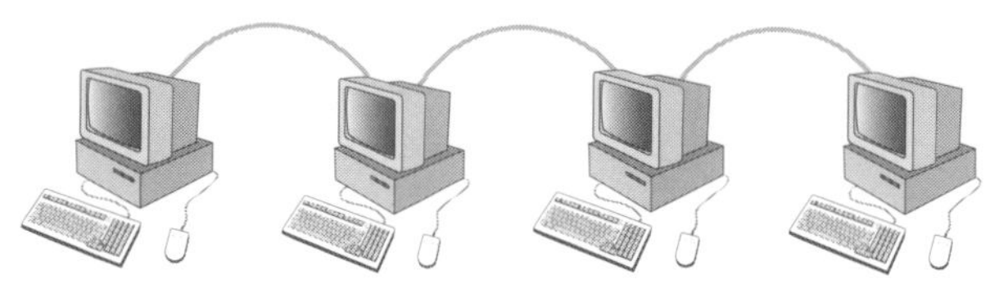

FIGURE 4-16

A peer-to-peer network.

Client/Server Networks

A client/server network differs from a peer-to-peer network in that in a client/server network, the computers have different roles (see Figure 4-17). A client/server network includes special computers (called **servers**) that basically run errands for and perform specific chores for the other computers (the clients). For example, a client/server network might include a server that does all of the work associated with printing documents. If you work on such a network and issue a command to print a document, your computer doesn't send the document to the printer—it dumps the document on the server's plate and asks the server to print it.

Client/server networks can be wonderfully powerful tools. And they allow people to do many types of tasks. For example, you need a client/server network with a designated mail server to send **e-mail** across a network. You also need a client/server network and a server in charge of the network to add security features and monitor **passwords** for the network. Note, however, that client/server networks are both challenging and expensive to operate. The hardware you need to set up a client/server network is the same as the hardware to set up a peer-to-peer network, but a client/server network requires additional special **software**—software that isn't cheap.

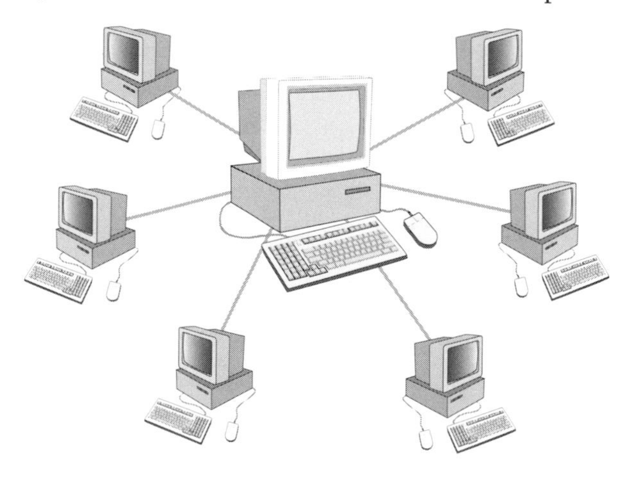

FIGURE 4-17

A representation of a client/server network.

Working with Files and Folders on a Network

To view the files, folders, and disks available to you through a peer-to-peer or client/server network, use the Network Neighborhood window (see Figure 4-18). To open this window, double-click the Network Neighborhood shortcut icon on the Windows desktop.

FIGURE 4-18

The Network Neighborhood window lets you view the other computers connected to the network.

You can open the Network Neighborhood window even if you're not on a network. However, you won't see any computers listed unless your computer connects to a network and you've logged on to the network.

Initially, each of the computers on your network appears in the Network Neighborhood window. Each computer on a network gets a name, as shown in Figure 4-18. On the little network in my office, for example, we have eight computers named Bob, Felix, Gopher, Lola, Montana, Rover, Vinnie, and Westpark. To see which disks a network computer lets you view, double-click the computer. Figure 4-19, for example, shows the only disk available on the network from the computer named Rover is its C disk.

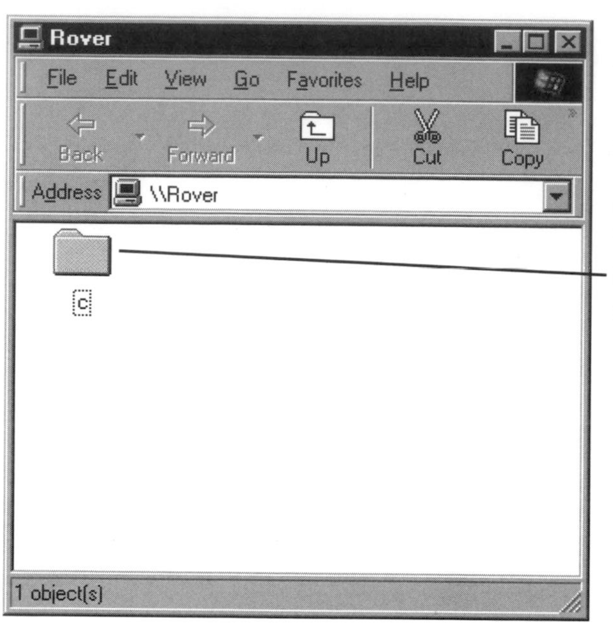

FIGURE 4-19

This Network Neighborhood window shows the computer disk that the networked computer named Rover will let you view.

Rover's shared C drive shows up as a folder.

The toolbar buttons in the Network Neighborhood window work the same way as those in Windows Explorer.

To see the folders and files that the C disk stores, double-click the C folder. Figure 4-20 shows the folders and files on C. Note that once you get to this Network Neighborhood window, you work with files and folders in the same manner as you work with files and folders on a local disk. (A local disk is just a computer disk that's inside the computer you're working on.)

FIGURE 4-20

This Network Neighborhood window shows the files and folders available on Rover's C disk.

You don't automatically get to do whatever you want with network disks. First of all, other people need to say it's okay to share their local disks in order to make them available to the network. And then, even after saying sharing is okay, what you can do over the network is usually limited. For example, you might be able to view a document or copy it, but you probably won't be able to delete it or rename it. If you have additional questions about how information sharing works on your network, consult the network administrator.

CHAPTER 5

Getting Your PC Just the Way You Like It

Microsoft Windows provides several ways in which you can customize your **PC** to fit your own individual needs and preferences. This chapter talks about how to use the tools that come with Windows to personalize your computing environment and includes the following topics:

- Changing your PC's date and time
- Changing your regional settings
- Customizing input devices
- Changing your PC's **folder** options
- Customizing a PC for people with disabilities
- Customizing the **Taskbar** and the Start menu
- Customizing the Quick Launch toolbar
- Customizing the StartUp menu
- Specifying a background for **windows** and the **desktop**
- Using an Active Desktop
- Using Desktop Themes
- Changing your display properties
- Using a **screen saver**

Changing Your PC's Date and Time

When you turn on your PC, it should have the correct date and time. But if these settings are ever incorrect, you can easily adjust your system clock to display the correct date and time. To change the date and time, follow these steps:

1 **Double-click** the clock on the right end of the Taskbar to display the Date/Time Properties **dialog box**, as shown in Figure 5-1.

FIGURE 5-1

The Date/Time Properties dialog box.

2. In the Date area, select the current month from the Month drop-down list box.
3. Select a year from the Year list box using the up and down arrows.
4. Click a date in the calendar to select it.
5. In the Time area, select the part of the time you want to change (the hour, minute, second, or AM/PM setting) and either type the correct setting or **click** the up and down arrows to change the setting.

The system clock keeps track of the date and time, even when power is off to your PC. The system clock remembers to add a day during leap years and even knows which day to spring ahead or fall back for daylight saving time.

6. Click OK to apply the new date and time and close the dialog box.

To change the time zone or to apply daylight saving time changes, follow these steps:

1. Double-click the clock on the right end of the Taskbar to display the Date/Time Properties dialog box.
2. Click the Time Zone tab, as shown in Figure 5-2.

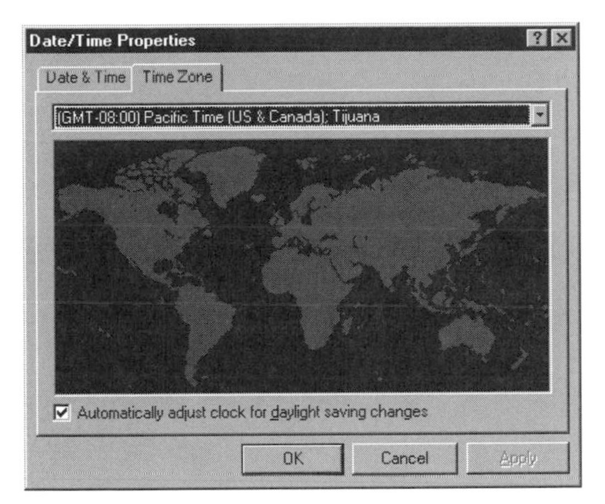

FIGURE 5-2

The Time Zone tab of the Date/Time Properties dialog box.

3 Select your location from the drop-down list box. For most locations, Windows already knows whether or not you observe daylight saving time. If the location you selected observes daylight saving time, Windows selects the Automatically Adjust Clock For Daylight Saving Changes check box. If this is incorrect, click the check box to clear it. If the location you selected doesn't observe daylight saving time, Windows grays out the check box at the bottom of the Time Zone tab.

4 Click OK to apply the new time zone and daylight saving time information.

Changing Your Regional Settings

You can change your PC's regional settings so Windows displays dates, numbers, and times the way you're used to seeing them. Many **programs** also make use of the regional settings you have selected. They not only display dates, numbers, and times the way you want, but they might also customize their dictionaries or offer special advice or features to users in your region.

To change your PC's regional settings, follow these steps:

1 Click the **Start button.**

2 Point to Settings.

3 Click **Control Panel** to open the Control Panel window, as shown in Figure 5-3.

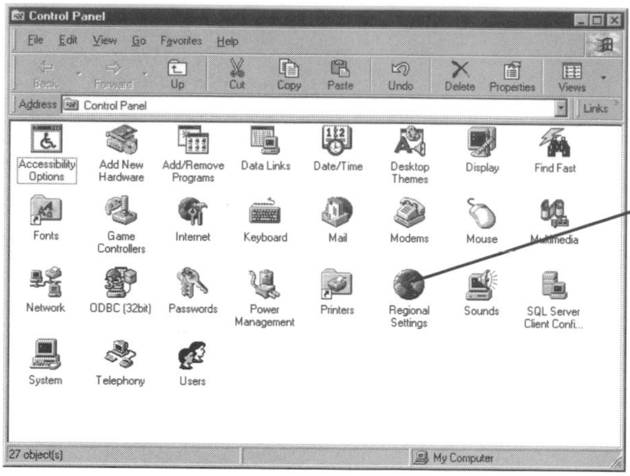

FIGURE 5-3

The Control Panel contains several tools that control the way your PC looks and works.

Regional settings.

4 Double-click the Regional Settings **icon** to display the Regional Settings Properties dialog box, as shown in Figure 5-4.

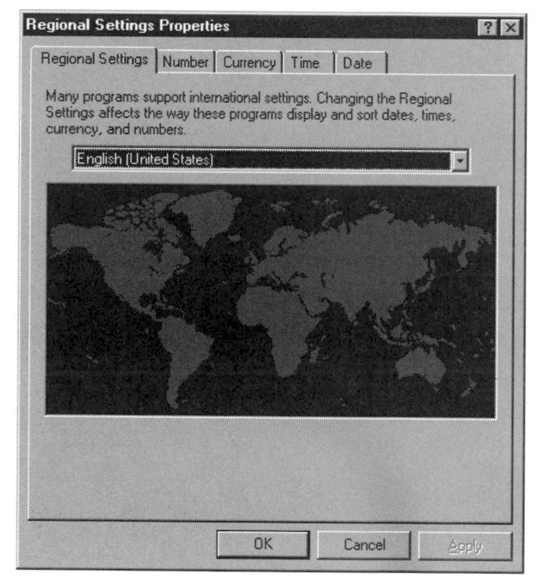

FIGURE 5-4

The Regional Settings dialog box.

5 Select the language you speak from the drop-down list box.

Notes *If the language you speak has more than one dialect, make sure you select the correct dialect.*

---

6 Click OK to apply the regional setting and close the dialog box. Windows then automatically adjusts the settings on the Number, Currency, Time, and Date tabs to reflect the standard preferences for your region.

You can manually adjust the settings in the following ways:

- Click the Number tab to specify the way decimals and negative numbers display, the way digits are grouped, the weight and measure system you use, and the symbol you use to separate items in a list.
- Click the Currency tab to specify the symbol your currency uses, where the symbol goes, how you want to express negative monetary amounts, how you want to use decimals for currency, and the way you want digits to group for currency amounts.
- Click the Time tab to tell Windows how many digits you want to use for clock displays, what symbol you want to use to separate hours from minutes, and how you want to express AM and PM.
- Click the Date tab to specify the calendar you use, which year you want your PC to use if you type in only two digits, and the shorthand and longhand ways you want your PC to display dates.

Customizing Input Devices

With Windows, you can customize the **keyboard** and the **mouse** so they work the way you want them to.

Customizing the Keyboard

Windows lets you customize the reaction time of the keyboard so it responds to your typing in the way you expect. Windows also lets you customize the layout of the keyboard for different types of keyboards (such as keyboards in languages other than English). To customize the keyboard, follow these steps:

1. Click the Start button.
2. Point to Settings.
3. Click Control Panel.
4. Double-click the Keyboard icon to display the Keyboard Properties dialog box, as shown in Figure 5-5.

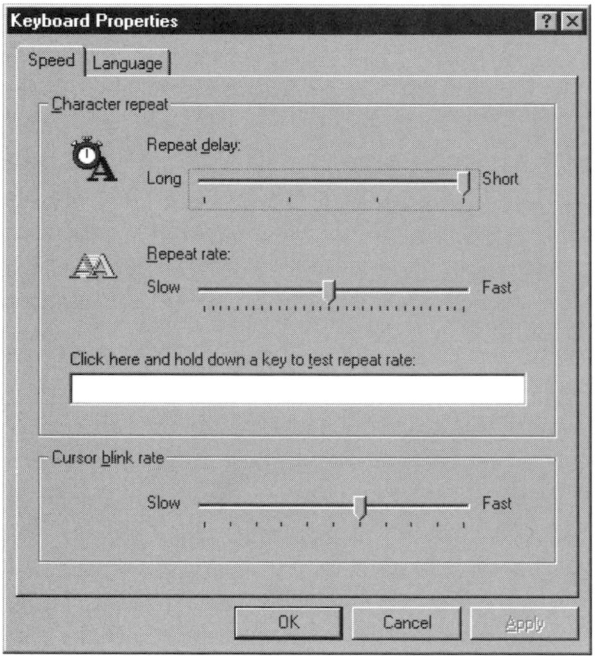

FIGURE 5-5

The Keyboard Properties dialog box.

5. **Drag** the Repeat Delay slider to tell Windows how long you want to hold down a key before it begins repeating the key.
6. Drag the Repeat Rate slider to tell Windows how fast you want it to repeat a character when you hold down a key.
7. Click the Test text box, and practice holding down a key to see whether you like the new settings.

8. Drag the **Cursor** Blink Rate slider to tell Windows how fast you want the cursor to blink.
9. To use a different type of keyboard with the PC, click the Language tab, as shown in Figure 5-6.

FIGURE 5-6

The Language tab of the Keyboard Properties dialog box.

10. To change the settings for your existing keyboard, click Properties.
11. Select a different keyboard layout from the drop-down list box, and click OK.
12. To add another keyboard, click Add.
13. Select the keyboard language from the drop-down list box, and click OK.
14. Insert your Windows CD, and click Apply.
15. Use the boxes and buttons at the bottom of the dialog box to set which language and keyboard layout you want to use by default, to describe how you want to switch keyboard layouts, and to specify whether you want the Taskbar to show which layout you're currently using.

Customizing the Mouse

Windows lets you customize the buttons, pointers, and speed of the mouse. To customize the mouse, follow these steps:

1. Click the Start button.
2. Point to Settings.
3. Click Control Panel.
4. Double-click the Mouse icon to display the Mouse Properties dialog box, as shown in Figure 5-7.

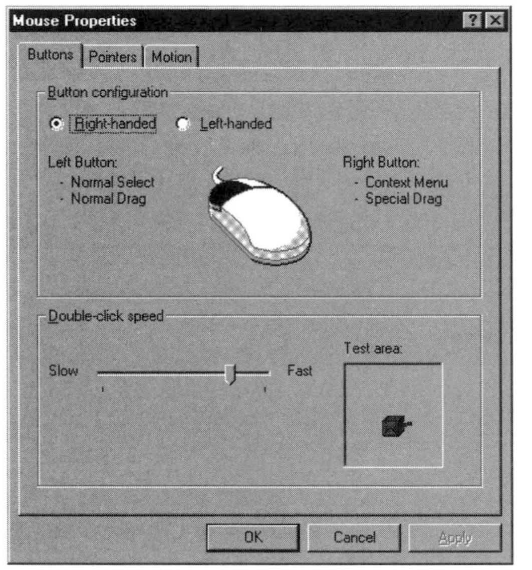

FIGURE 5-7

The Mouse Properties dialog box.

Notes

Figure 5-7 shows the dialog box for a generic mouse. If you have a special mouse, you might have more tabs that you can use for specifying options unique to that mouse. For example, you might have a tab for customizing the wheel or third button on your mouse or a tab for creating shortcuts to increase your productivity when using the mouse.

---

5. Click the Right-Handed or Left-Handed option button to tell Windows which mouse button you want to use for clicking.
6. Drag the Double-Click Speed slider to tell Windows how fast you want to click the mouse twice in a row in order for Windows to recognize it as a double-click.

7. Practice the new double-click speed by double-clicking the jack-in-the-box in the Test Area. If you don't like the new speed, drag the slider again and then double-click the jack-in-the-box to close him back in the box.
8. Click the Motion tab.
9. Drag the Pointer Speed slider to adjust the mouse's sensitivity to movement, as shown in Figure 5-8.

FIGURE 5-8

The Motion tab of the Mouse Properties dialog box.

10. Drag the Pointer Trail slider to adjust the length of the mouse pointer trail.

You probably don't want much, if any, of a mouse pointer trail. It just blurs the movement of the mouse on your screen so you can't tell its exact position.

Notes

If you're using desktop themes, the Mouse Properties dialog box includes a Settings tab that you can use to change the theme of the mouse.

Changing Your PC's Folder Options

Windows 98 and Internet Explorer 4 (or later) allow you to change the way you view and work with folders and icons. For instance, you can tell your PC to work like the **World Wide Web** so icons become **hyperlinks** that you click only once to open.

Specifying Web Style

To make your PC's folders and desktop look and work like the Web, follow these steps:

1. Click the Start button.
2. Point to Settings.
3. Click Folder Options to display the Folder Options dialog box, as shown in Figure 5-9.

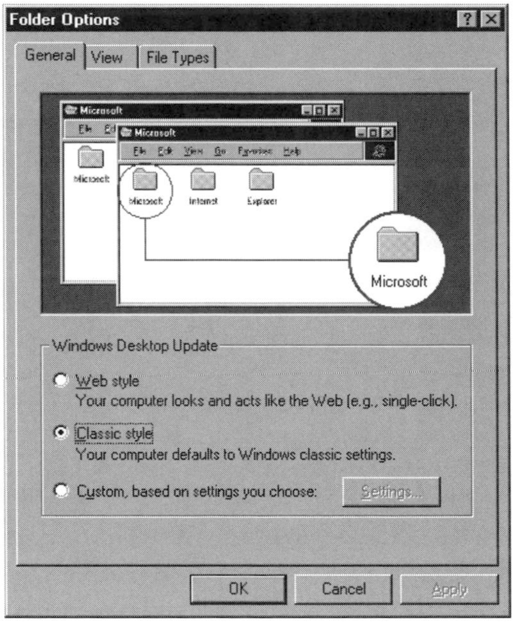

FIGURE 5-9

The Folder Options dialog box.

4 Click the Web Style option button to make working with your PC more like browsing the Web. When you choose this option, you need only point to objects in **Windows Explorer** or on the desktop to select them. (You don't need to click them.) To open the object you select, click it once instead of double-clicking it. With the Web Style option, you can also customize the look of folders as you display them, such as by using a **web page** as a background.

This book assumes you're using the Classic Style for working with your PC. If you decide to use the Web Style, you need to make a couple of mental notes. When this book describes tasks in Windows Explorer and on the desktop, you point to an object when this book says to click the object. And you click the object when this book says to double-click it.

5 Click OK.

Customizing a Folder

With Windows 98 or the Desktop Update feature in Internet Explorer 4 (or later), you can change the look of folders you display in Windows Explorer by adding background pictures or changing text color.

To customize the look of a folder, follow these steps:

1 Open Windows Explorer, and display the folder.

2 Choose the View **menu's** Customize This Folder command.

3 Click the Choose A Background Picture option button, and click Next to display the Customize This Folder dialog box, as shown in Figure 5-10.

*Although you can choose to create or edit an **HTML** document to change the appearance of your folder, don't choose this option unless you know HTML (the programming language used to create web pages).*

FIGURE 5-10

Selecting a picture to use as a background.

4 Select the picture you want to use as a background, or click Browse to locate a picture.

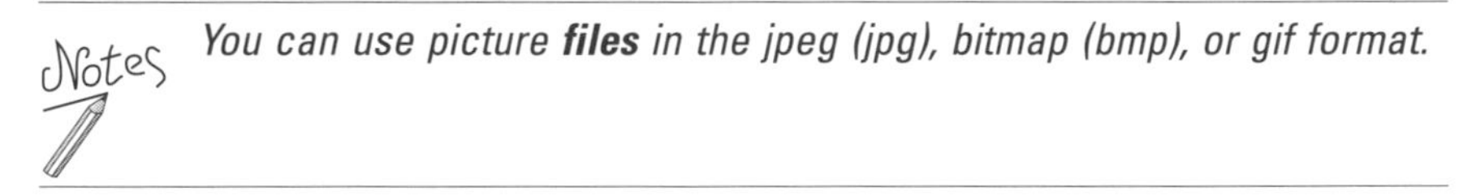

*You can use picture **files** in the jpeg (jpg), bitmap (bmp), or gif format.*

5 Click the Text button to open a color palette you can use to change the color of the text used to display file and folder names.

6 Click Next.

7 Click Finish. The folder displays with the new background, as shown in Figure 5-11.

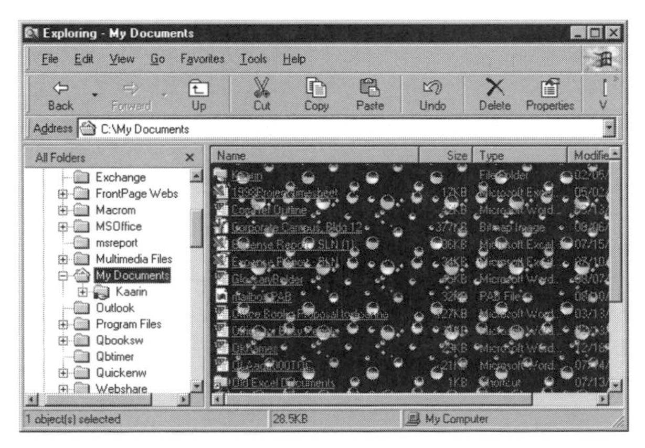

FIGURE 5-11

A customized folder.

After you customize the look of one folder, you can apply the new look to the rest of your folders. To do this, follow these steps:

1. Open Windows Explorer, and display the customized folder.
2. Choose the View menu's Folder Options command.
3. Click the View tab.
4. Click Like Current Folder to copy the design to your folders.
5. Click OK.

To reset all folders to their original appearance, click Reset All Folders in the Folder Options dialog box.

Customizing the Information that Windows Displays

Folder Options in Windows 98 and the Desktop Update feature of Internet Explorer 4 also allow you to customize the information you want to see when you work with Windows. For example, you can choose to hide or display your PC's system files and **file extensions** for the files it recognizes.

To specify view options in Windows, follow these steps:

1. Click the Start button.
2. Point to Settings.
3. Click Folder Options to display the Folder Options dialog box.
4. Click the View tab, as shown in Figure 5-12.

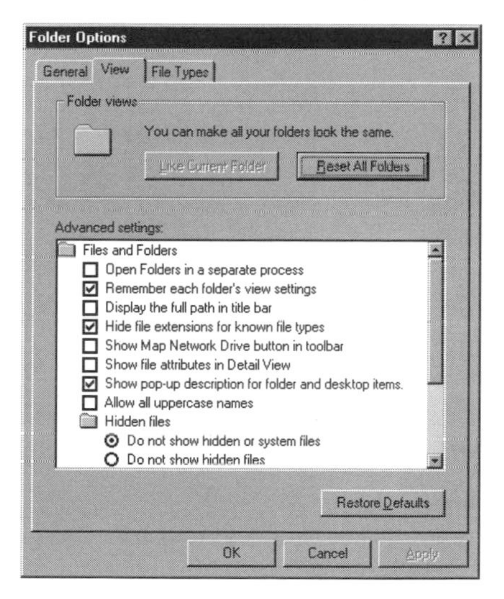

FIGURE 5-12

The View tab of the Folder Options dialog box.

5 Make your changes in the Advanced Settings list.

- Select the Display The Full Path In Title Bar check box if you frequently work with files that have the same name but are stored in different locations. This helps you keep track of which file you're currently working on.
- Clear the Hide File Extensions For Known File Types check box if you want to be able to view file extensions in Windows Explorer.
- Click one of the Hidden Files option buttons to tell Windows to display or hide the files you don't usually need to work with.

6 Click OK.

Notes *If you have a TrueType tab, this tab contains an option that lets you choose to display only TrueType **fonts** on your PC.*

Customizing a PC for People with Disabilities

Windows includes a variety of tools for customizing the computing environment for people with disabilities. Windows 98 includes the Accessibility Wizard, Microsoft Magnifier, and the Accessibility Options tool. Windows 95 also includes the Accessibility Options tool. The following section describes how to use these tools.

The Accessibility Wizard

The Windows 98 Accessibility Wizard guides you through the various adjustments you can make to your PC to make it better accommodate people with disabilities. To use the Accessibility Wizard, follow these steps:

1 Check to see whether you installed the Accessibility Wizard (which is really just a Windows **accessory**). Click the Start button, point to Programs, point to Accessories, and look for an Accessibility folder on the Accessories menu. If you see this folder, skip to step 9. If not, continue with the next step.

2 Click the Start button, point to Settings, and click Control Panel.

3 Double-click the Add/Remove Programs icon.
4 Click the Windows Setup tab.
5 Select Accessibility, and click Details.
6 Select both check boxes, insert your Windows 98 CD, and click OK twice.
7 Click the Start button.
8 Point to Programs, and point to Accessories.
9 Point to Accessibility, and click Accessibility Wizard.
10 Select the smallest text size you can read comfortably from the dialog box shown in Figure 5-13, and click Next twice.

FIGURE 5-13

The Accessibility Wizard.

11 In the next dialog box the wizard displays, select the options that describe your special needs. Select the I Want To Set Administrative Options button if more than one person works at the computer and you want to turn accessibility options on and off.
12 Go through the dialog boxes that the Accessibility Wizard displays to specify the accessibility settings you chose.
13 Click Finish when you reach the last dialog box to close the wizard and apply the new settings.

Microsoft Magnifier

Microsoft Magnifier allows you to magnify an area of your screen so you can better see what you're working on. Microsoft Magnifier comes with the Accessibility Wizard in Windows 98. To use Microsoft Magnifier, follow these steps:

1 Click the Start button, and point to Programs.
2 Point to Accessories, and point to Accessibility.
3 Click Microsoft Magnifier. This displays a special window at the top of your screen, as shown in Figure 5-14.

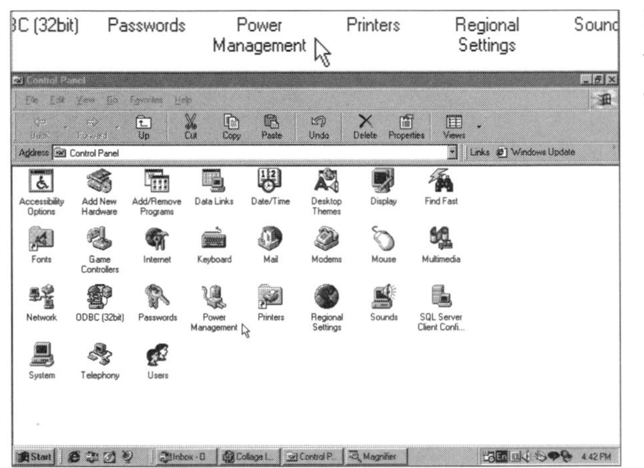

FIGURE 5-14

The Microsoft Magnifier window.

4 To magnify an area of your screen, move the mouse pointer to that area. The magnified area appears at the top of your screen in the Magnifier window.

The Accessibility Options Tool

Windows also comes with an Accessibility Options tool in the Control Panel. If you have Windows 95, you need to use this tool to set your accessibility options because you don't have the Accessibility Wizard. But even if you have Windows 98, you might prefer to use the Accessibility Options tool instead of the Accessibility Wizard. The tool provides less assistance, but it's quick to use for setting up the most common accessibility options. To use the Accessibility Options tool, follow these steps:

1 Click the Start button.

2 Point to Settings.

3 Click Control Panel.

4 Double-click the Accessibility Options icon to display the Accessibility Properties dialog box, as shown in Figure 5-15.

FIGURE 5-15

The Accessibility Properties dialog box.

5 Use the options on the Keyboard tab to specify your keyboard options. Enable StickyKeys if you have difficulty holding down two keys on the keyboard at once. Enable FilterKeys to reduce the sensitivity of the keyboard to brief touches or to keys held down too long. Enable ToggleKeys to hear a tone if Caps Lock or Num Lock are on.

6 Use the options on the Sound tab to have Windows display visual warnings to alert you to errors or to have programs display captions for speech and sound.

7 Use the options on the Display tab to make the fonts and colors Windows uses easier to read.

8 Use the options on the Mouse tab to tell Windows that you want to use the numeric keypad on your keyboard to move the mouse pointer.

9. Use the options on the General tab to specify how you want to turn the accessibility options on and off, or to install an alternate input device (something other than a mouse or keyboard).
10. Click OK.

Customizing the Taskbar and the Start Menu

You can customize the Taskbar and Start menu so they work best for you. For example, you can choose to hide the Taskbar so you have more room to see what you're working on. The Taskbar then pops up when you move the mouse pointer to the side of the screen where you last displayed it. You can also customize the Start menu to add or remove items or to clear the Documents menu.

The Taskbar

Windows lets you customize the Taskbar in a couple of ways. To customize the Taskbar, follow these steps:

1. Right-click a blank area of the Taskbar, and choose the shortcut menu's Properties command to display the Taskbar Properties dialog box, as shown in Figure 5-16.

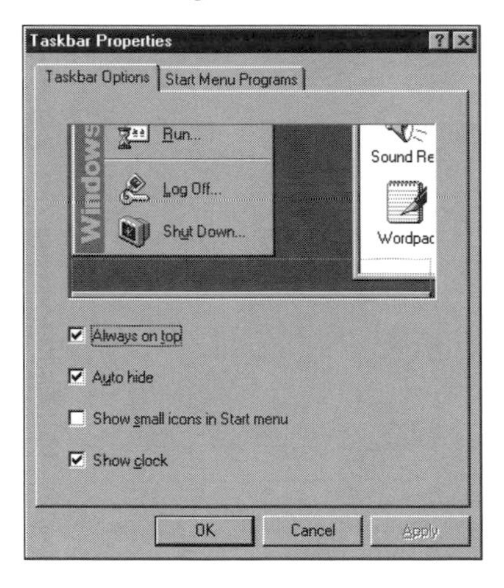

FIGURE 5-16

The Taskbar Properties dialog box.

2. Make sure the Always On Top check box is selected so you can still see the Taskbar when you maximize program windows.
3. Select the Auto Hide check box to make the Taskbar disappear unless you request it to come up by running the mouse pointer to the side of the screen where you lasted displayed it.

4. Select the Show Small Icons In Start Menu check box to use smaller icons on the main Start menu so the Start menu takes up less space on the screen.
5. Clear the Show Clock check box if you don't want to see the time as you work on your computer.
6. Observe the changes you made in the preview box.
7. Click OK to apply the changes and close the dialog box.

To move the Taskbar to a different edge of the screen, just drag it there. If you also use Auto Hide, you must run your mouse over that edge of the screen to redisplay the Taskbar.

The Start Menu

Windows lets you add shortcuts to the Start Menu so you can easily access the programs and tools you most frequently use. Windows also lets you clear the Documents menu to wipe the slate clean when you finish a project. To customize the Start menu, follow these steps:

1. Right-click a blank area of the Taskbar, and choose the shortcut menu's Properties command.
2. Click the Start Menu Programs tab, as shown in Figure 5-17.

FIGURE 5-17

The Start Menu Programs tab of the Taskbar Properties dialog box.

3. Click Add to add a program to the Start menu. Then, click Browse to locate the program. Select the program, click Open, and click Next. Then, select the folder in which you want to place the Start menu command, or click New Folder to create a new folder. Click Next. Enter the name for the way you want the program to appear on the Start menu, and click Finish.
4. To Remove a program from the Start menu, click Remove. Then select the command you want to remove from the Start menu, and click Remove and Close.

When you remove a program from the Start menu, you aren't removing it from your PC. You can still start the program in another way—such as by clicking its icon on the desktop or by double-clicking it in Windows Explorer. To remove a program from your computer, use the Add/Remove Programs tool as described in Chapter 10.

---

5. To clear the Documents menu of the **documents** you last worked on, click Clear.
6. Click OK.

Customizing the Quick Launch Toolbar

The Quick Launch toolbar is a handy tool you can use to quickly start the programs you use most.

You have the Quick Launch toolbar only if you're running Windows 98 or if you have Internet Explorer 4 or later installed. If you don't have Internet Explorer 4, see Chapter 7 for information on how to obtain and install it.

To customize the Quick Launch toolbar so it includes the buttons you need, follow these steps:

1. Open Windows Explorer.
2. Display the contents of the folder that contains the file for the program you want to add to the Quick Launch toolbar.

Many program files are stored in the Program Files folder or in one of its subfolders.

---

3 Click the plus sign next to your **hard disk's** icon in the folder list panc to display the folders on your hard disk.

4 Click the plus sign next to the Windows folder to display the **subfolders** contained in this folder.

5 Click the plus sign next to the Application Data folder.

6 Click the plus sign next to the Microsoft folder.

7 Click the plus sign next to the Internet Explorer folder. This displays a single folder, called Quick Launch.

8 Drag the program file to the Quick Launch folder in the folder pane.

9 Click the Quick Launch folder in the folder pane to display its contents, as shown in Figure 5-18.

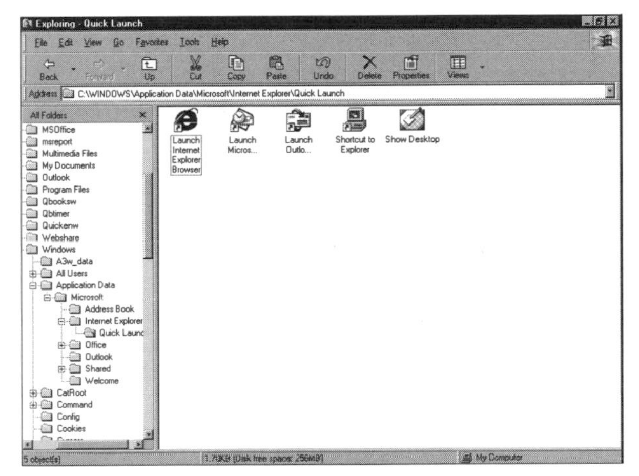

FIGURE 5-18

The contents of the Quick Launch folder.

10 To remove a Quick Launch button, select it and click the Delete **toolbar** button.

11 To rename a Quick Launch button, click it once, wait, and then click its name. Type a new name in the box, and press the Enter key.

If you've set up your computer for use by other people, each person can customize the Quick Launch toolbar. To work with your own Quick Launch toolbar, click the plus sign next to the Windows folder and the plus sign next to the Profiles folder. Then locate your profile, and continue with step 5.

Customizing the StartUp Menu

If you usually start the same programs every time you start Windows, you can tell Windows to automatically start these programs for you when you turn on your computer. To add a program to the StartUp menu, follow these steps:

1. Open Windows Explorer.
2. Display the contents of the folder that contains the program you want to start when you start Windows.
3. Click the plus sign next to your hard disk's icon in the folder list pane to display the folders on your hard disk.
4. Click the plus sign next to the Windows folder to display the subfolders contained in this folder.
5. Click the plus sign next to the Start Menu folder.
6. Click the plus sign next to the Programs folder.
7. Drag the program file you want to the StartUp folder in the folder pane.
8. Click the StartUp folder in the folder pane to display its contents, as shown in Figure 5-19.

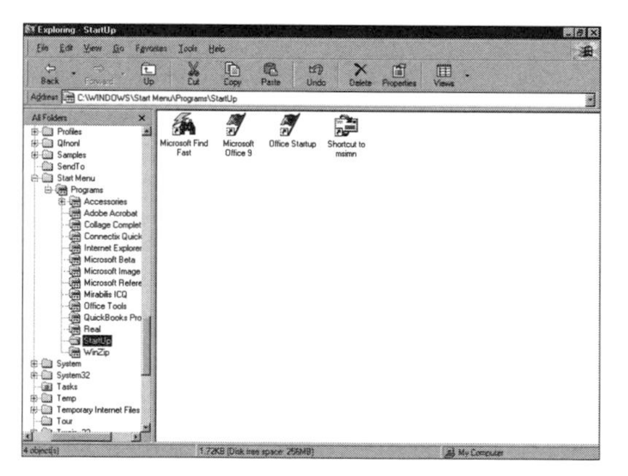

FIGURE 5-19

The contents of the StartUp folder.

9 To name the new StartUp shortcut, click it once, wait, and then click its name. Type a new name in the box, and press the Enter key.

Specifying a Background for Windows and the Desktop

Windows lets you wallpaper, paint, or add pictures to your desktop so it suits your style. For example, you might want to add a picture of your kids if you use your PC when you're away from home. To specify a background for your desktop, follow these steps:

1 Right-click a blank area of the desktop.

2 Choose the shortcut menu's Properties command to display the Display Properties dialog box, as shown in Figure 5-20.

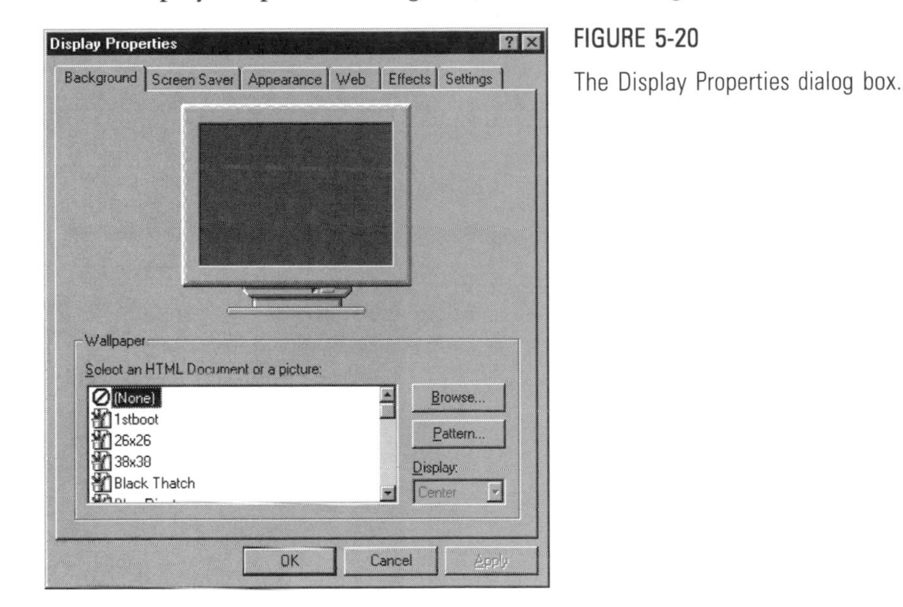

FIGURE 5-20

The Display Properties dialog box.

3 Select an HTML document or a picture from the list, or click Browse to locate an HTML document or picture you have saved on your computer.

You can preview how the document or picture will change the look of your screen by observing the picture of the ***monitor*** *on this tab.*

4. Select a layout for the picture from the Display drop-down list box. Select Center to center the picture in its original size in the middle of the screen. Select Tile to fill the entire screen with multiple copies of the picture. Select Stretch to stretch the single picture (regardless of its size) so it fills the entire screen.
5. If you choose to center the picture, click the Pattern box to specify a pattern you want to use as a frame around the picture.
6. Click OK.

Windows also lets you add pizzazz to program and document windows. You can tell Windows to display windows in your favorite colors and to display window names in wild and crazy fonts. To specify the look of windows, follow these steps:

1. Right-click a blank area of the desktop.
2. Choose the shortcut menu's Properties command to display the Display Properties dialog box.
3. Click the Appearance tab, as shown in Figure 5-21.

FIGURE 5-21

The Appearance tab of the Display Properties dialog box.

4 Select a scheme from the Scheme drop-down list box. A scheme is a design you apply to several window elements.
5 To change the look of an individual window item, select the item from the Item drop-down list box and use the Size, Color, and Font boxes to change the item's size, color, or font.

Notes

Which boxes you have available for changing the look of an item depends on the item you choose.

Desktop themes offer another way of applying a scheme, in this case a colorful and elaborate scheme that also includes a ***screen saver,*** *sounds, and mouse pointers. The "Desktop Themes" section later in this chapter describes how to install and add a desktop theme.*

Using an Active Desktop

Internet Explorer 4 or later and Windows 98 allow you to add web elements to your desktop. You can then have updated **Internet** content right there in front of you as you work. You can add active desktop items from two sources: from special **channel** web sites or from regular **web sites.** The way you add an Active Desktop item differs for these sources, so I describe each method in the following paragraphs. But before you can add Active Desktop items from any source, you first must specify that you want to use the Active Desktop. To do this, right-click a blank area of the desktop. Choose the shortcut menu's Active Desktop command and the Active Desktop submenu's View As Web Page command.

Chapter 7 describes channel web sites and how to work with them in more detail.

Notes

To use the Active Desktop, you must have Windows 98 or Internet Explorer 4 (or later) on Windows 95. You must also have an Internet connection set up. For help with Internet Explorer or an Internet connection, refer to Chapter 7.

Adding Active Desktop Items from Channel Web Sites

To add an Active Desktop item from a channel, follow these steps:

1. Click the Channel Guide button on the Internet Explorer Channel Bar on your desktop, or click the Channel Guide button on the Quick Launch toolbar.
2. Click Active Desktop Items on the web page that Internet Explorer displays.
3. If a site in the list on the left looks interesting, click that site's button. Otherwise you can search for a site, as shown in Figure 5-22.

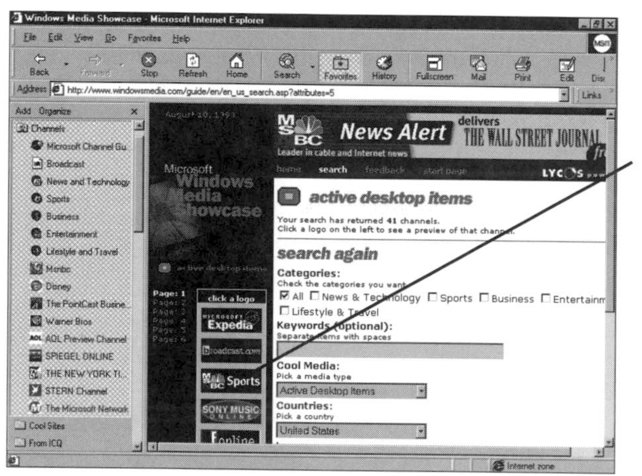

FIGURE 5-22

Using Active Desktop Items from channels.

Click a logo to preview a channel.

- Check a category box to see only channels with desktop items in that category.
- Enter a keyword to search for a channel that is related to that word.
- If you're looking for a desktop item from another country or in another language, select a country from the Countries drop-down list box or a language from the Languages drop-down list box.
- Click the Search button.
- When Internet Explorer displays a list of the channel sites that meet your specifications, click a site's logo to display the site.

4. Click the Visit Active Channel button to preview the channel.
5. Click the Add To Active Desktop button.
6. Click Yes in the message box that Internet Explorer displays.
7. Click OK to accept the schedule at which the desktop item updates.

Adding Other Active Desktop Items

To add an item from any other web site, follow these steps:

1. Open Internet Explorer, and display the web page containing the item you want to add to your desktop.
2. Right-click the item, and choose the shortcut menu's Set As Desktop Item command.
3. Click OK when Internet Explorer displays the message box shown in Figure 5-23.

FIGURE 5-23

Adding a desktop item from a regular web page.

4. Click OK.

Working with the Active Desktop

To customize the Active Desktop after you add web items, right-click a blank area of the desktop. Choose the shortcut menu's Active Desktop command and the Active Desktop submenu's Customize My Desktop command to display the Web tab of the Display Properties dialog box, as shown in Figure 5-24.

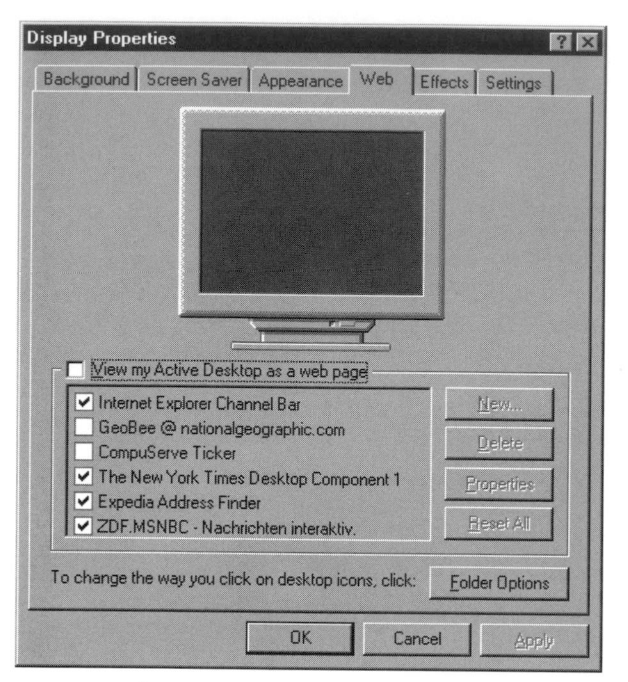

FIGURE 5-24

The Web tab of the Display Properties dialog box.

Select the check boxes for the Active Desktop items you want to display, and clear the check boxes for those items you do not want to display. To delete items you no longer want, select them and click Delete.

When you add Active Desktop items, you tell Internet Explorer to automatically update them so you don't have to. However, you can manually update Active Desktop items if you want. To do so, right-click a blank area of the desktop and choose the shortcut menu's Active Desktop command. Then choose the Active Desktop submenu's Update Now command.

To view an Active Desktop item's schedule for updating, click the down arrow in the upper-left corner of the item and choose the menu's Properties command. Then click the Schedule tab, and use its boxes and buttons to review or change the update schedule. Click the Download tab, and use its boxes and buttons to tell Internet Explorer what you want it to retrieve when it updates the item.

Using Desktop Themes

Windows 98 and the Plus! package that goes with Windows 95 include a feature called Desktop Themes. With Desktop Themes, you can customize your desktop background, the icons on your desktop, and even the sounds your computer makes so they all fit a theme. Windows 98 and Plus! for Windows 95 have several themes you can choose from, ranging from a science theme to a baseball theme to a tie-dye theme.

To apply a desktop theme to your computer, follow these steps:

1. Check to see whether you installed Desktop Themes. Click the Start button, point to Settings, and click Control Panel. If you see a Desktop Themes icon in the Control Panel window, skip to step 8. If not, continue with the next step.

Notes

*Although Desktop Themes make working at the computer a lot of fun, they also take up a lot of space on your hard disk. So if **disk** space on your PC is at a premium, you probably don't want to install Desktop Themes.*

2. Click the Start button, point to Settings, and click Control Panel.
3. Double-click the Add/Remove Programs icon.
4. Click the Windows Setup tab.
5. Select the Desktop Themes check box in the list of components.
6. Insert your Windows 98 or Plus! for Windows 95 CD-ROM, and click OK. (Close the CD-ROM's dialog box if it displays automatically.
7. Choose the View menu's Refresh command in the Control Panel.
8. Double-click the Desktop Themes icon to display the Desktop Themes window, as shown in Figure 5-25.

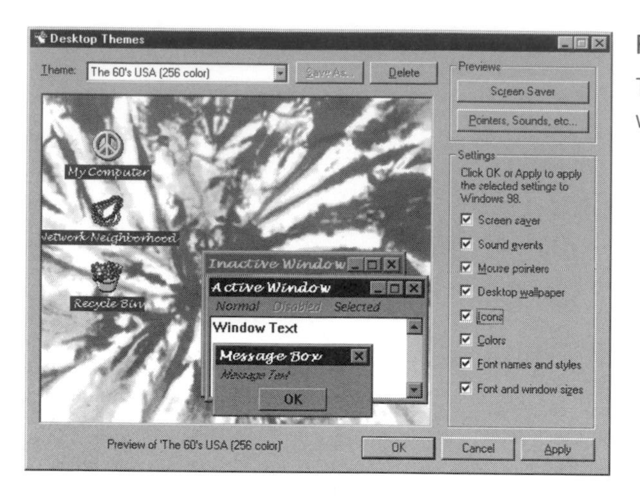

FIGURE 5-25

The Desktop Themes window.

9. Select a theme that intrigues you from the Theme drop-down list box. The theme's desktop is displayed in the Preview area.
10. Click Screen Saver to preview the theme's screen saver. Move the mouse to return to the Desktop Themes window.
11. Click Pointer, Sounds, Etc. to display the Preview dialog box, as shown in Figure 5-26.

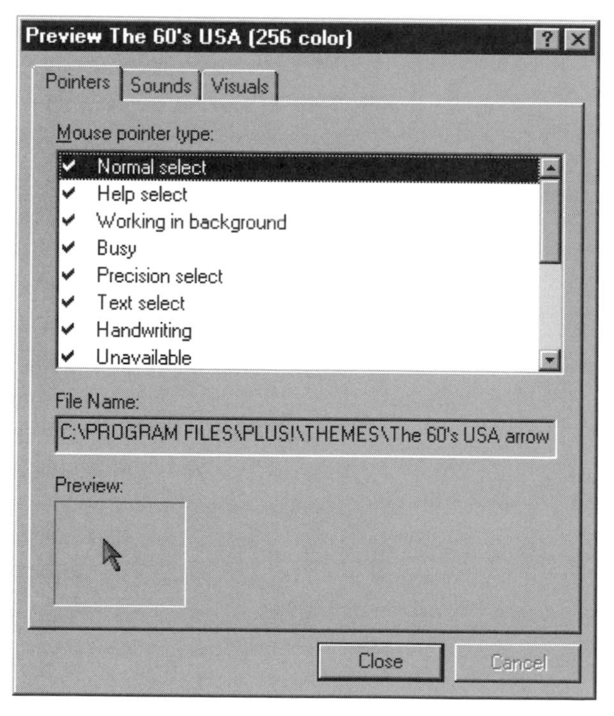

FIGURE 5-26

Use this dialog box to preview the theme's pointers and sounds.

12 Select an item from the Mouse Pointer Type list to view the mouse pointer in the Preview area.

13 Click the Sounds tab.

14 Select an event from the Sound Event list, and click the arrow next to the Icon box to hear the sound for that event.

15 Click the Close button.

16 Click OK in the Desktop Themes window to close the window and apply the theme.

Changing Your Display Properties

Windows also allows you to change the display properties of your monitor so you can see more or fewer colors and objects on your screen. To change your monitor's display properties, follow these steps:

1 Right-click a blank area of the desktop.

2 Choose the shortcut menu's Properties command to display the Display Properties dialog box.

3 Click the Settings tab, as shown in Figure 5-27.

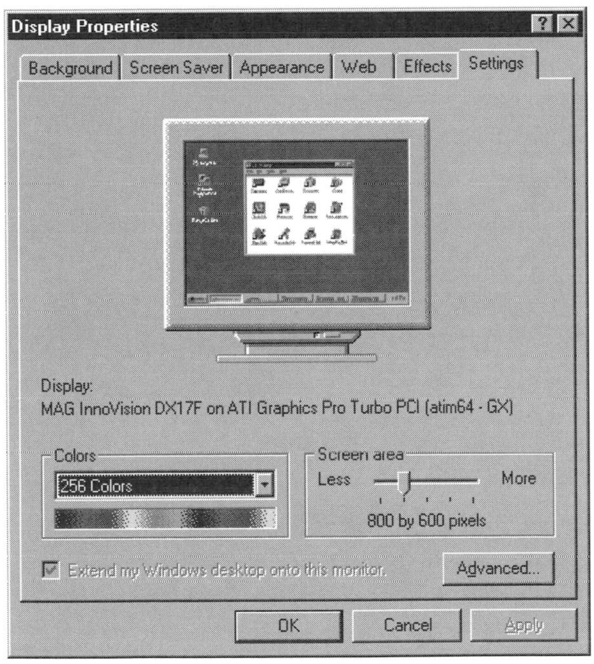

FIGURE 5-27

The Settings tab of the Display Properties dialog box.

4. Select the number of color variations you want your monitor to display from the Colors drop-down list box. The number of colors increases as you go down the list.

*You probably don't want to use 16 colors because your display won't look very good. You also probably won't be able to tell much difference between 16-**bit**, 24-bit, and 32-bit color.*

5. Drag the Screen Area slider to the left to make objects on your screen larger or to the right to make them smaller. By decreasing the screen area, you can better see what's on your screen, but you can't fit as much on your screen. By increasing the screen area, you can fit more on your screen (so you have to scroll less), but the reduced size of screen objects often makes the objects difficult to read.
6. Click OK.

Using a Screen Saver

A screen saver is a moving pattern or picture that's displayed to spice up your screen when your computer's idle. Windows comes with a variety of screen savers, or you can purchase or **download** other screen savers. To use a Windows screen saver, follow these steps:

1. Right-click a blank area of the desktop, and choose the shortcut menu's Properties command to display the Display Properties dialog box.
2. Click the Screen Saver tab, as shown in Figure 5-28.

FIGURE 5-28

The Screen Saver tab of the Display Properties dialog box.

3 Select a screen saver from the Screen Saver drop-down list box.

4 Click Settings to display a dialog box that lets you describe in detail how you want the screen saver to work.

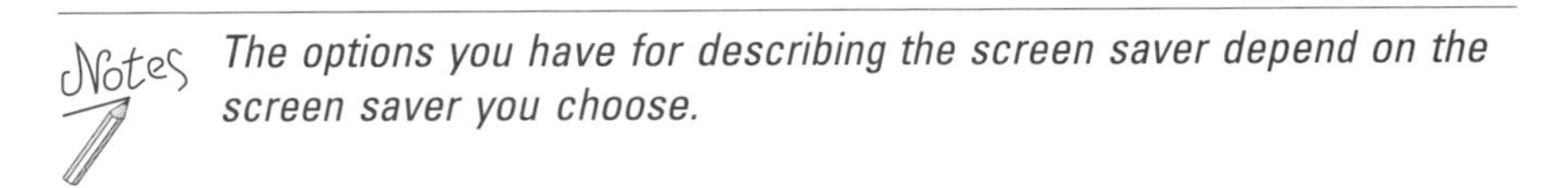

The options you have for describing the screen saver depend on the screen saver you choose.

5 Click Preview to preview the screen saver.

6 Select the Password protected check box if you want a person to have to log on after the screen saver displays.

7 Enter a number in the Wait box to describe how long you want the computer to sit idle before the screen saver comes on.

8 If available, use the energy savings options to limit the energy consumption of your monitor.

9 Click OK.

CHAPTER 6

Common Program Tasks

Programs help you accomplish the tasks you need to complete with your computer. You might sometimes use the programs that come with **Microsoft Windows**, and you will most likely use other, more advanced programs that either came with your **PC** or that you purchased separately. This chapter describes how you perform the following primary tasks that are common to almost all programs:

- Starting programs
- Creating new **files**
- Opening files
- Displaying files
- Sharing information between files and programs
- Correcting mistakes
- Saving files
- Printing files
- Closing files
- Exiting programs

Starting Programs

Most programs, regardless of whether they came with Windows or whether you purchased or obtained them separately, start in the same way. To start a program, follow these steps:

1. **Click the Start button.**
2. Point to Programs to display a list of the programs you have on your computer, as shown in Figure 6-1.

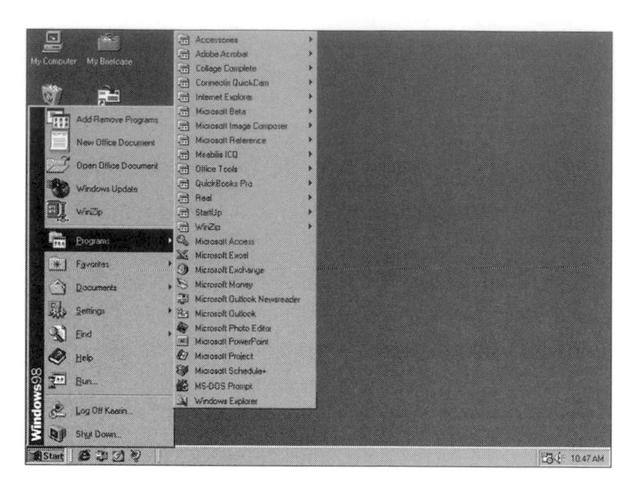

FIGURE 6-1

The Programs menu.

3 Click the program you want to start on the Programs menu.

Notes *If the program is a Windows **accessory**, it is listed under the Accessories folder. To display the Accessories folder, point to Accessories. If the program doesn't appear directly on the Accessories menu, it might be located under one of the Accessories subfolders. Click the subfolder to display its contents.*

Notes *Sometimes when you purchase a program, the program actually comes as a set with other programs. When this is the case, the program you're looking for might not appear directly on the Programs menu, but instead in a folder on the Programs menu. The folder might bear the name of the **software** manufacturer.*

You can also start some programs in two other, faster ways. You can start many programs by **double-clicking** their **icons** on the **desktop**, as shown in Figure 6-2. Not all programs automatically create desktop icons when you install them, but some do. And you can also start some programs by clicking their buttons on the Quick Launch toolbar, which is located next to the Start button.

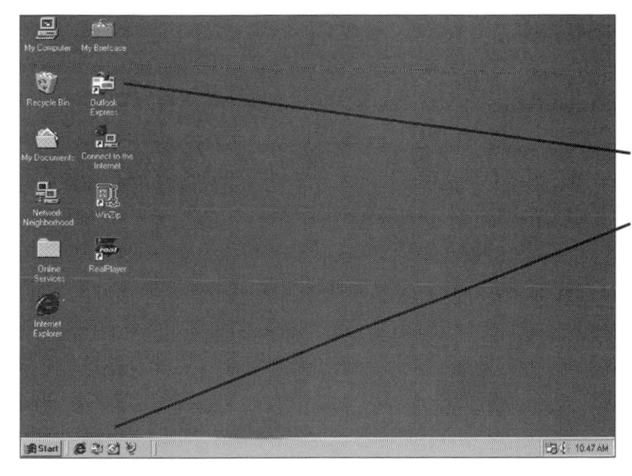

FIGURE 6-2

The quickest ways to start programs.

Double-click an icon on the desktop.

Click a Quick Launch toolbar button.

Notes *Chapter 5 describes how to create buttons on the Quick Launch toolbar.*

Creating New Files

Sometimes, as soon as you start a program, the program creates a new file for you. Other times, you must tell it that you want to create a new file. To create a new file in most programs, choose the File **menu's** New command. Often, when you choose this command, the program displays a **dialog box** in which you specify the type of file you want to create. For example, WordPad displays the dialog box shown in Figure 6-3 when you choose the File menu's New command.

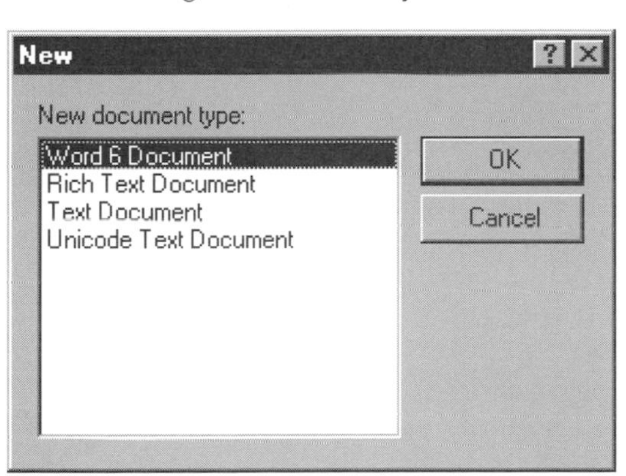

FIGURE 6-3

The New dialog box in WordPad.

New dialog boxes for other programs often allow you to select the template upon which you want to base your new file. A template is a file that contains formatting, blocks of stock text, or predesigned elements.

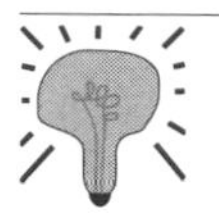

*Some programs include a button on the **toolbar** for creating a new file. This button usually creates the default type of file based on the default template.*

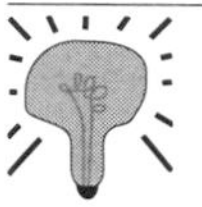

Some programs require you to further define the new file you want to create before you create it. Often, such programs display a dialog box or a series of dialog boxes in which you describe the specifications of the file you want to create.

Opening Files

Chapter 2 described how to open files from the Documents menu after clicking the Start button, and Chapter 4 described how to open files using **Windows Explorer.** But there is a third way to open files. You can also open files from within programs. To do this, choose the File menu's Open command. Doing so displays a dialog box similar to the one shown in Figure 6-4.

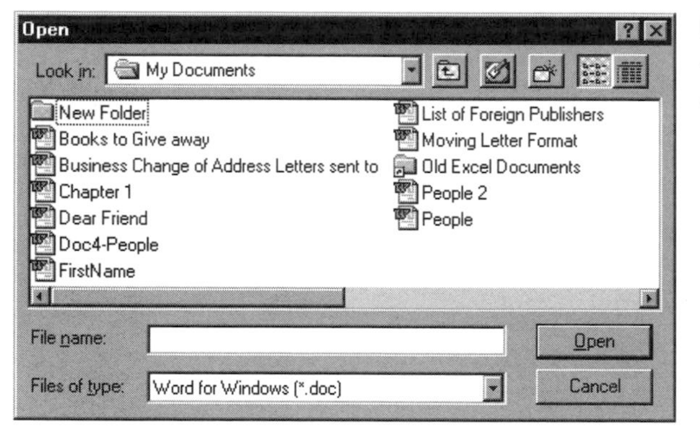

FIGURE 6-4

The Open dialog box in WordPad.

To use this dialog box, follow these steps:

1 Select the **disk** that contains the file you want to open from the Look In drop-down list box.

2 Locate the **folder** that contains the file you want to open in the large list box. Double-click the folder to view its contents.

You might need to repeat step 2 if the file you want to open is stored in a ***subfolder*** *of another folder.*

3 Click the file you want to open to select it.

4 Click Open.

If you have a lot of files in a folder and you're having difficulty locating the file you want to open, use the Files Of Type drop-down list box to display only files of the type you want to open.

If you accidentally try to open a file you already have open, the program might ask if you want to revert to the saved version of the file. To avoid losing the changes you've made to the file, click No.

Displaying Files

Sometimes when you have a file open, you still can't see it. This frequently happens when you open more than one file in a program. To display files that you have open (but not on top), use the program's Window menu. The Window menu lists the files you have open in that program. It also lists commands you can use to display more than one file in the program at once. To display a different file in the program, click the file's name. To display several files at once in the program, use one of the Window menu's commands for arranging or tiling the **windows.** Figure 6-5 shows two open files and the Window menu in the Microsoft Word program.

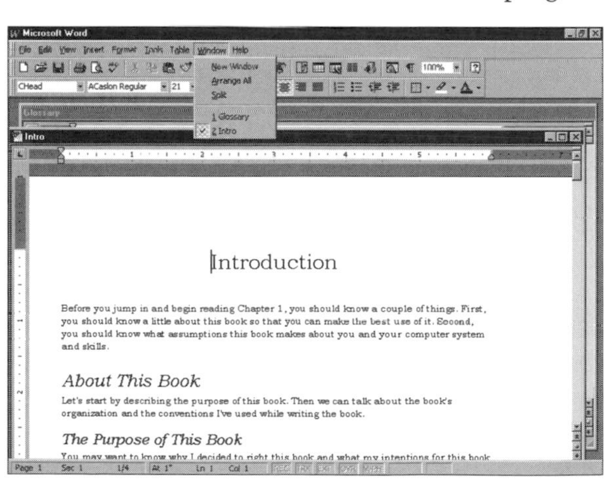

FIGURE 6-5

Displaying files in a program.

If you can see any part of a file's window on your screen, click anywhere within that window to display the file on top.

Sharing Information Between Programs and Files

With Windows, you can easily share information between different files. You can even share information between files created in different programs. The Windows **Clipboard** allows you to do this. The Clipboard holds information you place on it until you place something else on it or turn off your computer. With the Clipboard, you can accomplish three tasks for information sharing: cutting, copying, and pasting.

Cutting and Pasting

To move some object—an image, a block of text, or a table of numbers, for example—from one place to another, you use a technique called cutting and pasting. When you cut an object, you delete the object from its original location. Then you paste the object to place it in its new location. To cut and paste an object, follow these steps.

1 Open the file containing the object you want to cut. This file is called the source file.

2 Select the object you want to cut. In this example, it is a block of text.

Chapter 2 describes keyboard and mouse techniques for selecting different types of objects.

3 Choose the Edit menu's Cut command, as shown in Figure 6-6.

FIGURE 6-6

Cutting text in WordPad.

Notes: *Some programs might not have an Edit menu or a Cut command on that menu. Often, the Cut command changes names depending on what you have selected to cut. For example, if you want to cut an image, the menu command might be called Cut Image.*

4 Open the file into which you want to place the object. This file is called the destination file. (If you're cutting and pasting an object within a single document, you don't need to open a second file. The source file and the destination file are one and the same.)

Notes: *If the destination file is of the same type as the source file, you can open the destination file from the program, as described earlier in this chapter. If the destination file was created in another program, you need to start the other program. You can do this from the Start menu if you don't have the other program open already. Or if you've worked with the destination file recently, you might be able to open it from the Documents menu.*

5 Click the **mouse** to place the **cursor** where you want to paste the object.

6 Choose the Edit menu's Paste command.

Many programs have another command for pasting, called something like Paste Special. You can use the Paste Special command to specify the formatting of the object you cut and how you want the object pasted, for example, as a ***hyperlink.***

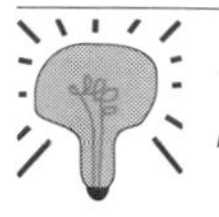

Many programs include buttons on the toolbar that you can use in place of menu commands for cutting and pasting. The button for cutting usually looks like a pair of scissors and is frequently called Cut. The button for pasting usually looks like a piece of paper on a clipboard and is frequently called Paste.

Another handy Windows technique for cutting is using **keyboard** shortcuts. Keyboard shortcuts accomplish the same thing as using the Edit menu's Cut command or the Cut toolbar button. But keyboard shortcuts are often available when no other Cut option is, for example, in dialog boxes. To use the keyboard shortcuts for cutting, select information you want to cut and then hold down the Ctrl key and press the letter X key (Ctrl+X). To paste information you've cut, hold down the Ctrl key and press the V key (Ctrl+V).

Copying and Pasting

Another technique for transferring objects from one file to another is by copying. When you copy an object, you leave the object in its original location and insert a copy of the object in the new location as well. To copy an object from one file to another, follow these steps:

1. Open the file containing the object you want to copy. This file is called the source file.
2. Select the object you want to copy. In this example, it is a block of text.
3. Choose the Edit menu's Copy command, as shown in Figure 6-7. Or press the keyboard shortcut keys Ctrl+C.

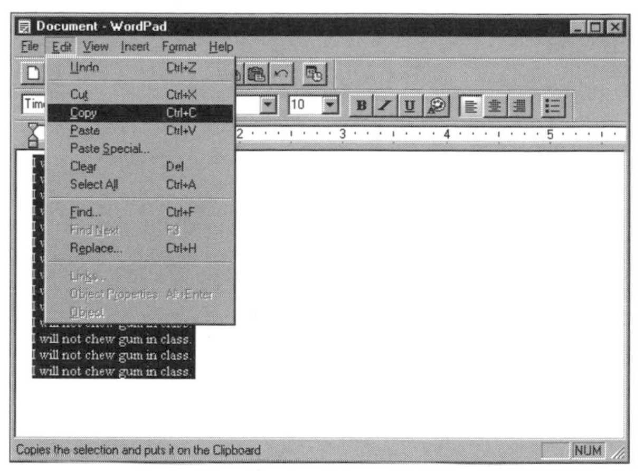

FIGURE 6-7

Copying text in WordPad.

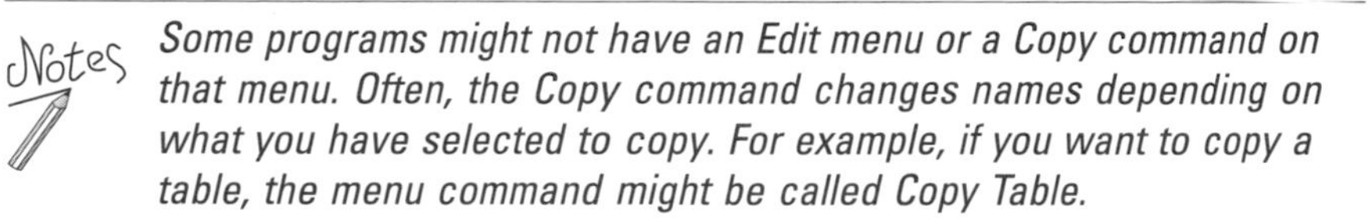

Some programs might not have an Edit menu or a Copy command on that menu. Often, the Copy command changes names depending on what you have selected to copy. For example, if you want to copy a table, the menu command might be called Copy Table.

4 Open the file into which you want to place the object. This file is called the destination file.

If you want to copy an object within a single file, you don't need to open a second file. The source file and the destination file are one and the same.

5 Click the mouse to place the cursor where you want to paste the object.

6 Choose the Edit menu's Paste command.

Many programs have another command for pasting, called something like Paste Special. You can use the Paste Special command to specify the formatting of the object and how you want the object pasted, for example, as a picture that floats over existing text.

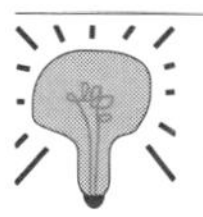

Many programs include buttons on the toolbar that you can use in place of menu commands for copying and pasting. The button for copying often looks like two loose pieces of paper and is frequently named Copy. The button for pasting often looks like a piece of paper on a clipboard and is frequently named Paste.

Importing and Exporting

If you want to work with a file using a program different from the one you used to create it, you often need to go through a two-step process of exporting and importing. Exporting a file means saving it in a format that another program can read. Importing a file means converting it from the common format. By exporting and importing a file, you can, for example, take a report you created using an accounting program and work with it in a **spreadsheet** program.

*The need to import and export commonly arises when you want to share information with people who use **operating systems** or programs that are different from yours. For example, you might want to share a file with someone using a Mac or a **word processor** that's different from yours.*

To export a file in one program and import it in another, follow these steps:

1. Open the file you want to work with in another program.
2. Choose the File menu's Save As command to display a dialog box similar to the one shown in Figure 6-8.

FIGURE 6-8

The Save As dialog box in WordPad.

Some programs have a special command on the File menu specifically for exporting. Usually, this command is named something like Export.

3. Specify the way you want to save the file in the Save As Type drop-down list box. For example, if you want to save a file so you can open it and work with it on a Mac, save the file in a Mac format.

Different programs have different file types available.

4. Optionally, specify a new location for storing the file. Click the down arrow in the Save In drop-down list box to display a list of the **drives** on your PC. Select the drive that contains the disk on which you want to save the file.
5. Locate the folder in which you want to save the file in the large list box, and double-click it.

If this is the first time you're saving the file, you need to also specify a filename using the File Name box. For more information on choosing a filename, see the "Saving Files" section later in this chapter.

6. Click Save.
7. Start the program you want to use to work with the file.
8. Choose the File menu's Open command to display a dialog box similar to the one shown in Figure 6-9. Use this dialog box to locate the file you want to import.

FIGURE 6-9

The Open dialog box in Microsoft Excel.

See the "Opening Files" section earlier in this chapter for more information on how to work with the Open dialog box.

9. Specify the type of file you're looking for in the Files Of Type drop-down list box.
10. Select the file, and click Open. The program might take you through a wizard to help you convert the file format.

Correcting Mistakes

No matter how careful you are, chances are that you'll make a mistake as you edit a file. Maybe you'll accidentally delete a paragraph you wanted to keep or click a formatting button and boldface or italicize text you didn't intend to. Luckily, correcting, or "undoing," a mistake is really easy in most programs. To undo the last change you made, choose the Edit menu's Undo command. Most programs also come with an Undo button on the toolbar. The Undo toolbar button usually looks like a curved arrow pointing to the left, as shown in Figure 6-10. Some programs keep track of a long list of the changes you make to a file. They then allow you to click the Undo toolbar button more than once to reverse several changes, starting with the change you last made.

Notes

Not all programs have an Edit menu with an Undo command. You might need to search the menus to find this command. The command might also change names depending on the change you last made to a file. For example, if you last changed the file by typing a sentence, the command might be named Undo Typing. If you last changed the file by formatting text, the command might be named Undo Formatting.

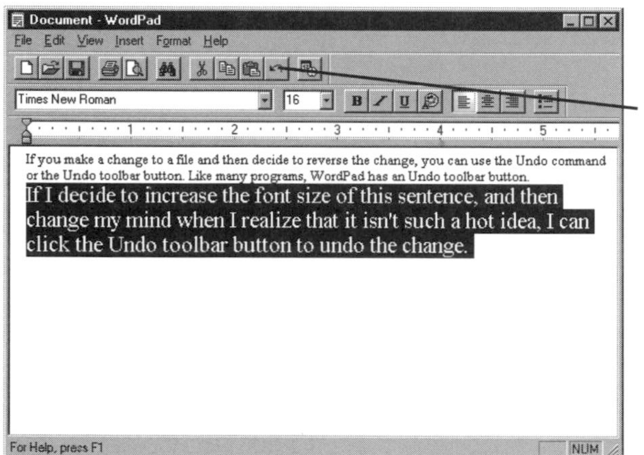

FIGURE 6-10

Undoing changes.

The Undo toolbar button.

In some programs, the Undo toolbar button might have a down arrow next to it. If you click this arrow, a list of the last changes you made to the file appears. You can then select from the list a number of changes to undo.

If no Undo command or toolbar button is available (for instance, if you're working in a dialog box), you can use a Windows keyboard shortcut to undo the last change you made. To do this, hold down the Ctrl key and press the Z key (Ctrl+Z).

If you accidentally reverse a change you didn't want to undo, you can reinstate the change by choosing the Edit menu's Repeat command or by clicking the Redo button on the toolbar. (The Redo toolbar button often looks like a curved arrow pointing to the right.) As with the Undo command, not all programs have Redo or Repeat commands, so you might have to search the menus available in the program.

Saving Files

Most programs don't save files after every change you make. Instead, many programs automatically save files periodically, say, every 10 minutes or so. However, you should save what you're working on periodically as well, just in case the program doesn't save it for you. It's a good idea to save a file at least every half hour. Then if the power should go out, or if your program or computer should **crash,** the most you lose is a half hour's work. When you're finished working on a file, most programs require you to save the file in order to keep your last changes. If you attempt to close a file without saving it, most programs prompt you to save the file.

To save a file, follow these steps:

1. Choose the File menu's Save command.

If you've saved the file before, choosing the File menu's Save command resaves the file with your changes. To keep the old copy of the file, you need to save the revised file under a new name by choosing the File menu's Save As command.

2. If this is the first time you've saved the file, the program displays a dialog box similar to the one shown in Figure 6-11. You use this dialog box to name the file, specify a file type, and choose a place to store the file.

FIGURE 6-11

The Save As dialog box.

3. Click the down arrow in the Save In drop-down list box to display a list of the drives on your PC.
4. Select the drive that contains the disk on which you want to save the file.
5. Locate the folder in which you want to save the file in the large list box.
6. Double-click the folder in which you want to save the file. (You might need to repeat this step to save a file in a subfolder within a folder.)

To make backing up your important files easier, save all of the files you create in the My Documents folder or in a subfolder within that folder. You can often even use the Save As dialog box to create such a subfolder by clicking the Create New Folder toolbar button.

7. Enter a name for the file in the File Name box.

Windows lets you name the file almost anything you choose. For example, if you want, you can create filenames that are really, really long (up to 255 characters including spaces). Only a few characters are off-limits for filenames—for example, slashes, quotation marks, colons, asterisks, and question marks. However, I don't recommend using long filenames because some operating systems and programs can read only eight-letter filenames. So try to stick to short filenames. If you do choose to use longer filenames, make sure that the first six letters of the filename clearly identify the file in case the long filename gets truncated.

*You don't need to enter a **file extension** as part of a filename. The program adds the file extension for you.*

8. If you want to save the file as a different type, select the file type from the Save As drop-down list box.

You might want to change the file type if you want to share the file with a person who uses an older version of the program, for example. The "Importing and Exporting" section of this chapter describes saving files in other formats.

9. Click Save.

Printing Files

It's easy to create a paper copy of a file you're working with. You simply tell the program that you want to print the file.

Preparing to Print

Before you waste a stack of paper printing a file incorrectly, it's best to preview the way the file will print first. To preview the printed version of the file, choose the File menu's Print Preview command or click the Print Preview toolbar button if the program includes one. The program often displays the file in a new window that includes a new toolbar for previewing the file. For example, the toolbar might have buttons for zooming or for displaying several pages of the file at once, as shown in Figure 6-12.

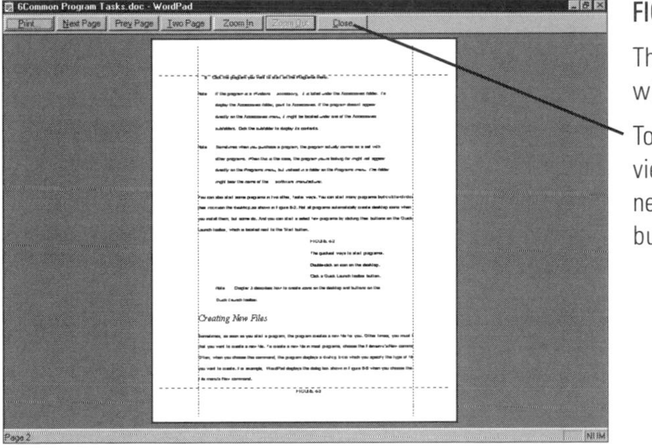

FIGURE 6-12

The Print Preview window.

To return to the normal view of the file, you often need to click a Close button.

To change the way a file prints, choose the File menu's Page Setup command. The dialog box that the program displays is different for each program. Most of the time, the Page Setup dialog box includes options for changing the page margins, selecting the paper size, and specifying whether the file is to print vertically or horizontally on the page, as shown in Figure 6-13.

FIGURE 6-13

The Page Setup dialog box in WordPad.

Printing the File

With most programs, you have two ways to print a file. If you want to print a file using all the default settings, you can usually click a button on the toolbar called Print. This button often looks like a little **printer**. If, on the other hand, you want to check or change the default settings before you print the file, you usually need to choose the File menu's Print command. When you do this, the program displays a dialog box similar to the one shown in Figure 6-14.

FIGURE 6-14

The Print dialog box.

The Print dialog box usually allows you to specify these options:

- Which printer you want to use for printing the file. If you have more than one printer installed on your computer, you can choose to print the file using a different printer by selecting a printer from the Name drop-down list box.
- Which pages you want to print. Most Print dialog boxes let you choose whether you want to print all the pages, only the pages you specify, or only the information you've selected.
- How many copies of the file you want to print. The default is usually set to one, but you can print more copies of a file.
- Whether you want to print the file on paper or create a special kind of file called a printer file. You probably won't have any need to create a printer file, so keep the Print To File check box clear.

Some Print dialog boxes also let you choose which elements of the file you want to print.

To use the Print dialog box with WordPad, follow these steps:

1. Select the printer that you want to use for printing the file.
2. Specify the pages you want to print.
    - Click the All option button to print all the pages of the file.
    - Click the Pages option button to print the page you have displayed.
    - Click the Selection option button to print the information you have selected.

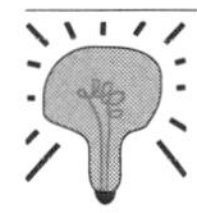

The Selection option button is usually only available if you select information before choosing the File menu's Print command.

3. Specify the number of copies you want to print. Type a number, or click an arrow in the Number Of Copies box to increase or decrease the number of copies to be printed.
4. Turn on your printer, and make sure it has the correct paper loaded.

Some printers require you to press their Online button before they print. If your computer has an online light, make sure this light is on.

5. Click OK.

Closing Files

After you're finished working on a file and you've saved your changes, you can close the file. Most programs don't require you to close one file before opening another, but some do. Even if a program doesn't require you to close a file, it often makes sense to do so. Closing the files you're not working on cleans up your workspace and makes your time spent at the computer more efficient.

If you want to keep the changes you make to a file, make sure you save the file before you close it.

You have two ways to close a file. Either way, you must first display the file you want to close. Then you can either click the file window's Close button or you can choose the File menu's Close command.

Exiting Programs

After you're finished using a program and have saved all the files you were working on in that program, you're ready to exit the program. Always exit any programs you don't plan to use for a while so your computer can operate faster for the tasks you are working on.

As with closing files, you have two ways to exit a program. You can click the program's Close button, or you can choose the File menu's Exit command.

Notes

Chapter 10 describes how to force stalled programs to close.

CHAPTER 7

Exploring the Internet

The **Internet**—it's all the rage. But what's it really all about? Why should you get connected, and what do you need if you want to connect? This chapter talks about the following subjects related to the Internet:

- What is the Internet?
- Installing Internet Explorer
- Connecting to the Internet
- A **World Wide Web** primer
- Using Internet Explorer
- Installing other Internet Explorer programs to work with the Internet
- Creating your own **home page** on the World Wide Web

What Is the Internet?

Let's start this chapter by describing what the Internet is and what it allows you to do. You can think of the Internet as a big, loosely organized **network** that connects millions of computers and networks from around the world. In other words, the Internet is enormous. People enjoy the Internet because it's a cheap, efficient, and entertaining means of sharing information. And because of the Internet's popularity, it just keeps getting bigger as more and more people connect.

Sometimes people refer to the Internet as the information superhighway. This is because it's much like a worldwide highway system—thousands of people enter from different on-ramps at any given moment, and from there, each person heads off in a different direction to one of millions of possible destinations.

The Internet has several aspects you can use to accomplish different tasks. Table 7-1 that follows outlines some of the most popular regions and what you can do in each one.

Area	What You Can Do There
E-Mail	Send and receive messages and **files.** As with regular mail, you can send individual personal messages to people, but you can also send and receive mass mailings. Chapter 8 describes using Outlook Express for **e-mail.** Chapter 9 describes using Netscape Messenger for e-mail.
Newsgroups	Post and read messages on electronic bulletin boards for several people to see. Chapter 8 describes **newsgroups**.
World Wide Web	View information in the form of colorful **documents** that businesses and individuals post for people to see.
Telnet	Connect to places such as your local library or a **server** at your place of work.
FTP	Post files for others to grab, or grab copies of files that other people have posted.
Conference Rooms	Hold private audio and/or video conferences with other people.

TABLE 7-1: A list of popular Internet resources.

This chapter can't cover all of these Internet resources. It introduces only one of the most popular ones, the World Wide Web. Chapter 8 discusses e-mail, newsgroups, and Internet conferencing.

Installing Internet Explorer

In order to browse the World Wide Web and to make use of other Internet resources, you need Internet **software.** This chapter talks about how you use Microsoft Internet Explorer, a free suite of **programs** that comes as a part of **Microsoft Windows** 98, later versions of Windows 95, and several popular Microsoft programs. If your **PC** came with Windows 98, or if you purchased Windows 98 and installed it yourself, your computer almost certainly has Microsoft Internet Explorer 4 or higher already installed on it. So you're ready to browse the Web and follow along with the discussion in this chapter. On the other hand, if you're running Windows 95 and want to follow along here, you need to install Internet Explorer 4 or higher if you haven't done so already.

Notes

*If you have another **web browser** installed on your PC (such as Netscape Navigator or a browser supplied by your **Internet service provider**), you don't need Internet Explorer to browse the web. As a matter of fact, even if your computer came with Internet Explorer 4 or higher, you're not limited to using it—you can easily download and try out another web browser. (You can download Netscape Navigator, the world's leading web browser, at http://www.netscape.com.) Chapter 9 tells you how to use Netscape Navigator.*

Your first step is to determine whether you have Internet Explorer 4 or higher installed on your computer. To do this, follow these steps:

1 First, take a look at your **desktop.** Do you see an **icon** of a blue letter "e" with the words Internet Explorer beneath it (see Figure 7-1)? If so, you have Internet Explorer 4 or higher installed on your computer.

FIGURE 7-1
The Internet Explorer icon on the desktop.

2 If you don't see an icon of a blue letter "e" on your desktop, take a look at the Windows **Taskbar.** (This is the bar with the **Start button.**) Do you see a toolbar on the Taskbar that includes a blue letter "e" button? If so, you have Internet Explorer 4 or higher installed on your computer.

FIGURE 7-2

The Internet Explorer button on the Quick Launch toolbar.

3 Click the Start button, and point to Programs. Do you see Internet Explorer on the Programs menu?

If you couldn't find Internet Explorer in any of these places, chances are you don't have it installed on your computer. In order to follow along with all the steps in this chapter, you need to install version 4 or higher. If you want to install Internet Explorer as quickly as possible (say, because you're eager to get going in this chapter), you can **download** the latest copy of Internet Explorer from the **web site** at http://www.microsoft.com/ie/. You can do this on your own computer (or have someone help you do this) if you have another browser currently installed. If you're having trouble with this, you can order a copy of Internet Explorer on CD by calling Microsoft at 1-800-485-2048.

Connecting to the Internet

Before you can begin using the Internet, you need to connect your PC to the Internet. Typically, the way that you do this is by using a telephone line and a **modem.** If this is the way you want to connect, you first need to specify how this connection will work and sign up for an account that lets you connect to the Internet.

Using the Internet is free, but connecting to it usually isn't. Certain companies, called Internet service providers, or ISPs for short, let you access the Internet for a monthly fee. If you think of the Internet as an information superhighway, the ISPs charge entrance fees at the on-ramps. Once you get on, however, you can go anywhere you want—regardless of whether your destination is New York or Nigeria—for free. Only a few destinations charge visiting fees.

Notes

*You can use a variety of modems to connect to the Internet, including regular old modems, **ISDN** modems, and even fast new cable modems. For simplicity's sake, you'll probably want to use a regular old modem and not one of the special new modems. But ask your ISP about your modem choices, and refer to Chapter 1 about purchasing a modem if you have questions.*

If you work on a computer that provides a permanent connection to the Internet, such as through a local area network, you don't need to dial using a modem in order to use the Internet. You're already connected to the Internet. If you have questions about how this permanent connection works, ask your network administrator.

You can use the Internet Connection Wizard that comes with Windows 98 and Internet Explorer to set up an Internet connection. To do so, follow these steps:

1. Click the Start button.
2. Point to Programs, Internet Explorer, and then click Connection Wizard to start the wizard you'll use to set up and describe your Internet connection (see Figure 7-3).

If you have a Connect To The Internet icon on your desktop, you can also ***double-click*** *this icon to start the Connection Wizard.*

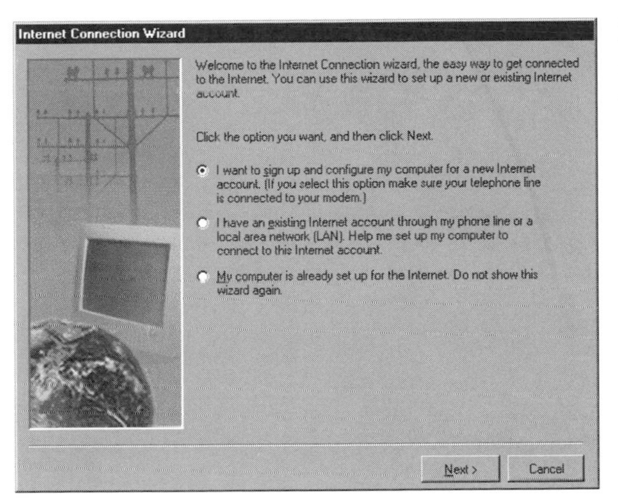

FIGURE 7-3

You use the Connection Wizard command to set up and describe an Internet connection.

3. If you've never used the Connection Wizard before, Windows might display an introductory **dialog box**. Click Next.
4. Click the option button that indicates you want to choose an ISP and set up a new Internet account. Then click Next.
5. Click Next again. The Connection Wizard connects to the Internet using a toll-free number to retrieve a list of ISPs that provide service to your area, as shown in Figure 7-4.

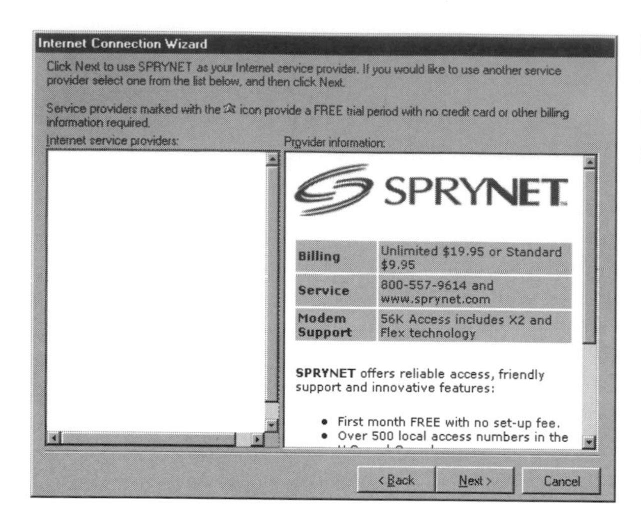

FIGURE 7-4

The Connection Wizard lists ISPs that provide service to your area.

When the Connection Wizard displays its list of ISPs, read through the descriptions, click to select the one you want, and then click Next.

The Internet service providers listed in the Connection Wizard most likely make up only a fraction of the Internet service providers available in your area. You don't have to choose one of the ISPs listed if someone recommends a different ISP. It's a good idea to ask around before choosing an ISP. You have several factors to consider before you choose an ISP. First, you want to make sure that whoever you choose provides good service. This means that the provider's computers run smoothly so you can dependably make your connection. It also means that you can reach your ISP's technical support technicians when you need help. Second, you want to determine the costs of making your connection. This means confirming that the connection requires only a local telephone call (not a long distance call). Third, you need to consider cost. Most ISPs offer inexpensive plans, but these plans usually include only a few hours of connection time. Consider one of the unlimited usage plans if you anticipate that you, your co-workers, or your family members will spend a lot of time connected to the Internet. And last, if you think you might want to establish your own presence on the World Wide Web (described later in this chapter), you need to make sure that your account includes space on the ***server*** *to host a* ***web page.***

If you decide to choose an ISP not listed in the Connection Wizard, you can still use the Connection Wizard to set up your connection. Just click the second option button when you start the Connection Wizard, and then follow the steps to provide the information that your ISP gave you. If you have any questions, contact your ISP.

6 Follow the Connection Wizard's on-screen instructions. You'll be asked to provide your name, address, and credit card number, as well as some other information. Once you complete these instructions—and different ISPs have you step through a slightly different process—you've set up the Dial-Up Networking connection you'll use to connect to the Internet.

Think carefully about the e-mail name you request. You want to pick a name that you can easily describe or provide. For example, something like "steve" is good because you'll later be able to say, "Oh, my e-mail name is 'steve'." Something cryptic like "stphnlnlsn" is not good because you'll often find it difficult to provide this name to people.

You usually don't need to do anything special to initiate your new Internet connection. When you start a program that frequently works with an Internet connection (such as Internet Explorer or Outlook Express), the program prompts you to make a connection. For example, it might require you to log on by entering your account name and **password.** After you log on the first time, you can usually check a box to have Windows remember your username and password so you don't have to.

If a program doesn't prompt you to connect to the Internet and you want to initiate a connection, see if the program has a command for connecting to the Internet. Many programs have a command called something like "Connect" on the File **menu.**

If you can't find a Connect command and you want to make a manual connection, follow these steps:

1 Click the Start button, and point to Programs and Accessories.

2 Point to Communications if you see it listed on the Accessories menu.

3 Click Dial-Up Networking to display the Dial-Up Networking window, as shown in Figure 7-5.

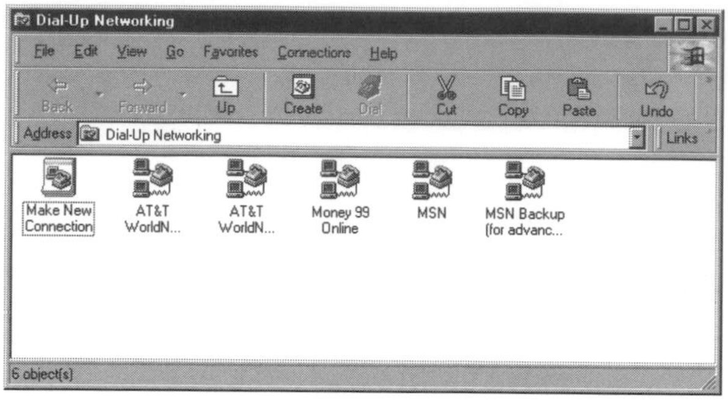

FIGURE 7-5

The Dial-Up Networking window.

4 Double-click the icon for the connection you want to make to display the connection's Connect To dialog box, as shown in Figure 7-6. Note that the connection you want to make might have two icons—one is for a primary number, and the other is for a backup number (for use if the first number is busy). The icon for the backup connection usually has "2" or "backup" in its name. Try the primary connection first.

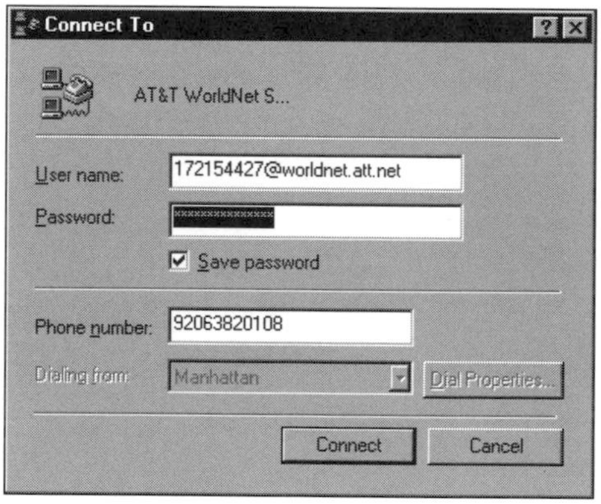

FIGURE 7-6

The Connect To dialog box for the AT&T connection.

5 Confirm your username and password, and click Connect.

A World Wide Web Primer

Let's open the discussion about the Internet with the most talked about part of it—the World Wide Web. The World Wide Web lets you view special files, called web pages, that are connected to each other with clickable **hyperlinks.** The Web is very easy to use—much easier than e-mail, for example. However, just to make sure you're comfortable with the concepts, let's go over a few points.

Understanding the Web

As noted above, the Web consists of web pages connected by hyperlinks. To understand this definition, you need to know the meaning of two key terms, *web page* and *hyperlink*.

A web page is a file that commonly uses multiple media for communicating information. For example, text is one medium. Pictures are another. Sound is still another. So web pages are files that use text, pictures, and sometimes even sound. Figure 7-7 shows a web page provided by Barnes & Noble. Note that it uses multiple media—both text and pictures. Web pages are the building blocks of the Web. A group of web pages linked together and stored in the same place make up a web site. For example, the Barnes & Noble web site is made up of several web pages. Some pages list books, some list magazines, and others let you place orders.

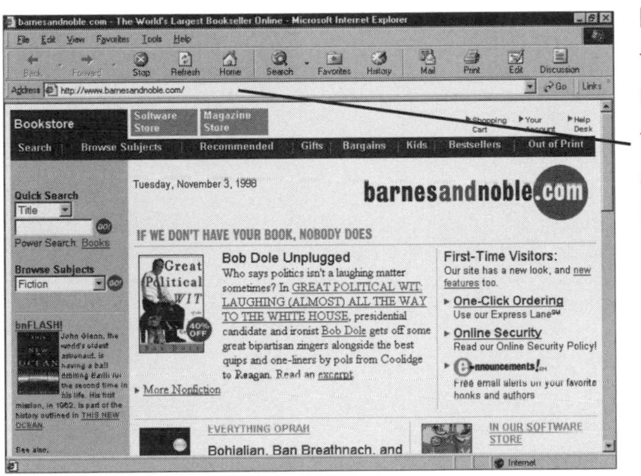

FIGURE 7-7

The main web page of the Barnes & Noble web site.

Notes

*Web pages are frequently written in a language called **HTML,** or hypertext markup language, and so are often called HTML documents. Another common type of web page is an ASP, or active server page. An active server page is a web page with a small program included in it so the web page can customize itself for you before you request to see it.*

The unique feature of web pages is that they also include hyperlinks. A hyperlink, essentially, is an address that points to another web page. When you click a hyperlink, you're actually telling Windows to retrieve and then display the web page identified by the hyperlink. In Figure 7-7, for example, there are several hyperlinks. The buttons across the top of the web page are hyperlinks. All of the underlined segments of text are hyperlinks as well. If you scroll down the page, you'll see a hyperlink to barnesandnoble.com's collection of Oprah's Picks. If you click this hyperlink, Windows retrieves a web page listing Oprah's Book Club™ picks, as shown in Figure 7-8.

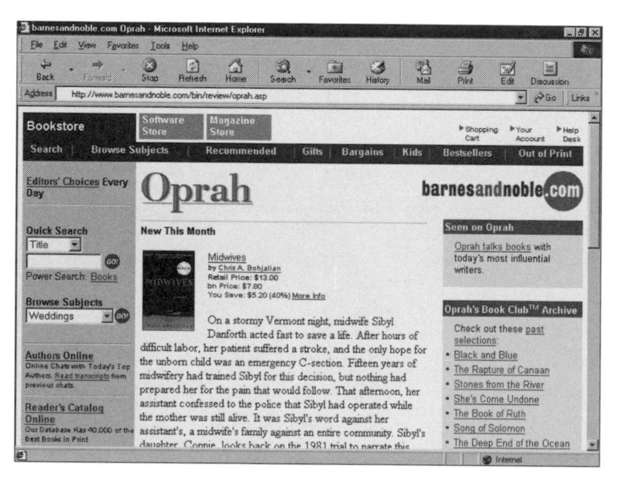

FIGURE 7-8

This web page appears if you click the Oprah hyperlink.

You now know how to view web pages and work with hyperlinks. No kidding. But there's one final point we should talk about. You should learn how addresses work so you can use them as you browse web pages.

A web page address is made up of four parts:

- A code that identifies the address as a World Wide Web page
- The name of the computer, called a web server, that stores the web page
- The **folder** location of the web page
- The web page name

If you look at Figure 7-8, you'll notice that its address is

http://www.barnesandnoble.com/bin/review/oprah.asp

The *http://* part of this address is the code that identifies the address as a World Wide Web page. The *www.barnesandnoble.com* part of the address is the name of the Barnes & Noble web server. (Remember that this is just the computer that stores the web page.) The */bin/review* part of the address is the folder and **subfolder** holding the web page. Finally, *oprah.asp* is the actual web page name. (If you display this web page, you might notice that the address includes a bunch of other numbers and symbols following the web page name. This is because this web page, as an ASP file, customizes itself for you and includes the number it uses to identify you.)

Notes

Web page addresses are also known by the term uniform resource locator, *or* ***URL.***

Basic World Wide Web Navigation Techniques

To view a web page, start your web browser. If you want to use Internet Explorer, you can start it by clicking the Internet Explorer Quick Launch toolbar button. If you aren't connected to the Internet, Windows might prompt you for the information it needs to make this connection. You might, for example, need to supply a password.

In any event, your web browser will soon begin loading a home page such as the one shown in Figure 7-9. A home page is simply a default web page.

FIGURE 7-9

The Microsoft Network (MSN) home page.

You can also move to another web page by entering a new URL here.

If you click this hyperlink, you move to another web page.

Notes

You can start Netscape Navigator and most other web browsers by clicking their icons on the desktop or by using the Start menu. Chapter 6 describes these techniques.

To move to another page, click a hyperlink. As noted earlier, hyperlinks often appear as underlined text. They also appear as clickable buttons. You can always tell whether some bit of text is a hyperlink, however, by pointing to it. If you point to a hyperlink with the **mouse**, Windows changes the mouse pointer to a pointing finger.

You can also move to another web page by typing the web page's address, or URL, in the Address box. Table 7-2 that follows provides a short list of web pages you can use if you want to begin exploring the World Wide Web. Note that you can return to your home page at any time by clicking the Home **toolbar** button.

When entering URLs, you don't need to enter the entire address. Web page addresses almost always begin with http://, so you can leave this part out. You can also leave out the / if it is the last character in the address.

Web Address	What It Provides
http://www.whitehouse.gov/	A **multimedia** tour of the White House. This web site is a good one to visit to get familiar with the mechanics of browsing web pages and clicking hyperlinks.
http://www.hotbot.com/	A special type of web site, called a **search engine**, that allows you to search various parts of the Internet. For example, you can search for a World Wide Web page by keyword or browse sites by category.
http://www.expedia.com/	A one-stop source for a wealth of vacation-planning information and tools. You can use this web site to locate flights, compare prices, and even reserve hotel rooms and purchase tickets **online.**
http://www.microsoft.com/	A large web site that's of interest to anyone running Windows or Windows software, which includes you.
http://www.cnn.com/	Perhaps the best news web site there is.
http://bigfoot.com/	An online White Pages listing everybody in the United States. You might be able to find your long-lost friend from school using this directory. Maybe.

TABLE 7-2: Interesting web pages for people new to the Internet.

If you don't know the address for a site you want to visit on the World Wide Web, you can often successfully guess it. Here's how:

- Many URLs begin with the letters www. Enter this first, followed by a period.
- Enter the name of the business, organization, or institution next, followed by a period. Don't include spaces. If the name is very long, it's probably abbreviated. Think of any likely abbreviations.

- For U.S. web pages, enter the **domain** .com for a commercial organization, .gov for a governmental organization, .edu for an educational institution, .org for a nonprofit organization, or .mil for a military web page. Or if the page you want to display is international, enter the country's two-letter domain code.

This might take a few tries, but with a little trial and error, it often works.

Let me give you a couple of examples. Let's say you want to see the home page for the University of Washington. Here are a few URLs you might want to try:

www.universityofwashington.edu

www.uofw.edu

www.uw.edu

www.washington.edu

If one doesn't work, your web browser either displays an incorrect page or beeps at you. You can then try the next URL. In this case, the fourth time's a charm.

Here's another example. Let's say you want to visit the Canadian Broadcasting Corporation web site in Canada. Here's what you might try:

www.cbc.ca

And you'd be right!

You can also move between web pages in Internet Explorer and in most other web browsers (such as Netscape Navigator) by clicking the two toolbar buttons labeled Back and Forward (see Figure 7-10). You can move to a web page you've previously viewed by clicking the Back toolbar button. After you click the Back toolbar button, you can move to the page you viewed before clicking Back by clicking the Forward toolbar button.

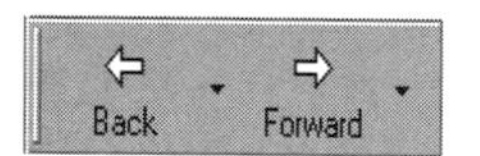

FIGURE 7-10

The Back and Forward buttons.

To tell your web browser to stop loading a web page, click the Stop toolbar button. You might want to stop loading a web page if retrieving the page is taking a long time—too long for you to wait.

To grab an updated copy of a web page, click the Refresh toolbar button. You might want to do this if you're viewing a web page with information that changes frequently, or if you had to click Stop because the web page was taking too long to appear.

FIGURE 7-11

The Stop and Refresh buttons.

Notes *In Netscape Navigator, the button you click to update the web page you're viewing is called Reload. And the Stop button looks like a traffic light.*

Using Internet Explorer

This next section describes how to work with some of the special features of Internet Explorer. You also can accomplish many of the tasks I'm about to describe using a different web browser, since the way in which you accomplish them is quite similar.

Designating a Home Page

If you don't like the web page that appears each time you start Internet Explorer, you can tell Internet Explorer to display a different page (called a home page or a start page) at startup.

Notes *The term* home page *has three separate meanings. First, home page can describe the web page that initially appears when you start a web browser. Second, you can create your own web page (described later in this chapter) and call it your home page. And third, people and businesses who create multipage web sites use the term home page to describe the main web page of their web sites. This section of the chapter refers to home page by the first definition.*

To change your home page, follow these steps:

1 Choose the View menu's Internet Options command to display the Internet Options dialog box, as shown in Figure 7-12.

2 In the Home Page area, enter the address of the web page you want to use as your home page in the Address box.

3 Click OK.

FIGURE 7-12

The Internet Options dialog box.

4 To display your home page, click the Home toolbar button.

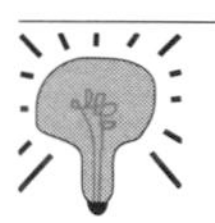

It's usually best to pick a web page for your home page that you most frequently visit or that you can easily use as a springboard to browse the World Wide Web. Many web sites allow you to customize your home page by choosing which information and hyperlinks you want included on the page.

To change your home page in Netscape Navigator, choose the Edit menu's Preferences command. Then select Navigator from the Category list on the left side. In the Home Page area, enter the address of the web page you want to use as your home page in the Location box.

Searching the Internet

Once you've spent a bit of time working with the Internet, you'll discover that with millions of resources available, you can't always easily find what you want. To address this problem, you'll want to learn how to use a search engine. Click Search to open the Search bar in Internet Explorer, as shown in Figure 7-13. The Search bar lets you use a selected search engine or display a web page to choose from a list of popular search engines.

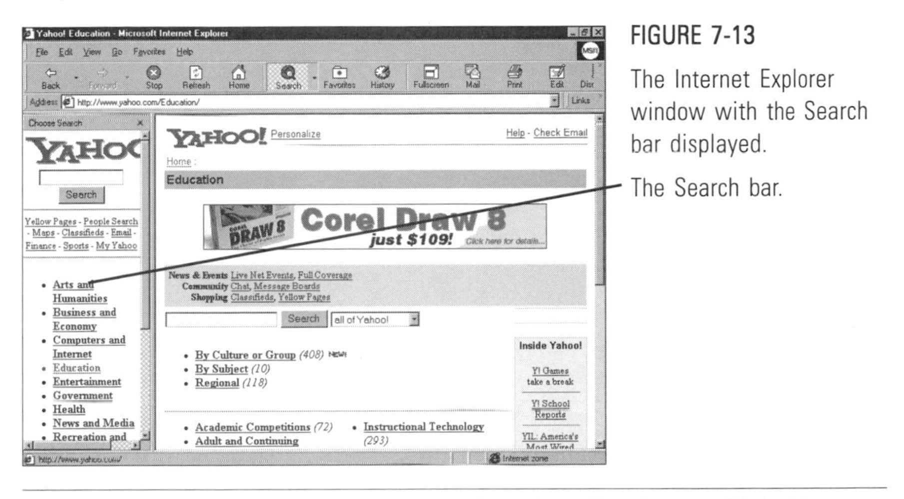

FIGURE 7-13

The Internet Explorer window with the Search bar displayed.

The Search bar.

Netscape Navigator also has a Search toolbar button. Click this button to display a Netscape page that includes a search engine and hyperlinks to other popular search engines.

There are two types of search engines: directory-style search engines and index-style search engines. Directory-style search engines work like the Yellow Pages. You search through alphabetical lists organized by category. One of the most popular directory-style search engines is Yahoo!, which you can visit by entering its web page address, http://www.yahoo.com, in the Address box. Yahoo! has nowhere near an all-inclusive list of web sites, but instead it filters web sites and focuses on the largest and most popular.

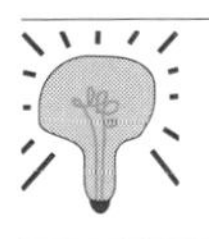

Experiment on your own using Yahoo!'s categories to find a web page that provides content related to a hobby of yours or perhaps a school project of your kids.

Index-style search engines build **databases** of keywords included in web pages, rather than sorting and filtering web pages by topic. One popular index-style search engine is HotBot, which you can visit by entering its web page address, http://www.hotbot.com, in the Address box, as shown in Figure 7-14.

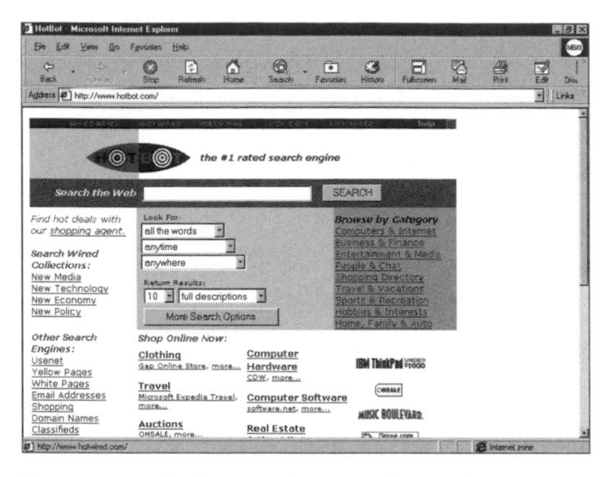

FIGURE 7-14

HotBot provides a web form you use to supply the word or phrase you want to look up.

To use an index-style search engine, type a word or phrase, click Search, and then wait for the search engine to build a list of web pages that use the word or phrase you typed. Figure 7-15 shows the first portion of a list of web pages that use the phrase "sea kayaking." To visit a web page, just click its hyperlink.

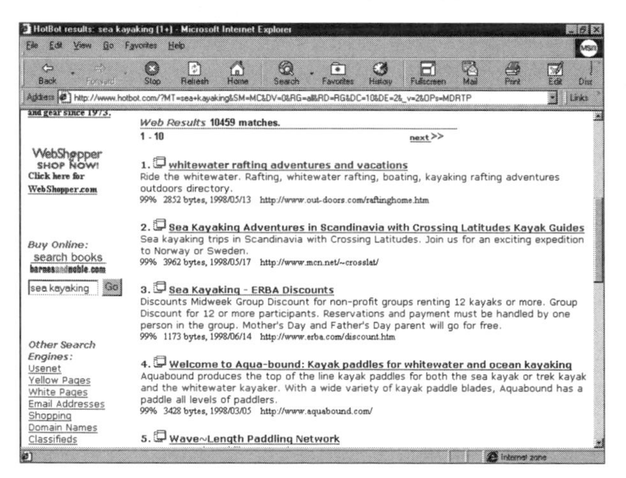

FIGURE 7-15

An index-style search engine builds a list of web pages that use the word or phrase you supplied.

Let me make a couple of final comments about search engines. First, a powerful search engine actually indexes millions and millions of web pages. Therefore, you commonly get a list of hundreds of web pages that use the word or phrase you supplied. Typically, an index-style search engine prioritizes the web pages it finds. It might, for example, list 25 web pages with the closest match on the first page of search results, 25 more web pages on the second page, and so on. In all cases, you usually need to do a bit of digging to find what you're looking for.

At the bottom of each page of search results are hyperlinks that let you move to another page.

Second, numerous search engines exist. I've mentioned some already in this chapter, but there are many others. Table 7-3 lists some of the most popular search engines. You might want to visit and experiment with more than one of them.

Search Engine	Web Page Address
AltaVista	http://www.altavista.digital.com
Excite	http://www.excite.com
HotBot	http://www.hotbot.com
InfoSeek	http://www.infoseek.com
Lycos	http://www.lycos.com
MetaCrawler	http://www.metacrawler.com
WebCrawler	http://www.webcrawler.com
Yahoo!	http://www.yahoo.com

TABLE 7-3: Web page addresses of popular search engines.

As you might expect, different search engines work differently. Learn as much as you can about how to work with a specific search engine. To do this, look for a hyperlink on the search engine's page that refers to "Help" or "Instructions." Most search engines, for example, require that you enclose a phrase or term that has spaces in it, like "state tax forms," in quotes. Otherwise, the search engine will not know to match the phrase exactly. Other search engines have a drop-down list box or button that lets you specify this.

Keeping a List of Favorite Web Pages

You can add a web page address to a special folder of favorite web pages. By designating a web page as a favorite, you can easily access it in the future without needing to type its URL. This is especially useful for web pages you frequently visit that have long URLs. To make a web page a favorite, follow these steps:

1. Display the web page in Internet Explorer.
2. Choose the Favorites menu's Add To Favorites command to display the Add Favorite dialog box, as shown in Figure 7-16.

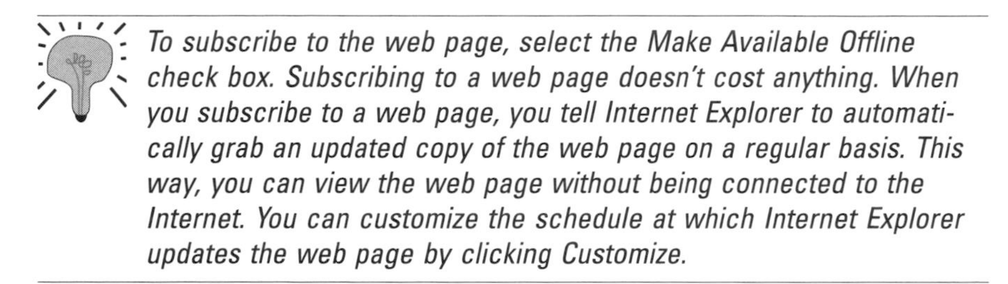

To subscribe to the web page, select the Make Available Offline check box. Subscribing to a web page doesn't cost anything. When you subscribe to a web page, you tell Internet Explorer to automatically grab an updated copy of the web page on a regular basis. This way, you can view the web page without being connected to the Internet. You can customize the schedule at which Internet Explorer updates the web page by clicking Customize.

3. Click OK.

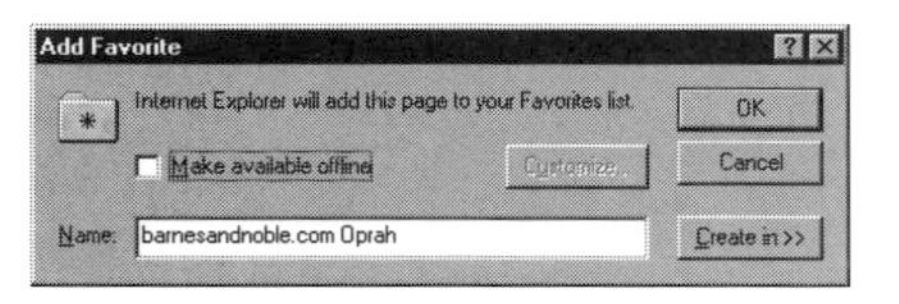

Figure 7-16

The Add Favorite dialog box in Internet Explorer 5.

If you're using Internet Explorer 4 (instead of 5), the Add Favorite dialog box includes a couple of other options. If you choose the second option, Internet Explorer checks for and notifies you of changes to the web page since you last viewed it. If you choose the third option, you subscribe to the web page.

To view your list of favorite web pages, click the Favorites toolbar button. This displays the Favorites bar, as shown in Figure 7-17. Click a button on this bar to display a favorite web page.

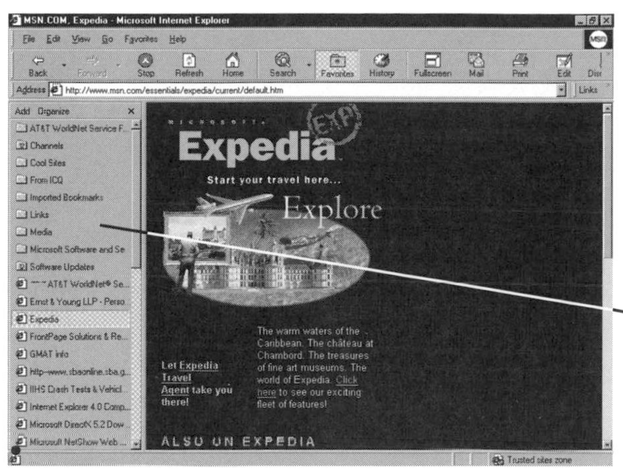

FIGURE 7-17

The Favorites bar lists web pages you've identified as favorites—and a handful of web pages your web browser or ISP has marked as useful or interesting.

The Favorites bar.

Notes

Netscape Navigator calls your favorite web pages ***bookmarks.*** *Click the Bookmarks toolbar button to display a menu of commands for adding, organizing, and displaying bookmarks.*

Viewing a History Log of Web Pages You've Visited

If you click the History toolbar button in Internet Explorer, it opens the History bar, which lists the web pages you've recently visited, grouped by web site and the day or week on which you visited them, as shown in Figure 7-18. To return to a web page you visited in the past 20 days, follow these steps:

1. Click the button for the day or week on which you visited the web page.
2. Click the hyperlink for the web site containing the web page. This displays a list of the web pages you viewed at that site.
3. To display the web page, click its hyperlink in the list.

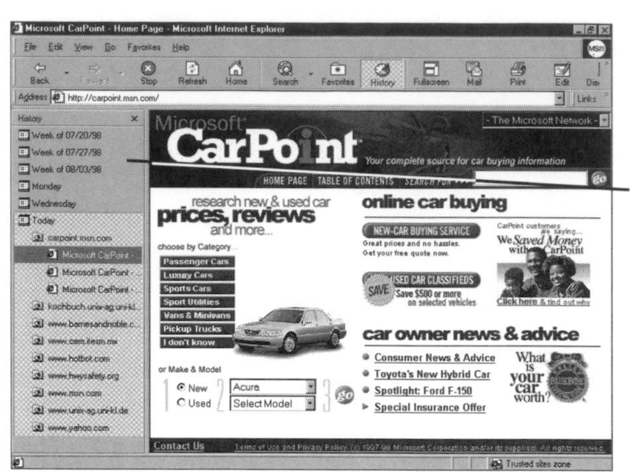

FIGURE 7-18

The History bar shows a record of the web pages you've recently viewed.

To close the Search, Favorites, or History bar, click its Close button.

To delete a web page listed in the History bar, right-click it and then choose the shortcut menu's Delete command.

If you want to erase your history log, follow these steps:

1. Choose the View menu's Internet Options command to display the Internet Options dialog box, as shown in Figure 7-19.
2. Click Clear History.

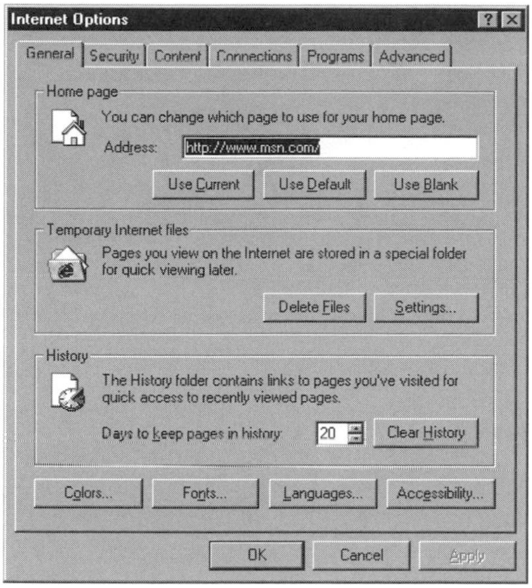

FIGURE 7-19

The Internet Options dialog box.

Using Channels

Channel web sites are special web sites that are set up to automatically deliver content to your computer. By subscribing to a channel, you can view the channel web site's content while offline.

Notes *To subscribe to Netscape channels, you use Netscape Netcaster.*

To subscribe to a channel using Internet Explorer, follow these steps:

1. Click the Channels toolbar button. (If you're using Internet Explorer 5, click the Favorites toolbar button, and click Channels on the Favorites bar.)
2. Click the channel button that describes the content category you're interested in. For example, if you're interested in a news web site, click the News And Technology button. Internet Explorer expands the bar to show the top channels available under that category (see Figure 7-20).
3. Click a channel site to preview the channel.
4. Click the Add Active Channel button to subscribe to the channel.

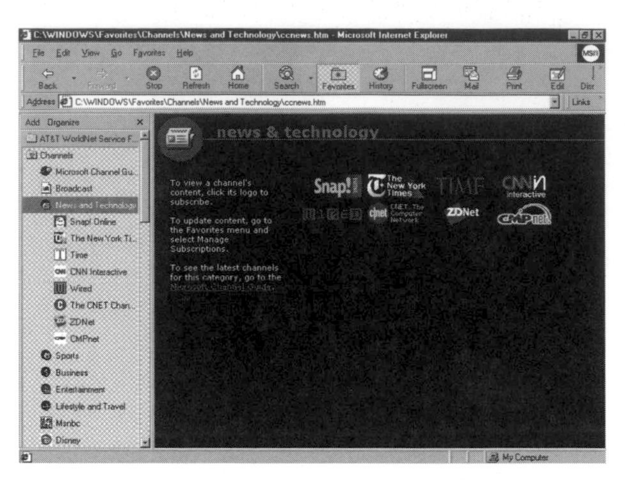

FIGURE 7-20

Internet Explorer lists categories of channel sites and specific channels within the selected category.

To see a longer list of channels available in a category, click the Microsoft Channel Guide button.

Expanding to a Fullscreen View

To display only a web page and a small toolbar in Internet Explorer, click the Fullscreen toolbar button. When you do this, Windows removes the program window title bar and menu bar and replaces the Standard toolbar with a smaller toolbar, as shown in Figure 7-21.

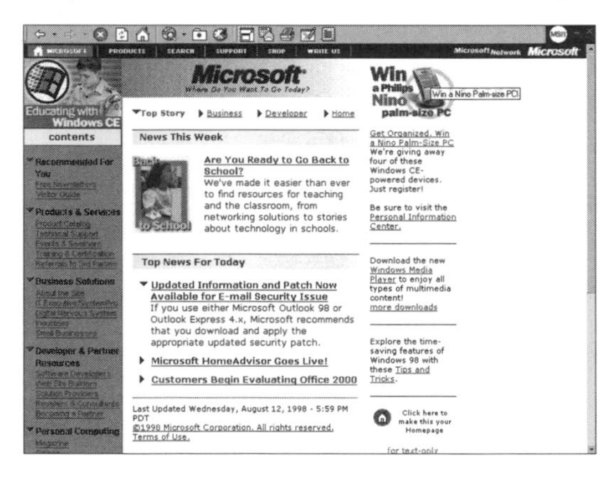

FIGURE 7-21

The Microsoft home page displayed in a Fullscreen view.

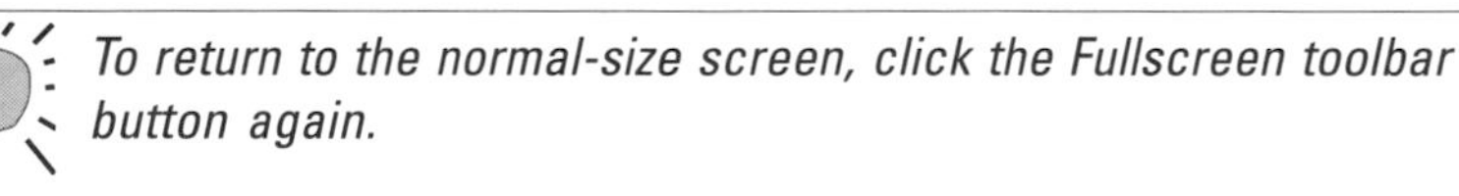

To return to the normal-size screen, click the Fullscreen toolbar button again.

Printing and Saving a Web Page

You can print and save the web pages you view. To print a web page, click the Print toolbar button. When Windows displays the Print dialog box, use it to describe how you want the web page printed.

Notes

If you need more information about printing, refer to the "Printing Files" section in Chapter 6. You print web pages in the same manner as you print other files.

To save a web page, choose the File menu's Save As command. When Windows displays the Save As dialog box, use it to name the web page file and specify where you want the file saved.

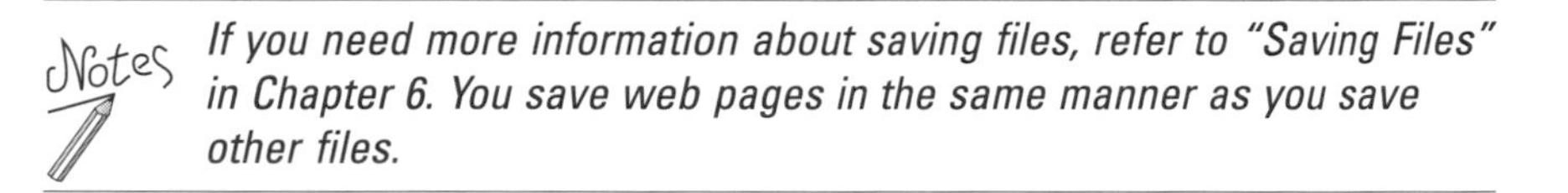

If you need more information about saving files, refer to "Saving Files" in Chapter 6. You save web pages in the same manner as you save other files.

Installing Other Internet Explorer Programs to Work with the Internet

Depending on how you obtained and installed your copy of Windows and Internet Explorer, you might or might not have a number of programs that come with Internet Explorer preinstalled. You probably have Microsoft Outlook Express installed, an Internet e-mail and newsgroup reader discussed in Chapter 8. But you might not have Microsoft FrontPage Express (a web-page creation program described in the next section), Microsoft NetMeeting (an Internet conferencing program introduced in the next chapter), or several other free Internet Explorer components installed. To install such programs, follow these steps:

1. Click the Start button.
2. Point to Settings.
3. Click Control Panel.
4. Double-click the Add/Remove Programs icon.
5. Select Internet Explorer from the list of installed programs, and click Add/Remove.

6 When Windows displays the Internet Explorer Active Setup dialog box, click the Add A Component To Internet Explorer option button and click OK, as shown in Figure 7-22. This starts Internet Explorer and connects you to the Internet.

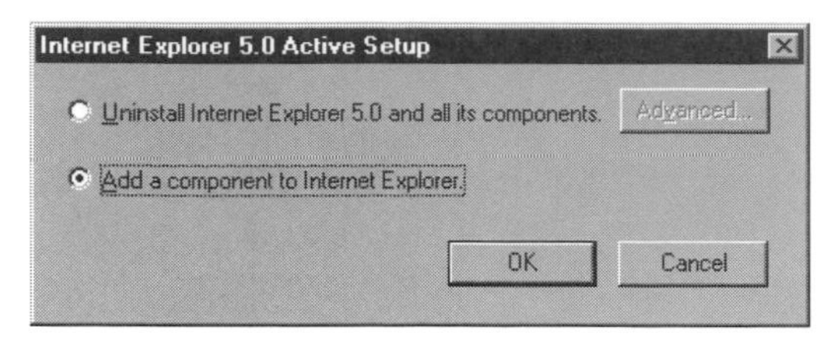

FIGURE 7-22

Adding an Internet Explorer component.

7 Click Yes when Internet Explorer asks if it can take a peek at your computer to see which components and file versions you have installed.

8 Check the Internet Explorer program or component you want to install, as shown in Figure 7-23, and follow the instructions to download and install the component.

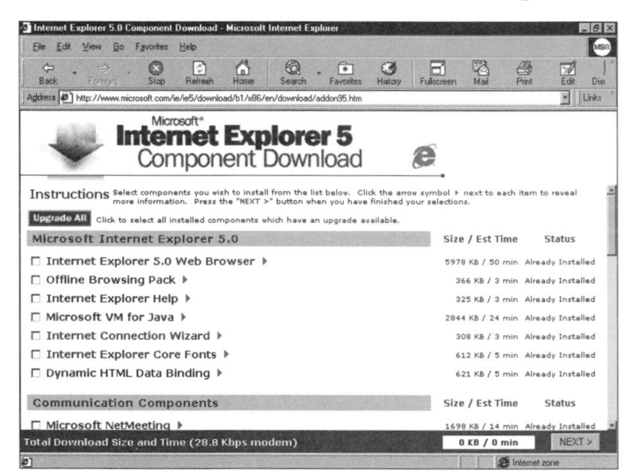

FIGURE 7-23

Downloading and installing a component.

Creating Your Own Home Page on the World Wide Web

Internet Explorer comes with a program called FrontPage Express that you can use to create a web page. FrontPage Express is a nice little program because it's easy to use. With FrontPage Express, you don't need to know how to write in HTML—you can use toolbar buttons to add various elements to your web page and create the effects you want.

Just because FrontPage Express comes as a free Internet Explorer component doesn't mean you are limited to using it to create a home page. Many other web authoring tools exist. As a matter of fact, if you know HTML, you can create a web page using a simple text editor like Notepad. You can also download or purchase other web authoring software such as Adobe PageMill, Claris Home Page, Corel WebMaster Suite, Microsoft FrontPage, or Netscape Composer. These products vary widely in functionality and price.

In order to post the web page you create on the World Wide Web so other people can see it, your ISP needs to offer space for its customers to post web pages. Many ISPs offer a nominal amount of space, enough for a small web page. Check with your ISP to find out if your account includes web hosting space.

To create a web page using FrontPage Express, follow these steps:

1. Click the Start button, and point to Programs and Internet Explorer. Then click the FrontPage Express item. This opens FrontPage Express with a blank page for you to use, as shown in Figure 7-24.

FIGURE 7-24

A blank web page in FrontPage Express.

You can create a web page from scratch as described in these steps, or you can use one of the FrontPage Express wizards to base your web page on one of the FrontPage Express predesigned pages.

2 To add text to the web page, just begin typing it. To format the text, use the Formatting toolbar. Table 7-4 describes what each toolbar button does. Note that you can tell which button is which by running the mouse pointer over the buttons to display their names. Figure 7-26 shows a web page with some formatted text.

Button	What It Does
Change Style	Applies a predefined web page style to the selected text
Change Font	Changes the **font** of the selected text
Increase Text Size	Increases the size of the selected text to the next largest size
Decrease Text Size	Decreases the size of the selected text to the next smallest size
Bold	Boldfaces the selected text
Italic	Italicizes the selected text
Underline	Underlines the selected text
Text Color	Opens a palette you can use to change the color of the selected text
Align Left	Aligns the text along the left side of the page
Center	Centers the text across the page
Align Right	Aligns the text along the right side of the page
Numbered List	Turns the selected paragraphs into a numbered list
Bulleted List	Turns the selected paragraphs into a bulleted list
Increase Indent	Indents the entire paragraph by another ½ inch
Decrease Indent	Moves an indented paragraph back by ½ inch

TABLE 7-4: The FrontPage Express Formatting toolbar buttons.

Entering and formatting text in FrontPage Express works much like entering and editing text in a ***word processor.***

Underlined text is usually reserved for hyperlinks, so you probably won't need or want to use the Underline toolbar button.

3 Add pictures to your web site by clicking the Insert Image toolbar button to display the Image dialog box, as shown in Figure 7-25. Click the Other Location tab, click the From File option button, and then click Browse. Use the next Image dialog box to locate the image file you want to insert. When you find it, select it and click Open.

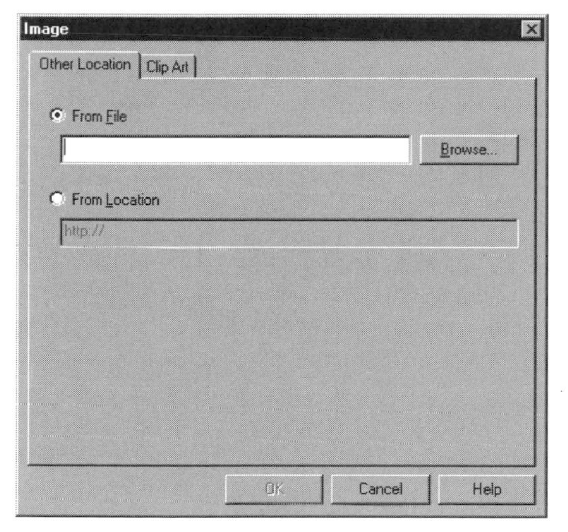

FIGURE 7-25

The Image dialog box.

4 Edit the picture as necessary. To resize a picture, click it to select it. Then **drag** one of the image's corner boxes to increase or decrease the image's height and width proportionally. To increase or decrease only the height or width, drag a box on one of the image's sides. Figure 7-26 shows a picture sized so it fits well on the page.

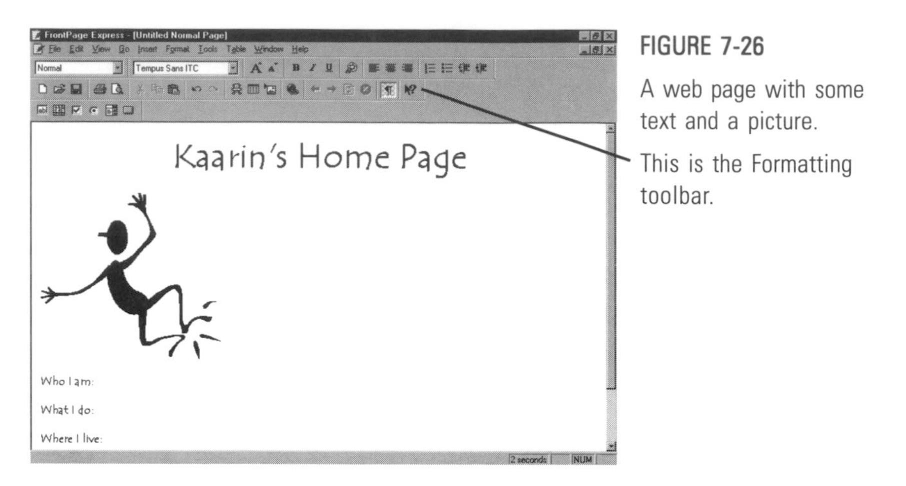

FIGURE 7-26

A web page with some text and a picture.

This is the Formatting toolbar.

5 Add hyperlinks to the web page. Hyperlinks are an integral part of the World Wide Web. You want to make sure that your web page includes some hyperlinks so people can quickly move to other pages that you think might interest them. To add a hyperlink, select the text or picture that you want to turn into a link to another web page. Then click the Create Or Edit Hyperlink toolbar button to display the Create Hyperlink dialog box, as shown in Figure 7-27. Click the World Wide Web tab, enter the address of the web page to which you want the text or picture to link in the URL box, and click OK.

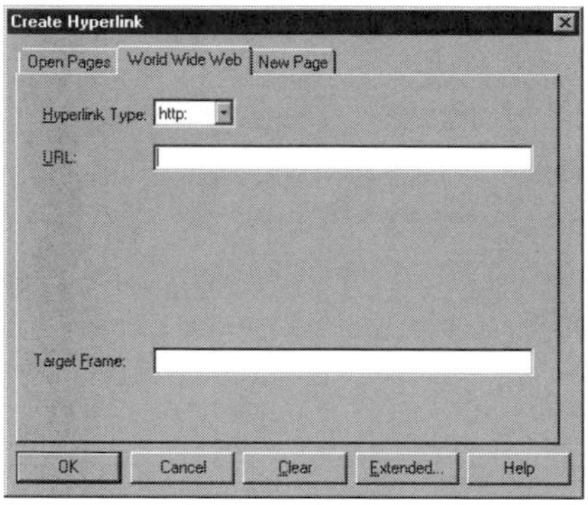

FIGURE 7-27

The Create Hyperlink dialog box.

6 Optionally, spice up your web page by changing the colors of the background and the various textual elements. To do this, choose the Format menu's Background command to display the Page Properties dialog box, as shown in Figure 7-28. On the Background tab, specify a background image or select a background color to use for the web page. Specify the colors you want to use for the textual elements on the web page in the Text box and the three Hyperlink boxes.

FIGURE 7-28

The Background tab of the Page Properties dialog box.

Keep legibility in mind when you select colors to use for text and background. Not all ***monitors*** *have the same color capabilities as yours might have, so it's important to pick common, contrasting colors.*

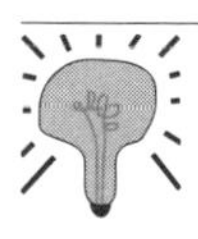

FrontPage Express offers several other features you can use to add special elements to your web page. For example, you can choose the Insert menu's Marquee command and use the Marquee Properties dialog box to add text to your web page that scrolls across the page.

7 Publish the web page. Click the Save toolbar button. This displays the Save As dialog box as shown in Figure 7-29. Enter a title for the page in the Page Title box and enter the URL to which you want to post the page in the Page Location box. (If you're publishing the web page on the World Wide Web, your ISP or web space provider provides you with the URL.) Click OK. If FrontPage asks you if you want to save the images in the web page as part of the web page, click Yes or Yes To All. Windows launches the Web Publishing Wizard shown in Figure 7-30.

Click As File to save the web page as a file on a local disk instead of publishing it immediately. You can then reopen it and edit it before publishing it.

Save As
Page Title:
A web page
Page Location:
http://www.stephenlnelson.com
Tip
Please be sure your page has a title.
Click OK to save this page to the web.
OK
Cancel
Help
As File...

FIGURE 7-29

Saving and publishing a web page.

8 Proceed through the Web Publishing Wizard's dialog boxes to publish the web page. The Web Publishing Wizard asks a little about the web server on which you're publishing the web page. It also asks you to name the URL for the new web page and describe your Internet connection for posting the web page.

FIGURE 7-30

The Web Publishing Wizard.

CHAPTER 8

Corresponding Over the Internet

One of the most popular features of the **Internet** is electronic mail, or **e-mail** for short. The popularity of e-mail and other forms of Internet correspondence stems from two facts: they're fast and they're cheap. When you correspond over the Internet, you can send messages across the world in the blink of an eye. And it costs next to nothing. You only need an Internet connection and some free **software.** This chapter describes how to use Microsoft Outlook Express, a slick little e-mail and **newsgroup** program that comes with both **Microsoft Windows** 98 and Microsoft Internet Explorer. This chapter covers the following topics:

- How e-mail works
- Setting up your PC for e-mail
- Using e-mail
- Working with newsgroups
- An introduction to audio and video conferencing with NetMeeting

Notes

You don't need to use Outlook Express for your electronic correspondence. There are several other good (and often free) e-mail programs available, such as Eudora and Netscape Messenger. You can download a copy of Eudora at http://www.eudora.com. You can download Netscape Messenger at http://www.netscape.com. Chapter 9 describes how you use Netscape Messenger.

Notes

*Chapter 7 describes how to set up an Internet connection and how to use another popular area of the Internet, the **World Wide Web,** to share information.*

How E-Mail Works

E-mail works like this. You use a program such as Outlook Express or Netscape Messenger to create your message. Then you tell your e-mail program to send the message to your e-mail post office (which, technically, is called a mail **server**). Your e-mail post office then sends the message to the recipient's e-mail post office (technically, another mail server). The next time the recipient's e-mail client "visits" the e-mail post office and checks his or her mailbox, the recipient receives the e-mail message.

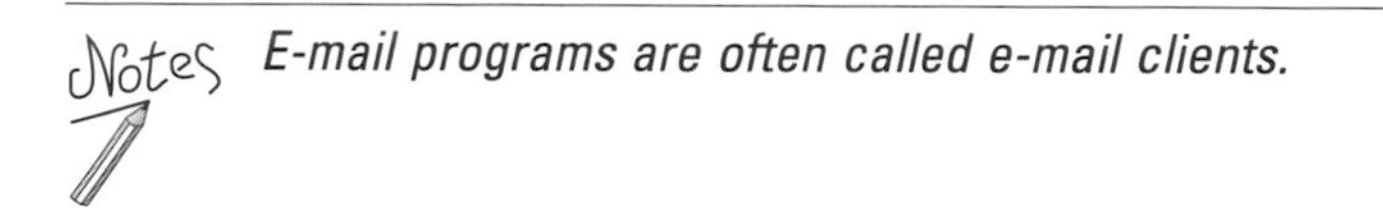

E-mail programs are often called e-mail clients.

Before you can send someone an e-mail message, you need to know the person's e-mail name and address. This e-mail name and address identifies both the person you're sending the message to and, in essence, the mail server that the person uses to pick up his or her e-mail messages. This all sounds rather complicated, but an example will show how simple it is.

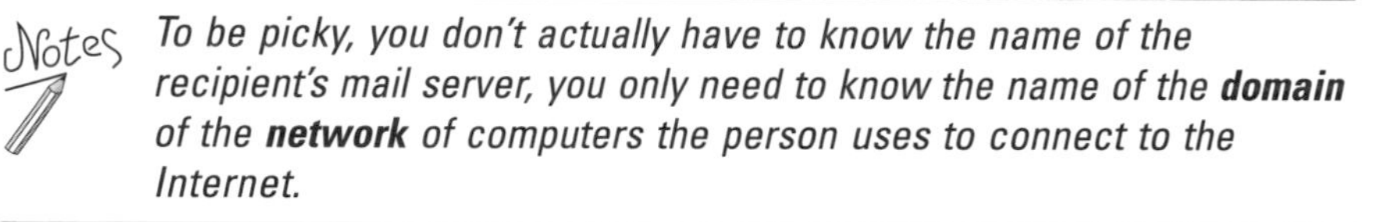

*To be picky, you don't actually have to know the name of the recipient's mail server, you only need to know the name of the **domain** of the **network** of computers the person uses to connect to the Internet.*

Suppose you want to send a message to the president of the United States. To do this, you need to know the domain name that the White House uses for its e-mail and you need to know the e-mail name that the White House uses to identify the president's e-mail mailbox. It turns out that the president's full e-mail name and address is president@whitehouse.gov. So the president's e-mail name is "president," and the White House domain name is "whitehouse.gov." The e-mail name and the domain name are separated by the "@" symbol.

When someone verbally gives an e-mail name and address, they say "at" in place of the @ symbol and "dot" in place of a period. So to describe the president's e-mail name and address, say "president at whitehouse dot gov." Note, however, that the actual e-mail name and address you type is president@whitehouse.gov.

That's really all you need to know to understand and use e-mail. To review, you use e-mail to send and receive text messages. To send someone an e-mail message, you need to know the person's e-mail name and address. Figure 8-1 shows a sample e-mail message created using Outlook Express.

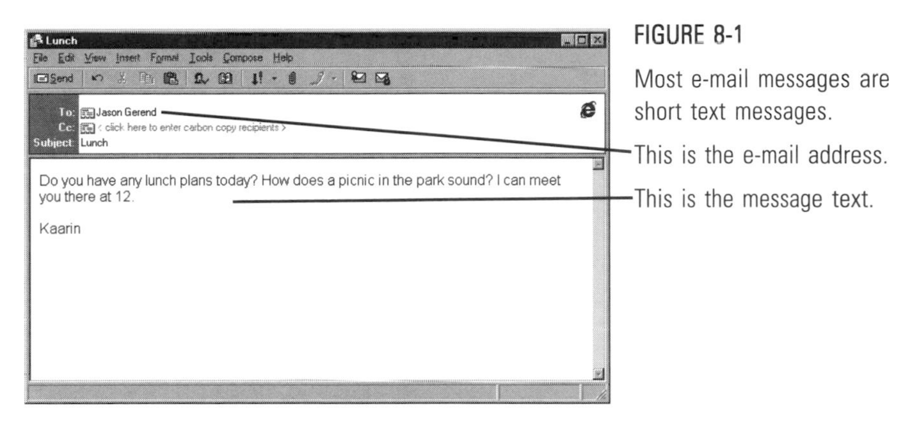

FIGURE 8-1

Most e-mail messages are short text messages.

Setting Up Your PC for E-Mail

Before you can begin enjoying the benefits of e-mail, you first need to set up your PC for e-mail. This process has a couple of steps. First, you need to install an e-mail program such as Outlook Express. Then you need to set up an e-mail account.

You also need to have an Internet connection set up on your PC. Chapter 7 describes how to do this.

If you're running Windows 98, Outlook Express is almost surely installed and ready to go on your computer. If, on the other hand, you're running Windows 95, you need to install Internet Explorer to use Outlook Express. Outlook Express installs by default when you install Internet Explorer.

Chapter 7 describes how to install and use Internet Explorer to browse the web. Chapter 7 also describes how to add Internet Explorer components, such as Outlook Express, to your computer if you didn't install them when you installed Internet Explorer.

To be able to send and receive e-mail messages, your e-mail client needs to know a little about you. For instance, it needs to know the name of your electronic "post office," or mail server. It also needs to know the name of your mailbox. If you have an account with a large ISP such as America Online, the Microsoft Network, Compuserve, or AT&T WorldNet, the ISP's software sets up your e-mail account for you. When you first start your e-mail client, you also often go through a wizard to provide the client with the information it needs. If you don't know what to enter in one of the wizard's dialog boxes, contact your ISP.

Using E-Mail

After you install and set up an e-mail client, you're ready to begin using e-mail. This section describes how to use Outlook Express to accomplish the most important e-mailing tasks: reading e-mail messages, creating and delivering e-mail messages, building a list of e-mail contacts, replying to and forwarding e-mail messages, deleting e-mail messages, and e-mailing files messages. Keep in mind that you don't need to use Outlook Express as your e-mail client. You can use other e-mail clients to accomplish these same tasks. The steps for doing so vary only slightly.

Reading E-Mail Messages

To read your e-mail messages in Outlook Express, click the Inbox folder. Outlook Express lists your messages in the Folder Contents pane and shows a message in the Preview pane, as shown in Figure 8-2.

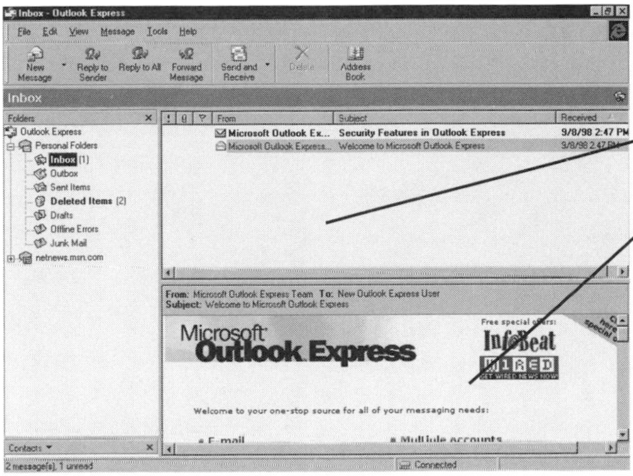

FIGURE 8-2

The Outlook Express program window.

This is the Folder Contents pane.

This is the Preview pane.

If you want to open a new window especially for a message—perhaps so you can see more of the message—double-click the message in the Folder Contents pane. Outlook Express opens a window for the message. After you read the message, click the Close button.

Creating E-Mail Messages

To create an e-mail message using Outlook Express, follow these steps:

1 Start Outlook Express by **double-clicking** the Outlook Express **icon** on the **desktop** or by **clicking** the Outlook Express Quick Launch toolbar button on the Windows **Taskbar.** This displays the **window** shown in Figure 8-3. Note that as you start Outlook Express, Windows might also display the Connect To **dialog box** so you can connect to the Internet. If this happens, you can click Connect if you want to retrieve new messages immediately. However, if you want to compose a message, you can wait and connect later.

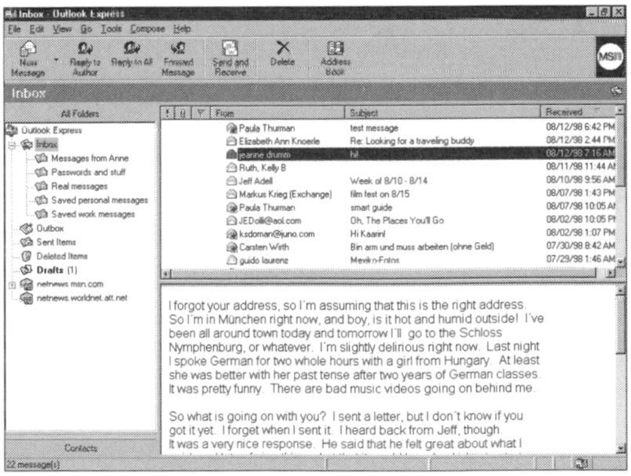

FIGURE 8-3

The Outlook Express program window.

2 Click the New Message **toolbar** button. Windows displays the New Message window, as shown in Figure 8-4.

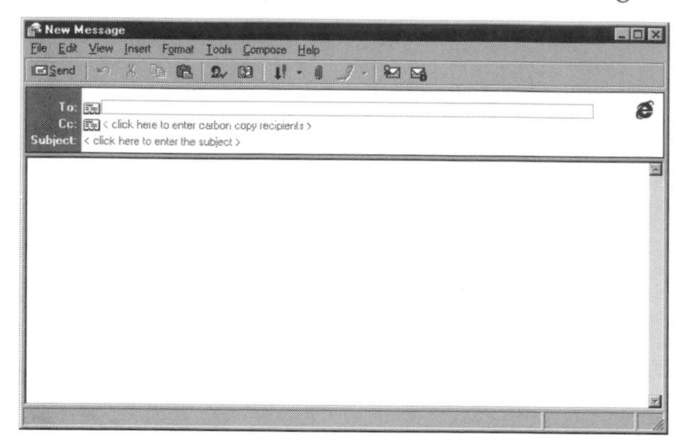

FIGURE 8-4

The empty New Message window.

3 Enter the e-mail name of the message recipient in the To box. For example, if you're sending the president of the United States an e-mail message, type *president@whitehouse.gov* in the To box.

4 Optionally, if you want to send a copy of the message to someone else, enter the e-mail name of the message copy recipient in the Cc box.

You can send a message or message copy to more than one recipient. To do this, enter the e-mail names separated by semicolons.

5 Type a brief description of your message's subject in the Subject box.

6 Type your message in the large text box. Figure 8-5 shows a partial message.

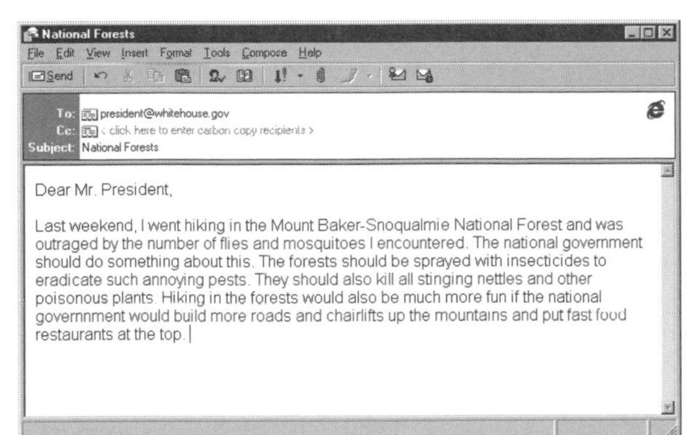

FIGURE 8-5

A partial message to the president of the United States.

7 Optionally, use the Message window's toolbar buttons to format your message. Note, however, that the recipient must use an e-mail client program (like Outlook Express) that understands how to display any formatting you apply. For this reason, it's often best not to format messages.

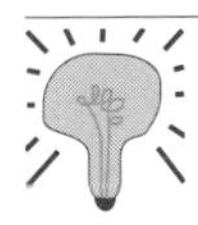

To check the spelling in your message, choose the Tools ***menu's*** *Spelling command. If Outlook Express finds an incorrectly spelled word, it will display a dialog box that lets you correct the misspelling.*

8 When you finish typing your message, click the Send toolbar button to place the message in your Outbox folder. After you click Send, Windows might display the Connect To dialog box to ask, in essence, whether it should connect you to the Internet so you can send the message. If you want to connect, click Connect.

Placing a message in the Outbox folder doesn't actually send the message. You need to connect to the Internet and deliver the message to your mail server in order to actually send the message.

Delivering E-Mail Messages

To deliver the messages in your Outbox folder to your outgoing mail server, click the Send And Receive toolbar button or choose the Tools menu's Send And Receive command. If your computer isn't currently connected to the Internet, Windows makes the connection. Then Windows delivers your outgoing messages and retrieves any incoming messages.

If you've already connected your computer to the Internet—perhaps you've been browsing the Web as described in Chapter 7—Outlook Express might automatically deliver your messages when you click the Send toolbar button on the Message window.

Creating and Using an Address Book

As soon as you start working with e-mail in Outlook Express, you'll want to begin building an Address Book, which you'll use to address the e-mail messages you want to send. Using the Address Book to store names and e-mail addresses makes the task of addressing the e-mail messages you create much quicker and reduces your chances of incorrectly addressing a message. You can add a name to your Address Book in two ways.

To add a person's e-mail name and address to your Address Book if you've received a message from the person, follow these steps:

1. Double-click the message in the Folder Contents pane. Outlook Express opens a Message window for the message.
2. Right-click the From e-mail name and address information.
3. Choose the shortcut menu's Add To Address Book command, as shown in Figure 8-6.
4. When Outlook Express displays the Properties dialog box, press the Enter key or click OK.

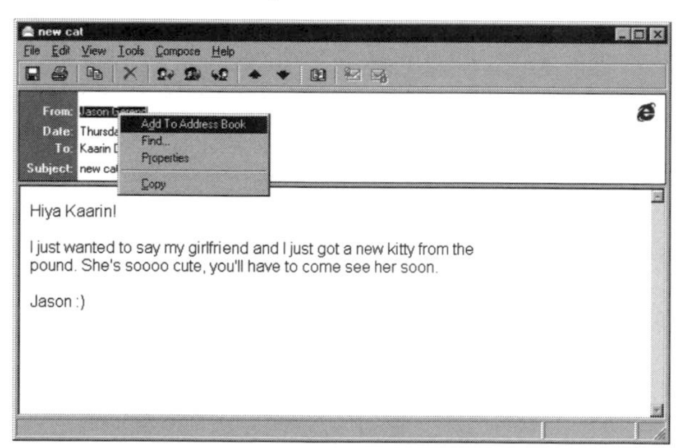

FIGURE 8-6

A Message window with the shortcut menu displayed.

To add a person's e-mail name and address to your Address Book if you haven't received a message from the person, follow these steps:

1. Click the Address Book toolbar button, or choose the Tools menu's Address Book command to display the Address Book dialog box, as shown in Figure 8-7.

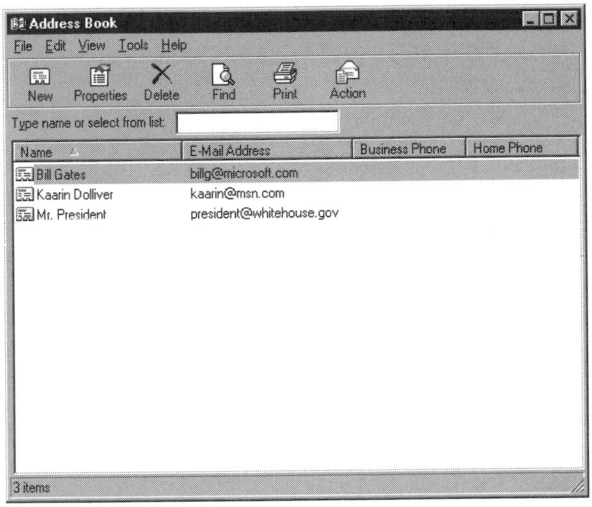

FIGURE 8-7

The Address Book dialog box shows the e-mail names and addresses you've collected.

2. Click the New or New Contact toolbar button (depending on your version of Outlook Express) to display the Properties dialog box, as shown in Figure 8-8.

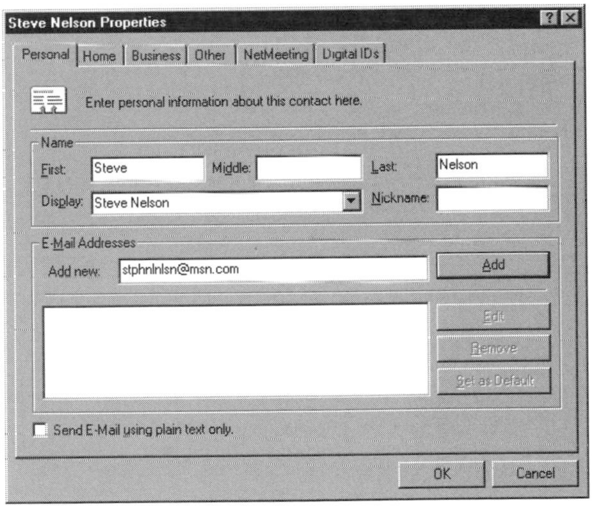

FIGURE 8-8

The Properties dialog box.

3 Enter the person's name in the Name boxes—First, Middle, and Last. Enter the person's full e-mail name and address in the Add New box.

4 Click Add. Outlook Express adds the e-mail name and address to your Address Book.

5 Click OK. Outlook Express displays the Address Book dialog box, which now shows the new name.

To use a name you've entered in the Address Book, follow these steps:

1 Click the New Message toolbar button. Windows displays the New Message window.

2 Click the To card icon to display the Select Recipients dialog box, as shown in Figure 8-9.

As along as a recipient's name is in the Address Book, you can enter it in the To box simply by typing the first couple of letters in the name. If Outlook Express recognizes the name, it enters the name for you.

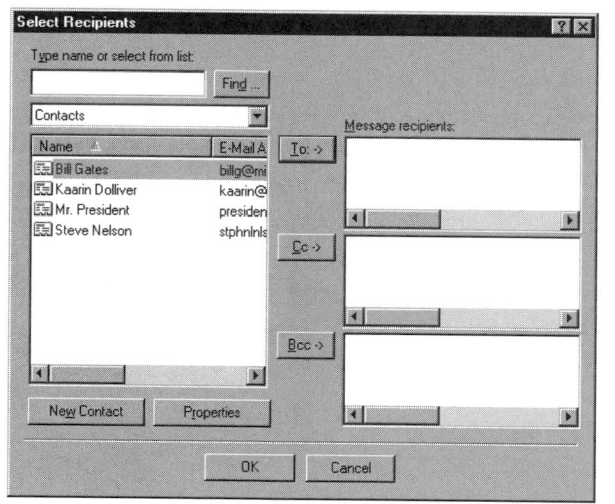

FIGURE 8-9

The Select Recipients dialog box shows the e-mail names and addresses you've collected.

3 To add a name to the To box, click the name to select it and then click To.

4 To add a name to the Cc box, click the name to select it and then click Cc.

5 To add a name to the Bcc box, click the name to select it and then click Bcc.

6 Click OK when you've finished collecting names from the Address Book. Then create your message in the usual way.

Replying to E-Mail Messages

You can send a reply message to someone who's sent you a message. To reply to a message, follow these steps:

1 Open the message.
2 Click the Reply To Author toolbar button, or choose the Compose menu's Reply To Author command. When you do this, Outlook creates a new message for you, filling in the To box with the e-mail name and address of the person you're replying to, as shown in Figure 8-10. Outlook Express also fills in the Subject box for you and then copies the original message text.
3 Add any new text to the message.
4 Delete any unneeded text from the original message text.
5 Click the Send toolbar button.
6 Deliver the message in the usual way.

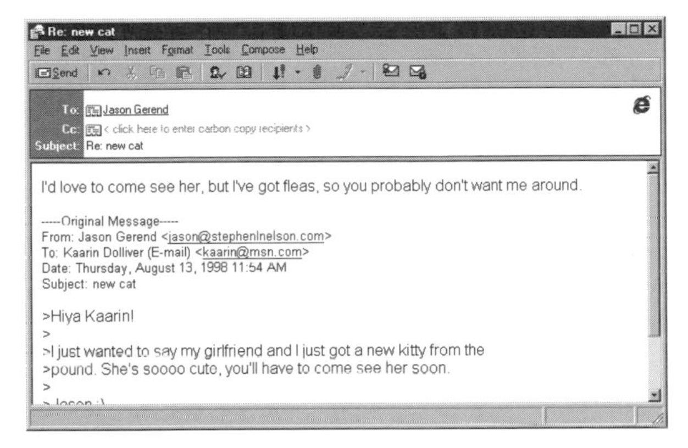

FIGURE 8-10

Reply to a message.

To reply to a message and send a copy of your reply to every recipient of the original message, click the Reply To All toolbar button or choose the Compose menu's Reply To All command.

Forwarding E-Mail Messages

You can easily forward a copy of any message you receive to someone else. To forward a message, follow these steps:

1. Open the message.
2. Click the Forward Message toolbar button, or choose the Compose menu's Forward command. When you do this, Outlook creates a new message for you, filling in the Subject box and then copying the original message text, as shown in Figure 8-11.
3. Enter the e-mail name and address of the message recipient in the To box.
4. Add any new text to the message.
5. Click the Send toolbar button.
6. Deliver the message in the usual way.

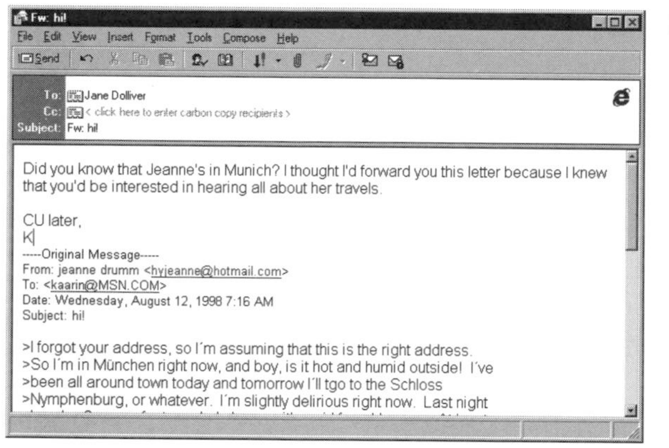

FIGURE 8-11

Forwarding a message.

The people you send messages to can also easily forward your messages to anyone else. For this reason, you probably don't want to say anything in an e-mail message that you don't want repeated in public.

Deleting Messages

To delete a message in one of the Outlook Express folders, select it and then click the Delete toolbar button or press the Delete key. You can also right-click the message and choose the shortcut menu's Delete command.

When you delete a message, Outlook Express moves the message to the Deleted Items folder. If you accidentally delete a message, you can still retrieve it. To retrieve a message, follow these steps:

1. Click the Deleted Items folder icon. Outlook Express opens the folder and displays its contents in the Folder Contents pane.
2. Right-click the message you want to retrieve.
3. Choose the shortcut menu's Move To or Move To Folder command to display the Move dialog box.
4. Select the folder from which you originally deleted the message, as shown in Figure 8-12. For example, if you originally deleted the message from your Inbox folder, indicate you want to move the message back to the Inbox folder. Then click OK.

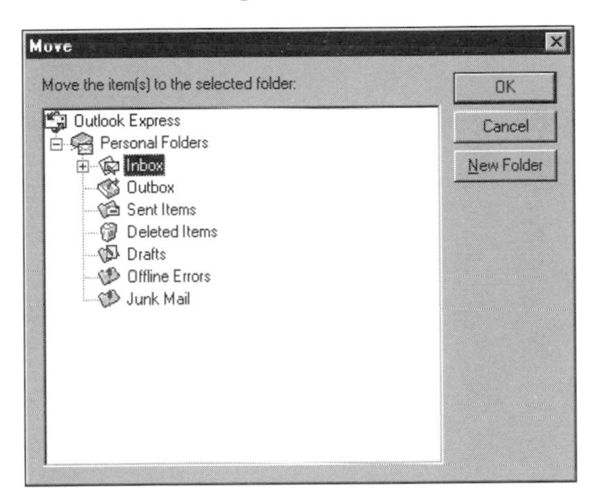

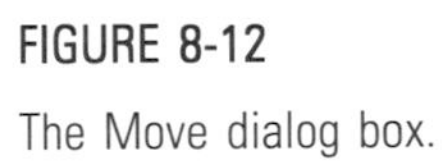
FIGURE 8-12

The Move dialog box.

Because every message you delete actually gets moved to the Deleted Items folder, the number of messages stored in this folder grows quickly. To empty the Deleted Items folder, follow these steps:

1. Right-click the Deleted Items folder.
2. Choose the shortcut menu's Empty Folder command.

Once you delete a message from the Deleted Items folder or empty the Deleted Items folder, the message is permanently lost.

E-Mailing a File Attachment

While most e-mail messages include only text, it's also possible to e-mail files. When you e-mail a file, you simply attach a copy of the file to the message.

To e-mail a file attachment, follow these steps:

1. Click the New Message toolbar button. Windows displays the New Message window.
2. Enter the e-mail name of the message recipient in the To box.
3. To send a copy of the message to someone else, enter the e-mail name of a message copy recipient in the Cc box.
4. Type a brief description of your message's subject in the Subject box.
5. Type your message in the message area beneath the Message window's Formatting toolbar.
6. Click the Attach toolbar button, or choose the Insert menu's File Attachment command to display the Insert Attachment dialog box, as shown in Figure 8-13.

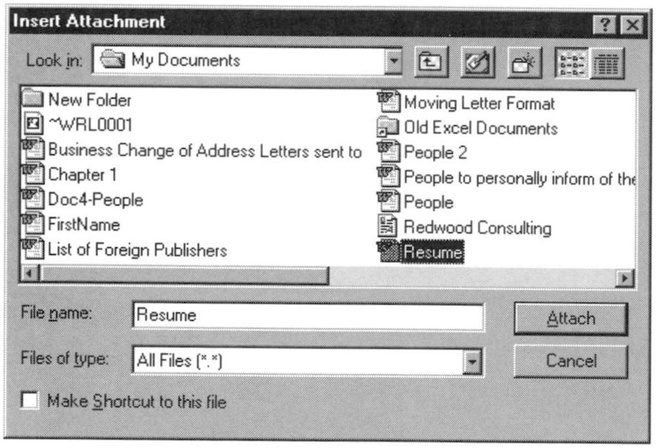

FIGURE 8-13

The Insert Attachment dialog box.

7. Select the **disk** that contains the file you want from the Look In drop-down list box, and locate and double-click the folder that contains the file you want to attach in the large list box.

8 Locate and double-click the file you want to attach to the message. Outlook Express attaches the file to the message, as shown in Figure 8-14.

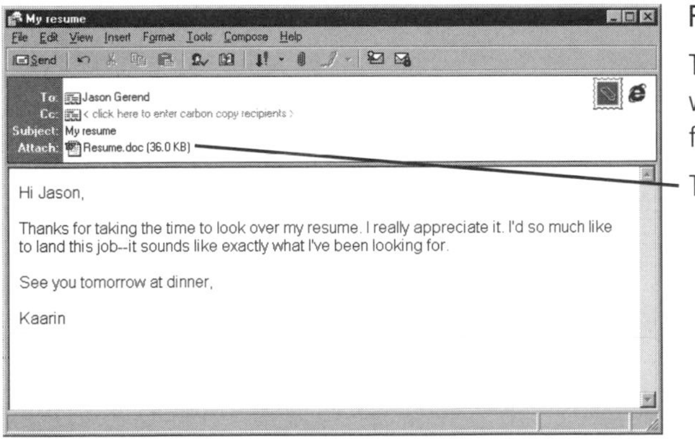

FIGURE 8-14

The Message window with message text and a file attachment.

The attachment.

To e-mail files, both the e-mail client programs and the mail servers need to know how to handle the file attachments.

If the message recipient uses different software than you do, you may need to convert the file to the correct format before you send it. For information about converting files to different formats, refer to the "Importing and Exporting" section in Chapter 6.

If you receive a message with a file attachment, you can detach the file attachment from the message and permanently save the attachment. To do this, follow these steps:

1 Double-click the message header in the Folder Contents pane to display the message in its own window.

2 Right-click the attachment icon.

3 Choose the shortcut menu's Save As command to display the Save As dialog box.

4 Name the file and specify in which **folder** it should be saved in the Save As dialog box. (If you don't specify a location, Outlook Express saves the attachment on your **hard disk** in the Windows folder's Temp **subfolder.**)

Notes

Chapter 6 describes in detail how to save files.

Notes

If you want to only open a file attachment—not save it—you can do so by double-clicking its icon.

Working with Newsgroups

Newsgroups are another way to share information over the Internet. In essence, a newsgroup works like a bulletin board that people use to post e-mail messages. Other people then read these messages. Typically, you use your e-mail client program to post messages and read messages posted on a newsgroup bulletin board. This section describes how to use Outlook Express, the e-mail client program that comes with Windows 98 and Internet Explorer. But you can use other newsgroup readers, such as Netscape Collaborator (which comes with Netscape Communicator), to work with newsgroups.

Because there are hundreds of thousands of people who post messages on thousands of different topics and millions of people who want to read these messages, each newsgroup contains only those messages that fall into a specific category. For example, there's a newsgroup for fans of the Spice Girls. There's a newsgroup for people who enjoy fly fishing. There's a newsgroup devoted to orchid-growing topics. And as you might expect, there are hundreds and hundreds of newsgroups for specialty computer topics.

Subscribing to a Newsgroup

You subscribe to a newsgroup so you can easily visit the newsgroup and read or post messages. To subscribe to a newsgroup—which doesn't cost you anything by the way—follow these steps:

1 Start Outlook Express, and connect to the Internet if you aren't currently connected.

2 Select your news server in the Folder pane.

3 Outlook Express lists all the newsgroups that your Internet service provider carries on that news server.

FIGURE 8-15

Outlook Express lists the newsgroups available on a news server.

If you're using Internet Explorer 4 instead of Internet Explorer 5, you need to click the Newsgroups toolbar button to display the Newsgroups dialog box, which lists the newsgroups available on the news server you selected.

4 Scroll through the list of newsgroups. When you find one you want to subscribe to, double-click it. You can subscribe to as many newsgroups as you want.

To find newsgroups that cover a topic you're interested in, enter a topic name in the Display Newsgroups That Contain box. A list of newsgroups with the topic name appears.

Unfortunately, there's not any way to know from a newsgroup name what the newsgroup messages are about. You'll need to experiment a bit—but that's supposed to be part of the fun.

Reading Newsgroup Messages

After you've subscribed to a newsgroup, you can then read the messages people have posted. To read a newsgroup's messages, follow these steps:

1 Click the newsgroup name in the All Folders list. If the news server branch of the list isn't expanded, you might need to do this by clicking the plus sign [+] to the left of the news server name. Outlook Express then retrieves a list of the newsgroup messages from the news server, as shown in Figure 8-16.

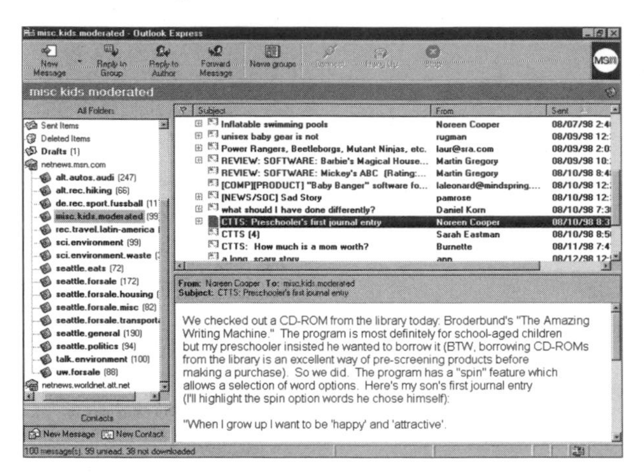

FIGURE 8-16

To read a newsgroup message, click or double-click the message.

2 Click the message you want to read in the Folder Contents pane. Outlook Express displays the message in the Preview pane. If you want to open a window for a message, double-click the message.

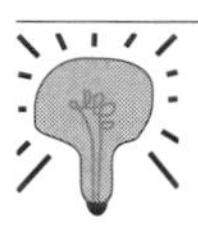

Some newsgroup messages include file attachments. To save the file attachment that's part of a newsgroup message, right-click the attachment and then choose the Save As command.

Posting a Newsgroup Message

To post a message to a newsgroup, first click the newsgroup name in the All Folders list. Next click the New Message toolbar button. When Outlook Express displays the New Message window, enter a subject description in the box provided and then enter your message. (The steps for creating a newsgroup message closely resemble the steps for creating a regular e-mail message.) When you're finished, click the Send toolbar button to post your message to the newsgroup.

If you post messages to newsgroups, you tend to receive lots of unsolicited e-mail from people who want to sell you various products and services—including many products or services that you might find offensive.

An Introduction to Audio and Video Conferencing with NetMeeting

Conferencing via computer is the newest way to use the Internet to communicate with other people. With Microsoft NetMeeting you can see and hear other people in real time. You can even share files and applications on your computer. In order for people to see you, you need a camera attached to and set up on your computer. In order for people to hear you, you need a **sound card** and a microphone plugged into your computer. And for you to hear what people say to you, you also need speakers attached to your computer.

To use NetMeeting, follow these steps:

1. Click the **Start button.**
2. Point to Programs, and point to Internet Explorer.
3. Click Microsoft NetMeeting. The first time you run NetMeeting, a wizard guides you through the process of setting it up. The wizard asks you to pick a primary server (which is basically an electronic conference room) where you want to hold your meetings. The wizard also asks a little about you and whether you intend to use NetMeeting for personal, business, or adult-only communication. NetMeeting uses the information you provide to list you on this server so others can find you. After you've provided all the information NetMeeting needs, the wizard conducts a test of your speakers and microphone to optimize the sound quality you hear, record, and send.
4. If you're working offline, you need to connect to the Internet. This might include completing your Internet service provider's **logon** procedure.

5 If you plan to meet someone on a server other than your default server, select a type of communication (Personal, Business, or Adult-Only) from the Category drop-down list box, and then select the correct server from the Server drop-down list box. If you aren't automatically logged on to the server, choose the Call menu's Log On To Name Of Server command to log on to the server you selected.

If you are trying to call someone using NetMeeting and it doesn't seem to be working, check to make sure you are still connected to the server by looking at the status bar in the lower-right corner of your screen. If it says you are "Not logged on," choose the Call menu's Log On To Name Of Server command until the status bar indicates that you are logged on.

6 To call someone listed on the server, select the person's name from the list and click the Call toolbar button (see Figure 8-17). Then click Call in the New Call dialog box. To call someone not on the list, enter the person's computer IP address, e-mail address, or username in the Address box and then click Call.

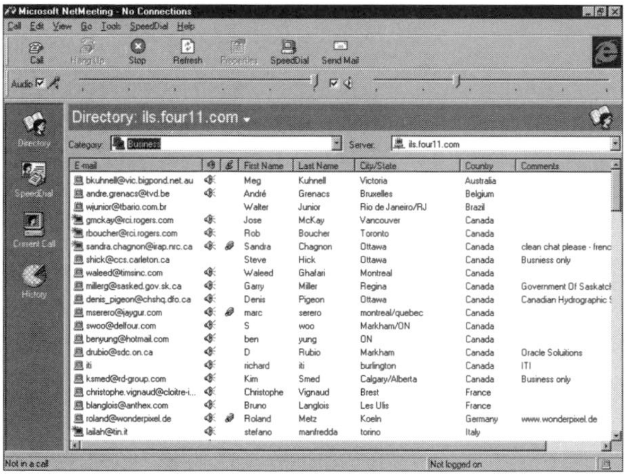

FIGURE 8-17

The list of people currently logged on to the server.

An IP address is a unique number that identifies a computer connected to the Internet. An IP address contains a series of four numbers (each having from one to three digits) separated by periods. That much said, you probably don't need to know about IP addresses because you may likely not even know your own IP address, much less someone else's. (Most ISPs assign you a different IP address each time you connect to the Internet.) The easiest way to call someone not on the directory list is by entering his or her e-mail address or NetMeeting username.

After you have conducted a NetMeeting call with someone, NetMeeting adds that person to the SpeedDial window so you can quickly and easily see if the person is ***online*** *and then place another call to him or her. Just click the SpeedDial icon on the bar on the left, select the person's name from the list, and click the Call toolbar button.*

7 If the call is accepted, NetMeeting opens the Current Call window, as shown in Figure 8-18. The windows on the right let you view video that you send and receive. Drag the Volume sliders at the top to adjust the incoming and outgoing volume.

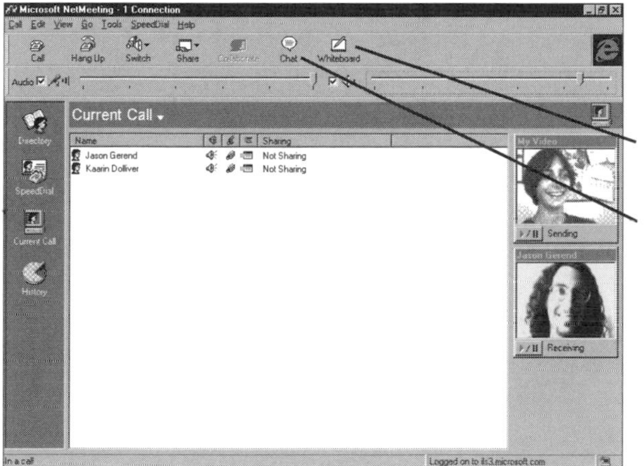

FIGURE 8-18

A NetMeeting call in progress.

The Whiteboard toolbar button.

The Chat toolbar button.

8 Click the Whiteboard toolbar button if you want to draw on a virtual whiteboard.

9 Click the Chat toolbar button if you want to write back and forth in real time.

10 If you want other people in the meeting to see a file on your computer, open the file and click the Share toolbar button. Then select the file you want to share from the pop-up menu. If you want other people in the meeting to be able to work with the file, click the Collaborate toolbar button.

CHAPTER 9

Using Popular Programs

You use **programs** to accomplish most of the tasks you perform on the computer. Your **PC** might have come with some extra programs preinstalled, but even so, at some point you'll still probably need to buy a few programs to accomplish other tasks. This chapter introduces several of the most common types of programs that people use and describes why you would use each type of program. It also provides some general instructions for working with each of the program types introduced. This chapter covers the following types of programs:

- **Word processors**
- **Spreadsheets**
- **Web browsers**
- **E-mail** clients
- Personal information managers
- Integrated programs
- Finance programs
- Tax preparation programs
- Antivirus programs
- Games
- Presentation programs

Many programs come in suites. For example, you can often purchase a word processor, spreadsheet program, presentation program, and even an e-mail client and web browser all in one box. While such a suite is expensive, you save money over buying all of the programs individually. Three of the most popular suites of programs are Corel WordPerfect Suite, Lotus Smartsuite, and Microsoft Office.

Word Processors

A word processor doesn't really "process" words—you use a word processor to write **documents** on your computer. **Microsoft Windows** comes with a very basic word processor, WordPad, but an advanced word processor provides many more tools for creating more complicated documents, which makes writing easier and more fun. Some of the most popular word processors are Corel WordPerfect, Lotus Word Pro, and Microsoft Word. This section describes how to use Microsoft Word, but the other word processors work in much the same way. They just look a little different on your screen and have a couple more features in one area and a few less in another.

As with WordPad, when you start Word, it displays a screen resembling a blank piece of paper all ready for you to begin writing. You can use this blank new document to create a document, but you can also use an existing document design, called a template, to create a new document. So instead of starting from scratch, you have predesigned forms that are ready for you to use to create different kinds of documents—business letters, faxes, memos, envelopes, mailing labels, and so on.

Notes

*Later versions of Word even include a template for creating **web pages.***

Let's say you want to write a letter. To do this with Word, follow these steps:

1. Choose the File **menu's** New command to display the New **dialog box.**
2. **Click** the Letters & Faxes tab, as shown in Figure 9-1.

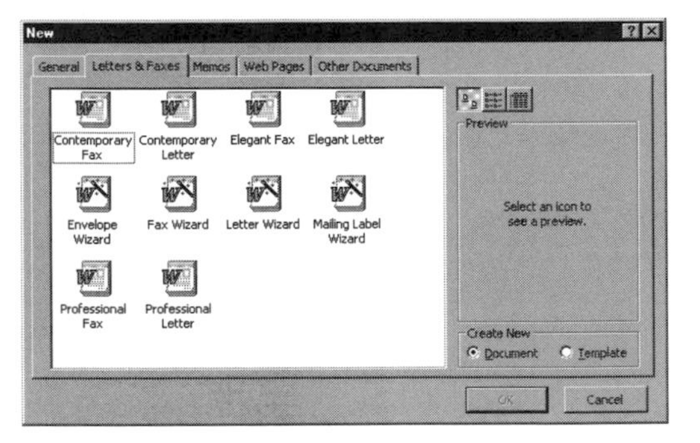

FIGURE 9-1

The Letters & Faxes tab of the New dialog box.

3 Click one of the letter **icons**, and preview that type of letter in the Preview box.

4 When you find a letter template you like, click OK. Word opens a new document **window** with the template for your letter, as shown in Figure 9-2.

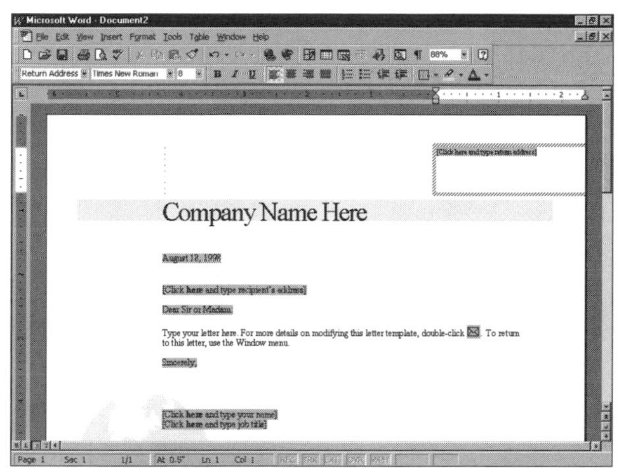

FIGURE 9-2

A new letter template.

5 Fill in the fields with the information the template requests—the name and address of the recipient, your name and address, and so forth.

6 To add formatting, use the Formatting **toolbar.** The Formatting toolbar works much like the Format bar in WordPad and the Formatting toolbar in FrontPage Express (as described in Chapter 7).

As you work on the letter, save your work every few minutes by clicking the Save toolbar button. The first time you click Save, Word asks you to name the document and specify a location.

Notes

As you type, Word corrects some common typos and misspellings. The ones it finds that it can't correct, it underlines with a wavy line. Word underlines what it sees as grammatical or punctuation errors (such as incomplete sentences or too many spaces between words) in green and spelling errors (any words it can't find in its dictionary) in red. To correct a section of green or red underlined text, right-click the text and select the correction.

7 Click the Print toolbar button to print the letter.

Word and other word processors work much like the WordPad **accessory** that comes with Windows. However, Word and the other word processors provide many more features. The following list describes some of the things that you can do in Word and cannot do in WordPad:

- Insert tables in documents
- Create columns of text
- Highlight text
- Use a toolbar's tools to draw pictures
- Show or hide nonprinting characters, such as carriage returns
- Look up words in a thesaurus
- Quickly copy formatting from one section of text to another
- Calculate the length of your document in characters, words, lines, paragraphs, or pages
- Merge infomation from a **database** to create form letters for mailing labels
- Use footnotes
- Add headers or footers to a document, such as page numbers

Spreadsheets

You use spreadsheet programs to enter data in a table format. You can then perform calculations and create charts from the data. People often use spreadsheets to build simple budgets. But they're also a handy tool for making most any type of table—even those that require no data or calculations. Some popular spreadsheet programs include Lotus 1-2-3, Quattro Pro, and Microsoft Excel. These programs work in much the same way. This section describes how to use Microsoft Excel to build a simple spreadsheet.

1. Start Excel. The program displays a blank document divided into a grid, as shown in Figure 9-3. This blank document is called a worksheet. At the bottom of the document window are three tabs: Sheet 1, Sheet 2, and Sheet 3. An Excel document (called a workbook), comes with three blank pages, called worksheets, by default. You can add or remove these pages as needed.

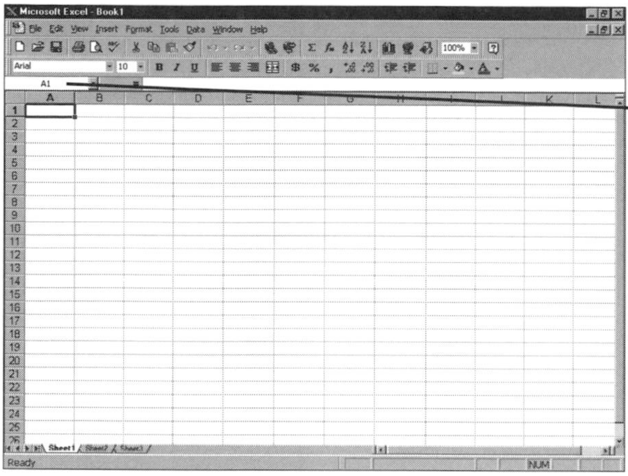

FIGURE 9-3

A blank Excel worksheet.

The Name box.

2 Click an empty box. These boxes are called cells. When you select a cell, Excel displays the cell's name (its column letter and row number) in the Name box.

3 Enter some text or a number, and press the Enter key. This enters the data in the cell and moves you to the next line.

4 To change the contents of a cell, select the cell and type something else.

5 Excel enters data automatically if it can detect a pattern in what you type. For example, if you enter *Sunday* in one cell and *Monday* in the next cell, Excel fills in the rest of the days of the week for you, as shown in figure 9-4. Just select the first cells you entered, and **drag** the small square in the lower-right corner of the selection to continue the pattern. This technique also works for series or patterns of numbers.

6 If you enter an equation (called a formula), Excel calculates the data. For example, to add up the data you entered in a row or column, click the AutoSum toolbar button. Excel places a blinking box around the cells it thinks you want to add. Press the Enter key to accept the range of cells. If you later change one of the added cells, the sum changes as well.

7 You can also enter your own equations in a cell. When you type an entry in a cell, precede the entry with an equals sign, and then type the equation. For example, if you type =5-3 in a cell, Excel displays the number 2.

8 To insert more complicated functions, such as financial functions, click the Paste Function toolbar button.

Microsoft Excel - Book1

H5 =SUM(H2:H4)

	A	B	C	D	E	F	G	H
1		Sunday	Monday	Tuesday	Wednesda	Thursday	Friday	Saturday
2	Breakfast	1020	340	450	450	480	250	600
3	Lunch	530	690	600	580	760	540	620
4	Dinner	980	990	850	830	770	920	810
5		2530	2020	1900	1860	2010	1710	2030

FIGURE 9-4

An Excel worksheet with some data and formulas.

This row of cells displays the sum of the column.

9 To create a chart, or graph, of your data, select the cells you want to include in the chart and click the ChartWizard toolbar button. The ChartWizard guides you through the process of creating a chart of your data, as shown in Figure 9-5.

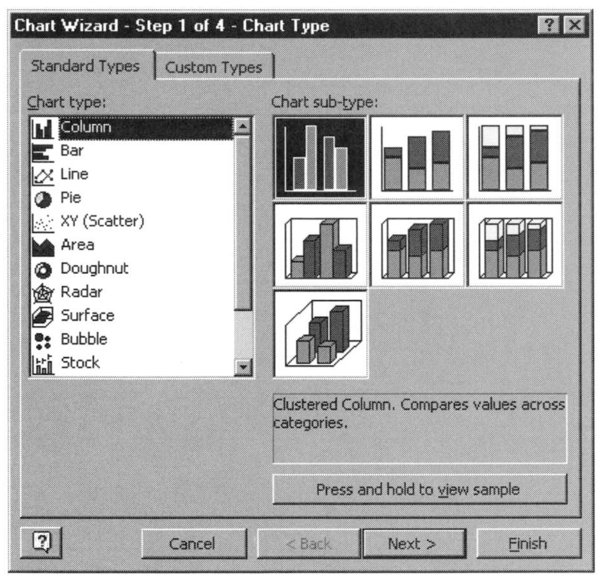

FIGURE 9-5

Use charts to visualize your data.

Web Browsers

You use a web browser to browse the **World Wide Web.** Windows 98 comes with Microsoft's web browser suite, Internet Explorer. But many people use other browsers for viewing web pages. The most popular of these web browsers is Netscape Navigator, which, like Internet Explorer, comes as a part of a free suite of **Internet** programs (in this case, Netscape Communicator). This section describes how to use Netscape Navigator to browse the World Wide Web.

1 Open Netscape Navigator to display your home page, as shown in Figure 9-6.

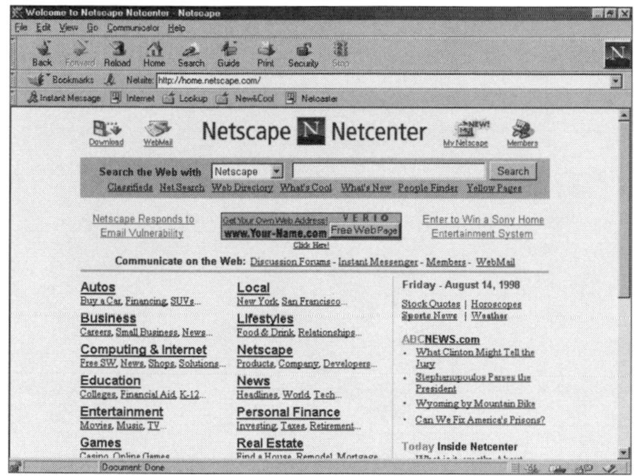

FIGURE 9-6

The Netscape Navigator window.

2 You can move to another page in a few basic ways:

- Enter a different **URL** in the Location box.
- Click a **hyperlink** on a page.
- Click the Home toolbar button to return to your home page.
- Click the Back and Forward toolbar buttons to go back and forth through the web pages you just visited.

3 You can also move to a different web page in a few more advanced ways:

- Click the Search toolbar button to display a Netscape page containing a list of hyperlinks to the most popular search engines.
- Click the Guide toolbar button to view the Netscape home page.
- Click the Bookmarks toolbar button and select a category and popular site to go to that site, as shown in Figure 9-7.
- Choose the Communicator menu's History command to display the History window, which lists the web pages you've recently visited. To return to a web page, **double-click** it in the History window.

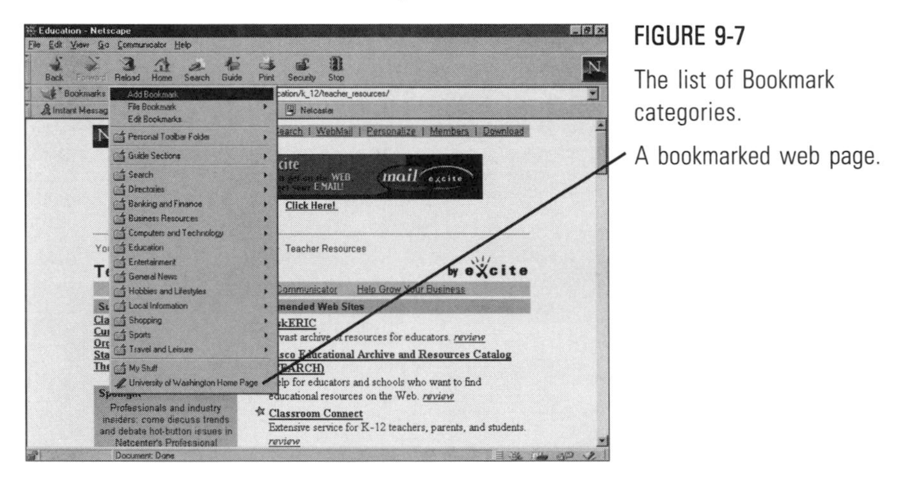

FIGURE 9-7

The list of Bookmark categories.

> *To add a web page to your list of Bookmarks, display the page, click the Bookmarks toolbar button, and choose Add Bookmark.*

E-Mail Clients

You use e-mail clients to send and receive electronic mail. Chapter 8 describes Outlook Express, the free e-mail client that comes with Windows 98 and Internet Explorer. But other popular e-mail clients exist, such as Eudora, Netscape Messenger, and Outlook (which also functions as a personal information manager, as described later in this chapter). E-mail clients function in much the same way. Since this book already describes in detail how you use Outlook Express, this section briefly describes Netscape Messenger, the free e-mail client that comes with Netscape Navigator, the leading web browser.

1 The first time you use Netscape Messenger, it asks you a few questions about yourself. Messenger uses the information you provide to set up your e-mail accounts.

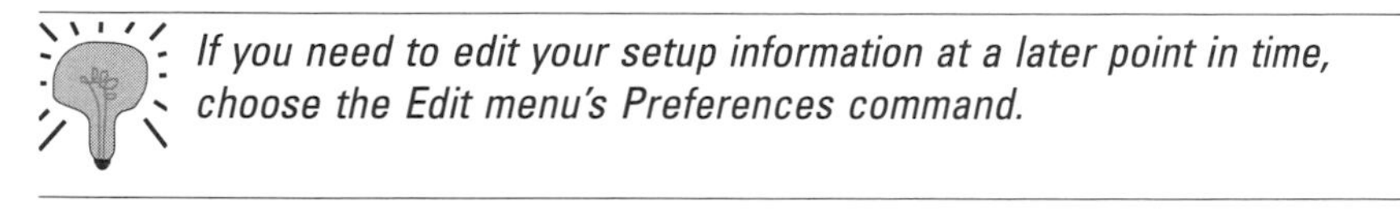

If you need to edit your setup information at a later point in time, choose the Edit menu's Preferences command.

2 To **download** messages from your mail **server**, click the Get Msg toolbar button. To display a message's text, select the message, as shown in Figure 9-8.

FIGURE 9-8

The Netscape Messenger program window.

3 To reply to or forward a message, select the message and click the Reply or Forward toolbar button. To add the sender's e-mail address to your Address Book, select the message, choose the Message menu's Add To Address Book command, and then choose the Sender command.

4 To add an address to your Address Book from scratch, choose the Communicator menu's Address Book command. This displays the Address Book window, as shown in Figure 9-9. Click the New Card toolbar button.

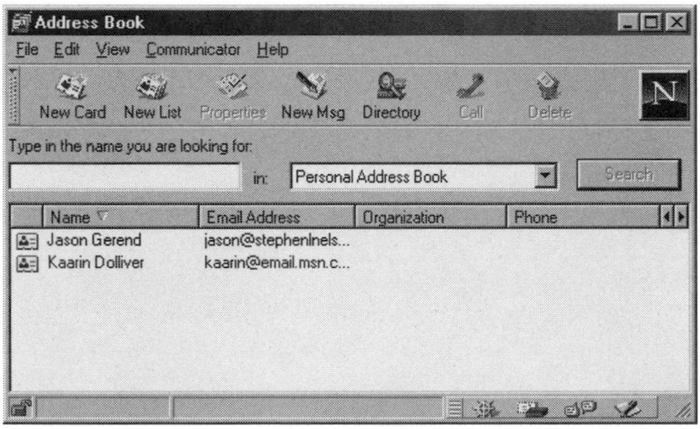

FIGURE 9-9

The Address Book window.

5 To write a new message, click the New Msg toolbar button. This opens a blank Composition window, as shown in Figure 9-10.

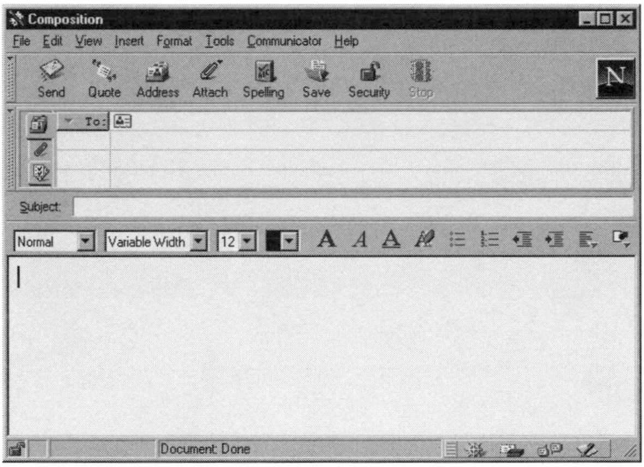

FIGURE 9-10

Use the Composition window for writing messages.

6 Enter the recipient's name on the To line and a subject in the Subject box.

Enter the recipient's name as you entered it in the Address Book. After you type a few letters, Netscape Messenger determines the name you're typing and completes the To line for you.

To send a message to someone you haven't added to your Address Book, enter his or her e-mail address on the To line.

7. Type the message body in the large text box.
8. To add an attachment, click the Attach toolbar button and select File, Web Page, or My Address Book Card depending on what you want to attach to the message. (By attaching your Address Book Card, you send the recipient your Address Book contact information on an electronic business card.)
9. Click the Send toolbar button to send the message.

To read and post ***newsgroup*** *messages, use Netscape Collabra. Just click the Discussion Groups button in the lower-right corner of the Netscape Messenger window.*

Personal Information Managers

People use personal information managers to manage their schedules. With a personal information manager, you can enter all of your appointments in your computer. You can also enter the dates you need to remember, such as birthdays and anniversaries. Personal information managers also let you build and prioritize To Do lists of the tasks you need to accomplish. The most popular personal information managers are Lotus Organizer, Microsoft Outlook, and Symantec ACT! This section describes Microsoft Outlook, but the other personal information managers work in much the same way.

1. To go to an Outlook folder, click that folder's icon on the Outlook bar. Choose from the following icons:
   - Click Inbox to work with e-mail messages
   - Click Calendar to add and work with appointments and events
   - Click Contacts to record contact information

- Click Tasks to work with To Do tasks
- Click Journal to record time spent on activities
- Click Notes to jot down notes to yourself

2 If you click the Calendar icon, Outlook displays the Calendar window, as shown in Figure 9-11.

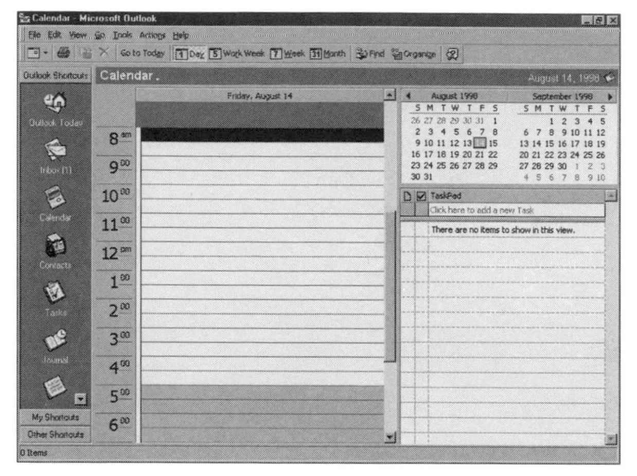

FIGURE 9-11

The Outlook Calendar.

3 Click the New Appointment toolbar button to display the New Appointment window, as shown in Figure 9-12.

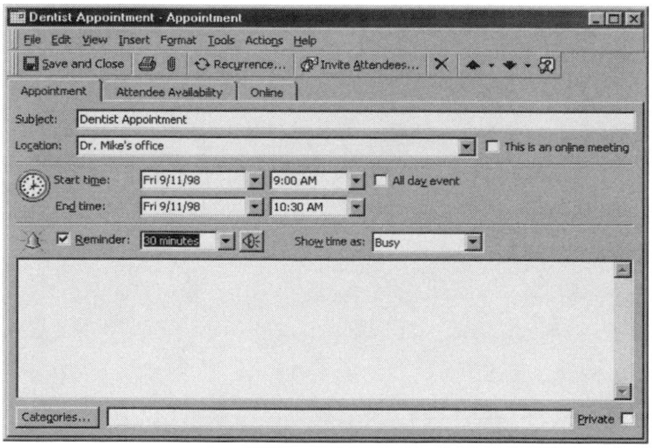

FIGURE 9-12

The New Appointment window.

4 Describe the appointment in the Subject, Location, Start Time, and End Time boxes. Select the Reminder check box and use the Reminder drop-down list box to set a reminder for the appointment. Click the Recurrence toolbar button if the appointment occurs on a regular basis.

5 Click the Save And Close toolbar button to record the appointment.

6 If you click the Tasks icon, Outlook displays the Tasks window, as shown in Figure 9-13. Enter a new task using the boxes at the top of the list. To mark an existing task as complete, select the check box beside the task.

FIGURE 9-13

The Outlook Tasks list.

Integrated Programs

As mentioned earlier in the chapter, you can buy several programs together in a package called a suite. If you're not an avid computer user though, you have another much less expensive option for purchasing word processing, spreadsheet, and other functionality in one package: buying an integrated program. With an integrated program, you get the basic functionality of programs in a suite, but not all of the features included in the full versions of the programs. The most popular integrated programs are Claris Works and Microsoft Works. Both function in much the same way. This section describes how to use Microsoft Works.

When you start Microsoft Works, it asks what type of document you want to create and allows you to create it using a template. To use a Microsoft Works template, follow these steps:

1 In the Works Task Launcher dialog box, select the task category and then select the individual task, as shown in Figure 9-14.

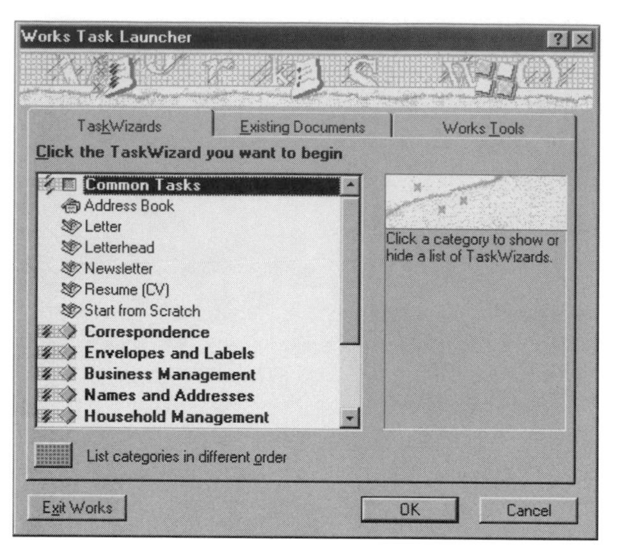

FIGURE 9-14

The Works Task Launcher dialog box.

2 Click OK, and then click the checkerboard button next to Yes, Run The TaskWizard to use the TaskWizard. Works displays the Works TaskWizard dialog box for the task you selected, as shown in Figure 9-15.

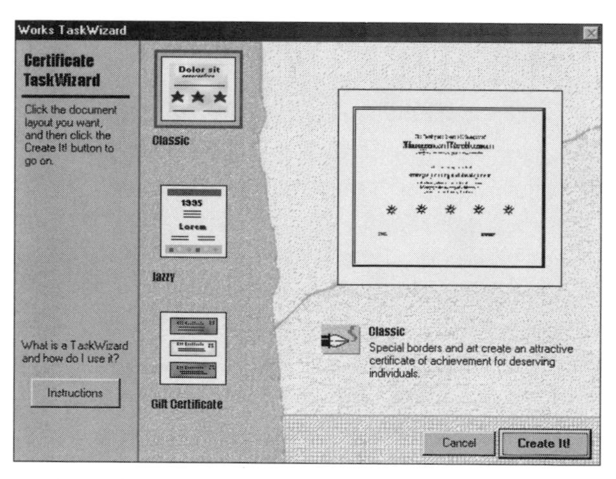

FIGURE 9-15

The Works Certificate TaskWizard dialog box.

3 Select the template you want to use, and click Create It! Works creates a new document based on the template you selected.

4 Edit the document as needed, as shown in Figure 9-16.

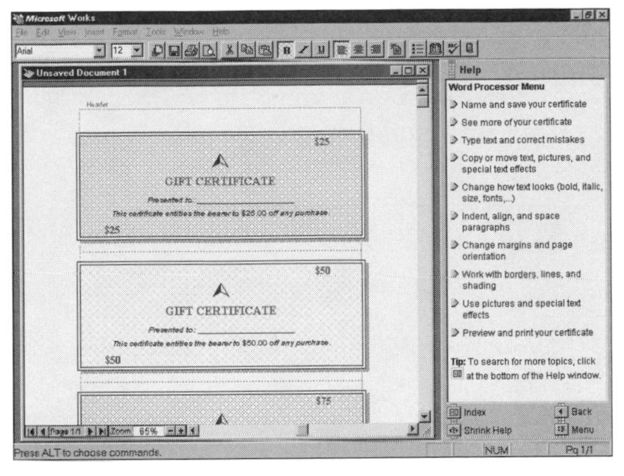

FIGURE 9-16

Working on a document in Works.

5. Click Save to save the document.
6. To open a document you've previously created from the Works Task Launcher, click the Existing Documents tab. You can open several documents at once within Works. You can even work with all the different types of documents Works creates within the same window, using the same menus and toolbar.

Finance Programs

Finance programs allow you to more easily keep track of your finances. With a finance program, you keep your checkbook on your computer. You enter information in an on-screen check register just as you would in a paper register. But with a finance program helping you keep your checkbook, balancing your checkbook at the end of the month is much simpler. And a finance program includes several tools to help you monitor your spending habits. Using the data you enter in your account registers, a finance program can, for example, create charts or reports showing your income and expenses. Most finance programs also include financial calculators to help you plan for the future or to create budgets. Two of the most popular finance programs are Quicken by Intuit and Microsoft Money. For small businesses, Quicken Small Business or QuickBooks are also good choices. This section describes how to use Quicken, but Money works in a similar fashion. To use some of Quicken's basic features, follow these steps:

1. When you install Quicken, the program asks you a little about yourself and your accounts. It's a good idea to have all of your bank, credit card, and other account statements and financial information (such as paycheck stubs) handy as you set up your first Quicken **file.**
2. To enter transactions in a register, click the Registr icon on the Iconbar. This displays a check register that resembles a paper check register, as shown in Figure 9-17.

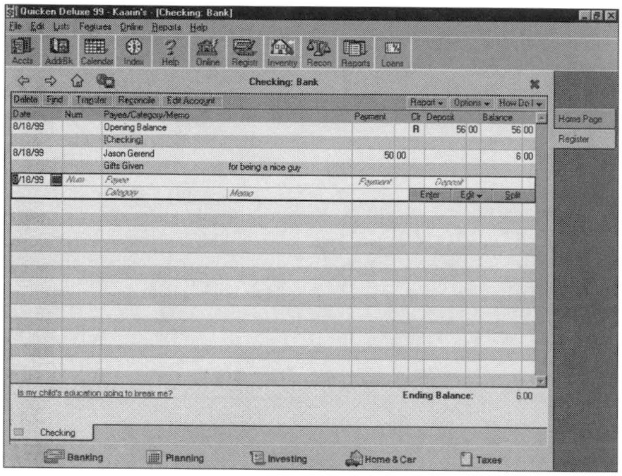

FIGURE 9-17

An account register in Quicken.

3. To see a report of your spending, click the Reports icon and choose the type of report you want to create, as shown in Figure 9-18.

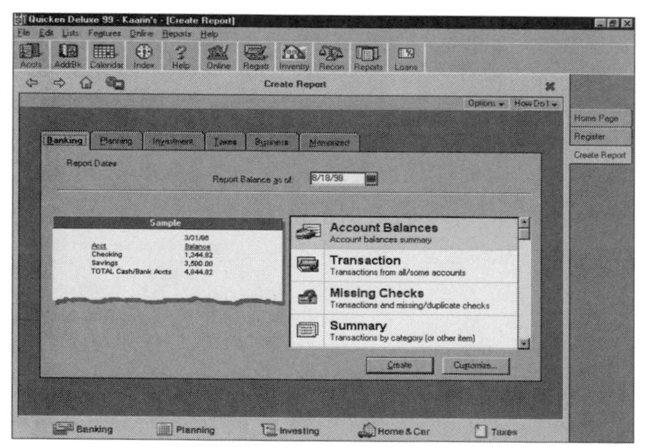

FIGURE 9-18

Creating reports.

4 To create a budget using Quicken, choose the Features menu's Planning command and the Planning submenu's Budgets command. You can create a budget from scratch or one based on your existing Quicken transactions. Figure 9-19 shows the Budget window in Quicken.

FIGURE 9-19

The Budget window.

Tax Preparation Programs

Tax preparation programs help you prepare your taxes. Popular tax preparation programs include Intuit's TurboTax and Kiplinger TaxCut. To use these programs, you just answer the program's questions by clicking buttons and entering information in boxes. The program helps you look for deductions and alerts you if it finds inconsistencies or possible errors in the amounts you enter. Figures 9-20 and 9-21 show what TurboTax looks like and how it works.

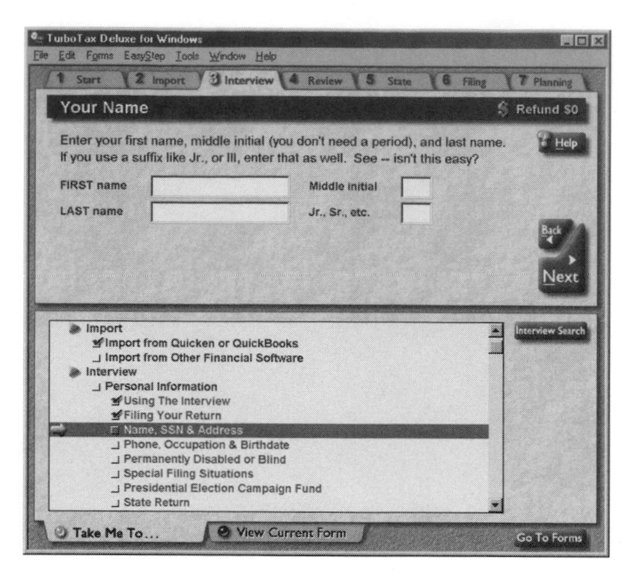

FIGURE 9-20

Click Next to go through TurboTax's tabs and enter information.

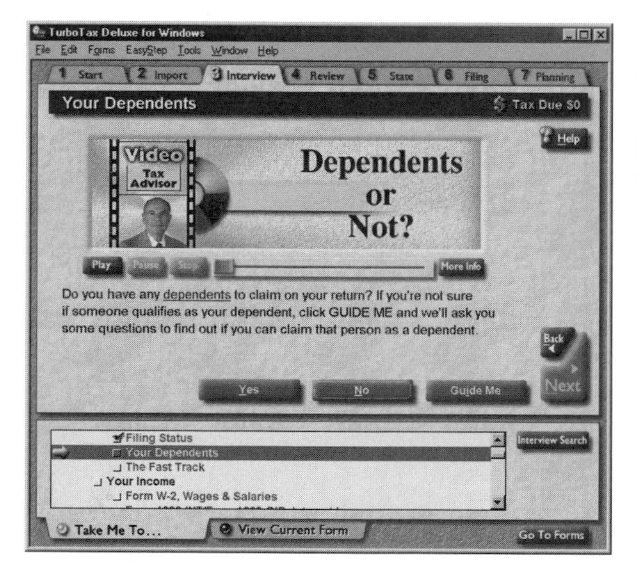

FIGURE 9-21

Some versions of TurboTax provide video assistance in deciding what to enter.

Antivirus Programs

Antivirus programs help to protect your computer from **viruses.** An antivirus program detects viruses, notifies you when a **disk** has a virus, and cleans your **hard disk** of viruses it finds. Popular antivirus programs include Dr. Solomon's Anti-Virus, McAfee VirusScan, and Norton AntiVirus. Most antivirus programs require little work on your part. After you install an antivirus program, you usually need to set a few options for how and when you want the program to run. Then the antivirus program scans your computer automatically, usually after you **boot** your computer or based on the schedule you specify. Now and again you probably need to download updates for your antivirus program so it protects you against new viruses. Figure 9-22 shows Norton AntiVirus in action scanning a hard disk.

Norton AntiVirus

Scanning files for viruses...

Folder: C:\WINDOWS\SYSTEM\RL\SOFT

Item	Scanned	Infected	Cleaned
Memory:	Yes	No	No
Master boot records:	1	0	0
Boot records:	1	0	0
Files:	421	0	0

Stop

FIGURE 9-22

Norton AntiVirus.

Games

Games are some of the most popular programs people buy for the computer. Because the purpose, strategy, rules, and procedures differ completely from game to game, I can't describe in general terms how you play games. I can, however, broadly describe a few of the different types of games available. For adults, one of the most popular types of games is the action game, represented by such classics as Quake, TombRaider, and UnReal. These games usually involve a single person (played by you), rampaging around killing things with increasingly realistic and sometimes dazzling graphics. Another popular type of game is the Strategy game. This type includes games such as Age of Empires and Diablo, and usually involves controlling vast quantities of people, weapons, and resources in the attempt to wage war against the computer or another player. A more subdued type of game is the Adventure game, represented by games such as Riven and the 11th Hour. These games usually have the most beautiful graphics and an involved story line, with you trying to solve puzzles and uncover some sort of mystery. Simulators, such as flight simulators, pretty much speak for themselves, as do Sports games, with games in each category trying to accurately re-create the actual experience of something. The last type of game worth mentioning are Puzzle games, where your goal is to simply solve puzzles or answer trivia. And, of course, there are several games geared especially for children, such as educational games.

Presentation Programs

People, especially traveling salespeople, use presentation programs to create presentation slides on the computer. With a presentation program and a laptop computer, you can take your presentation with you on business trips and even display your presentation slides on an overhead projector. Or you can print the slides and distribute them so audience members can take notes and follow along. Presentation programs also work well for simple desktop publishing tasks, such as printing fliers. Two of the most popular presentation programs are Corel Presentations and Microsoft PowerPoint. This section describes how to use Microsoft PowerPoint, but both programs work in essentially the same way. To use PowerPoint, follow these steps:

1 When PowerPoint displays the PowerPoint dialog box shown in Figure 9-23, click the AutoContent Wizard option button and click OK.

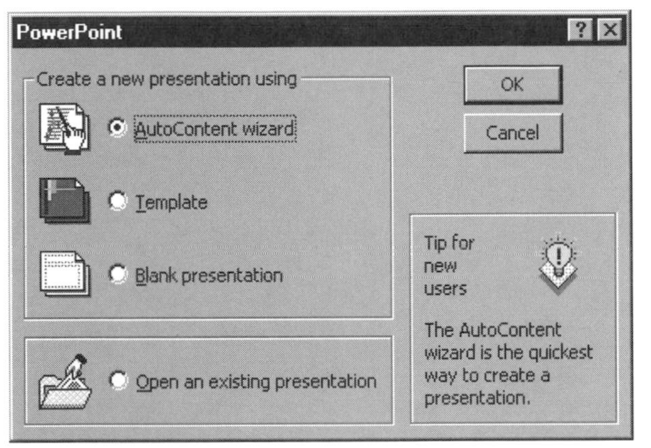

FIGURE 9-23

Starting PowerPoint.

2 Go through the AutoContent Wizard to select the type of presentation you want to create and how you want to present it, as shown in Figure 9-24.

FIGURE 9-24

Defining the presentation.

3 Click Finish to create the presentation.

4 Add the content, and use PowerPoint's toolbars to customize the presentation, as shown in Figure 9-25.

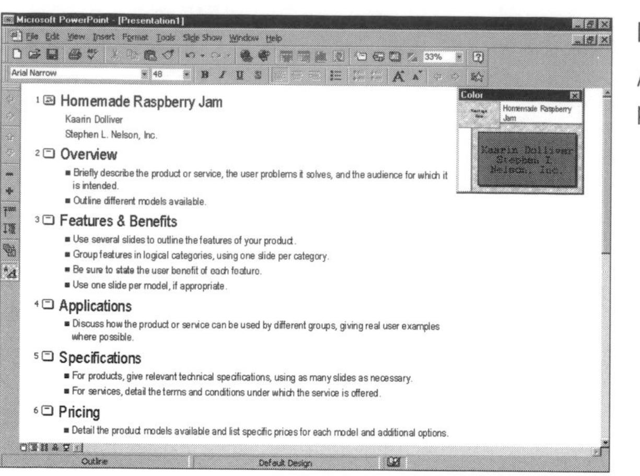

FIGURE 9-25

A PowerPoint presentation.

5 Use the Views buttons in the lower-left corner of the presentation document window to display the presentation in different ways. For example, click the Slide Show button to preview the presentation as a slide show. Click the **mouse** to proceed through the slides.

Here are some fun things you can do in a PowerPoint presentation:

- Animate text so it moves across the slide on demand and even makes sounds that accompany the movement
- Specify the transition between slides—how you want the slides to fade in and if you want a sound to accompany the change between slides
- Create a home page
- Rehearse the timing of a presentation
- Add clip art images

CHAPTER 10

Upgrading and Maintaining Your PC

Sooner or later you'll undoubtedly encounter a time when your **PC** doesn't perform the way you expect. In such a situation, you need to remember two things: First, don't worry. Chances are, the problem can be fixed within a couple of seconds. Second, it's probably not your fault. Even if you take good care of your PC as described in this chapter, your PC will on occasion stop working the way it should. This chapter covers the following topics related to maintaining and upgrading your PC to keep it at its optimum performance:

- Basic care of PC **hardware**
- Using Windows tools to maintain PC performance
- Do-it-yourself troubleshooting
- Upgrading your PC
- Finding technical help

Basic Care of PC Hardware

To avoid unnecessary problems with your PC and to help prevent data loss, keep your PC's parts and pieces as clean as possible, just as you would any other expensive item around the house.

Keeping the Mouse Clean

To keep your **mouse** clean, keep the mouse pad clean. (I'm assuming you're using the mouse on a mouse pad and not on the hard surface of your desk because it's easier on the wrist.) The best way to do this is to not eat at the computer. Also don't work at the computer when you have oily or sticky hands. Doing so can really gunk up the mouse pad and the mouse. If the mouse pad does get dirty, shake it upside down or wipe it with a damp cloth.

You can tell whether your mouse itself is dirty because when you move it, the mouse pointer sticks or doesn't move as quickly as it should. To clean your mouse, follow these steps:

1. Make sure your hands are clean.
2. Turn the mouse over.
3. Turn the disk around the mouse ball counterclockwise to remove it.
4. Turn the mouse back over in the palm of your hand so the ball falls out.
5. Wipe off any smudges on the ball with a clean damp cloth.
6. Clear out dust or particles on the inside of the mouse by gently shaking the mouse. If the inside of the mouse is very dusty or dirty, you can clean it out by blowing air into it. Computer stores and camera shops have pressurized air in cans with a nozzle you can use to direct the air and clear dust and dirt from the corners of the inside of the mouse.
7. Gently drop the ball back into the mouse.
8. Line up the disk around the ball so it falls in place.
9. Turn the disk clockwise until it locks in place.
10. Turn the mouse back over.

Keeping the Keyboard Clean

To keep your **keyboard** clean, once again it's best not to eat at the computer. Liquids, especially sticky juices or sodas, can ruin a keyboard. If you need to use your PC in a place where things get dirty (like a garage or a kitchen), buy a key guard to protect the keys. A key guard is pliable and fits snugly over the keys so you can still type with it on. In a typical office environment, protect the keyboard with a dust cover when you're not using it.

To clean your keyboard, turn it upside down and gently shake it at different angles so the dust and crumbs fall out. Wipe the surface of the keys with a damp cloth. If the keys still stick, buy a pressurized air can and use it to blow air between the keys and dislodge stuck particles.

Taking Care of Removable Disks and Their Drives

Here are some tips for taking care of **floppy disks** and compact discs and their respective **drives:**

- Keep all **disks** in cases when you're not using them. Don't let them sit on your desk for days and collect dust and particles.
- Keep disks away from heat or excessive cold, liquids, and magnets.
- Be careful not to scratch compact discs when you handle them. Always hold CDs and **CD-ROMs** by the outer or inner edges.
- Don't touch the thin black shiny disk under the metal slide on a floppy disk.
- If you have any trouble with a floppy disk, use a different one. A broken disk can ruin a drive. For example, if a floppy disk catches when you insert it in the drive, or if the metal slide becomes loose, save the disk's contents on a new disk and throw away the old disk. Floppy disks are the least reliable storage devices, but they are also the cheapest to replace.
- Always insert CDs and CD-ROMs with the blank side down. (If your CD-ROM drive opens vertically, use the clips to hold the CD in place and insert the CD with the blank side against the tray.) If your CD-ROM drive comes with a tray for inserting CDs, always use the tray.
- Keep your CD-ROM drive clean by purchasing a compact disc **laser** lens cleaner. (Make sure you insert this special disk according to the instructions.)
- Clean dust off compact discs by purchasing special compact disc wipes and using them according to the instructions on the package.
- Always insert floppy disks with the metal slide first and the arrow pointing forward. The metal circle in the center of the disk should face down.
- Don't use your drives for anything but inserting disks. Using the CD-ROM drive tray as a cup holder, plant stand, or what-have-you produces excess strain on the tray and will likely cause it to break.

- Don't insert more than one disk in a drive at a time.
- Don't remove a disk when the disk drive light is on.
- Don't insert a disk into a drive in which it doesn't fit. If the disk drive has a tray for a round disk, don't insert a square disk and vice versa. If a disk is too wide, narrow, thick, or thin for a drive, it doesn't belong in that drive.

*Floppy disks are handy for backing up data and sharing data with others, but avoid working off floppy disks. If you want to work with a **file** on a floppy disk, copy the file to your hard drive first. This not only reduces the wear and tear on the disk but it also dramatically increases the speed at which you can work with the file.*

Cleaning the Monitor, System Unit, and Other Devices

To keep your **monitor, system unit**, and other hardware devices clean, dust them regularly and keep them away from sources of dust, such as air vents. If needed, wipe the surface of the system unit, monitor, or **printer** with a damp rag, and protect them with dust covers when you're not using them. To clean the nooks and crannies of your PC that you can't get to, blow air into them with a can of pressurized air.

Keeping your monitor screen clean also helps to improve its display. To dust your monitor screen, use a lint-free cloth and a nonabrasive glass cleaner. Or use whatever cleaner your monitor manufacturer recommends.

Using Windows Tools to Maintain PC Performance

Just as it's important to keep the surfaces of your PC clean, it's also important to keep your **hard disk** tuned up so it runs smoothly. **Microsoft Windows** includes several handy **utilities** you can use to keep your hard disk in top shape. I describe these tools in the following sections.

Using the Disk Cleanup Utility

If your computer runs Windows 98, you can use the Disk Cleanup utility to rid your hard disk of unnecessary files and thereby gain file space and improve performance. To use this utility, follow these steps:

1. Save your work, and close any **programs** you're running.
2. **Click** the **Start button**, point to Programs, point to Accessories, and point to System Tools.
3. Click Disk Cleanup.
4. In the **dialog box** Windows displays, select the hard disk you want to clean up from the Drives drop-down list box, and click OK. Windows scans your hard disk and displays the Disk Cleanup dialog box, as shown in Figure 10-1.

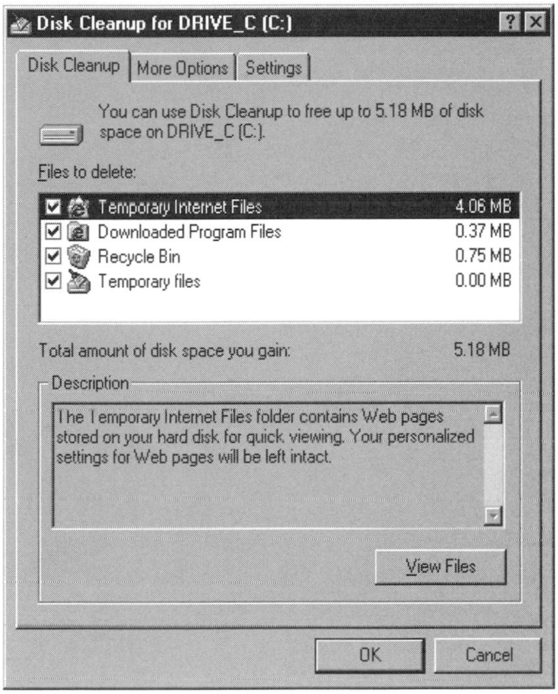

FIGURE 10-1

The Disk Cleanup dialog box.

5. Select the check boxes next to the locations from which you want to delete unnecessary files. To view the files before you delete them, select the location from the Files To Delete list box and click View Files.
6. Click Apply.

7 Click the More Options tab.

8 Click Clean Up in the Windows Components area to display the Windows Setup tab of the Add/Remove Programs Properties dialog box, as shown in Figure 10-2. Remove optional Windows components that you don't need, such as games or **desktop** themes you no longer use, from the drop-down list box.

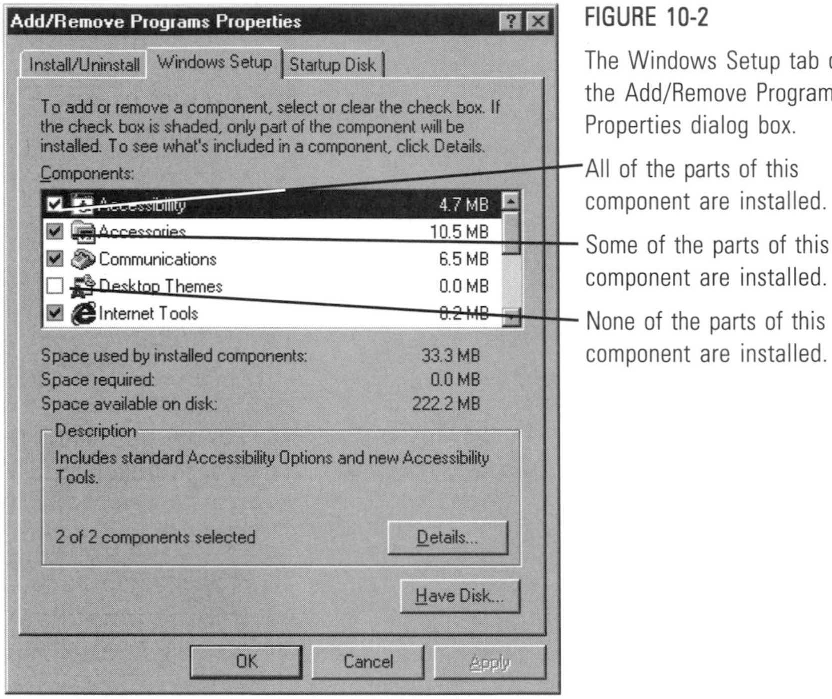

FIGURE 10-2

The Windows Setup tab of the Add/Remove Programs Properties dialog box.

All of the parts of this component are installed.

Some of the parts of this component are installed.

None of the parts of this component are installed.

9 To uninstall all the parts of a Windows component, clear the check box next to the component's name. To uninstall only some parts of a component, select the component and click Details. Then clear the check boxes by the individual parts you want to uninstall, and click OK.

10 Click OK.

11 Click Clean Up in the Installed Programs area to display the Install/Uninstall tab of the Add/Remove Programs Properties dialog box, as shown in Figure 10-3. To uninstall a program you no longer use, select it from the list and click Add/Remove to start a wizard that helps you uninstall the program. After you uninstall a program, Windows might ask you to restart.

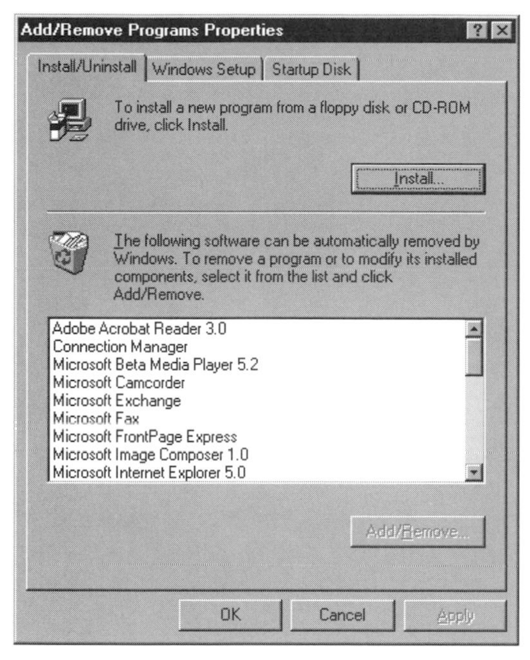

FIGURE 10-3

The Install/Uninstall tab of the Add/Remove Programs Properties dialog box.

Emptying the Recycle Bin

Windows 95 doesn't include the Disk Cleanup utility, so you need to perform the Disk Cleanup tasks individually. The most important task that the Disk Cleanup utility performs is emptying the **Recycle Bin.** The Recycle Bin can quickly take up a lot of space on your hard disk and slow down your PC. You have two ways of emptying the Recycle Bin manually with Windows 95 or Windows 98:

1. If you have Windows Explorer open, right-click the Recycle Bin in the left pane and choose the shortcut menu's Empty Recycle Bin command, as shown in Figure 10-4.
2. Or **double-click** the Recycle Bin **icon** on the desktop and choose the File menu's Empty Recycle Bin command.

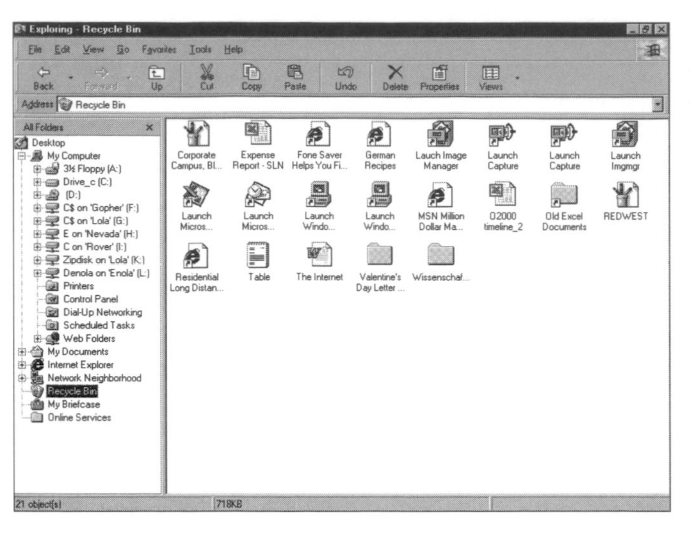

FIGURE 10-4

The Recycle Bin in Windows Explorer.

It's a good idea to empty the Recycle Bin about once a week so it doesn't take up too much space on your computer.

Emptying the Temp Folder

Another task that the Disk Cleanup utility performs that you can do manually in Windows 95 is that of emptying the Temp folder. To empty the Temp folder, follow these steps:

1 Save your work, and close any programs you're running.

2 Start **Windows Explorer**, and display the contents of your hard disk. (If you have more than one hard disk, display the contents of the hard disk on which you installed Windows.)

3 Display the contents of the Windows **folder.**

4 Display the contents of the Temp folder using Details view, as shown in Figure 10-5. Look through the list of files in the Temp folder. Sometimes programs save files to the Temp folder by default. See if you have any **document** files in the Temp folder that you have copies of somewhere else (such as in the My Documents folder.) If you find duplicate or old copies of document files in the Temp folder, select them and click the Delete **toolbar** button.

FIGURE 10-5

Viewing the Temp folder in Windows Explorer.

5 Select all of the files of the type TMP file, and delete these files. As you work, programs create temporary files, which they save in the Temp folder. When you close a document file and quit the program, the program should delete the temporary files it created. Sometimes, however, this doesn't happen, and when this is the case, the Temp folder fills up with old TMP files.

Because programs use Temp files as you work in them, it's important to close all document files and quit all programs as instructed in step 1. If you do this, you should have no problems deleting the TMP files stored in the Temp folder. However, if you select more than one file and one won't delete, just continue deleting the files you can.

Cleaning the Temporary Internet Files Folder

The last main task of the Windows 98 Disk Cleanup utility is cleaning the Temporary Internet Files folder of unnecessary files. If you have Windows 95, you can also accomplish this task manually in Internet Explorer. To do this, follow these steps:

1 Start Internet Explorer.

2 Choose the View **menu's** Internet Options command to display the Internet Options dialog box, as shown in Figure 10-6.

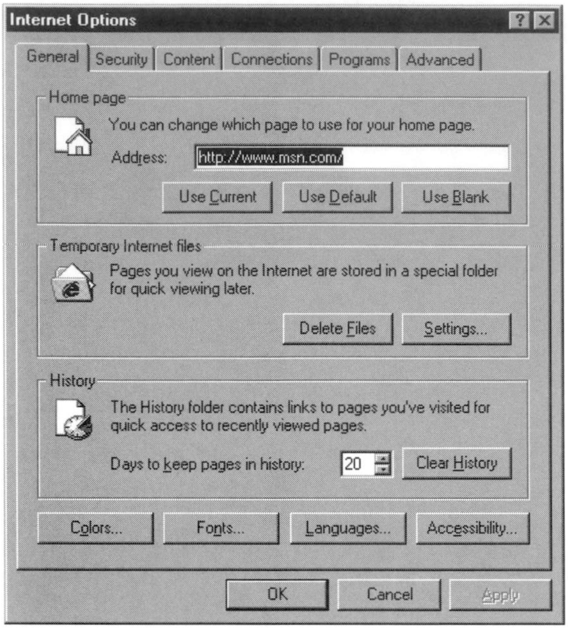

FIGURE 10-6

The Internet Options dialog box.

3 Click Delete Files in the Temporary Internet Files area. Clicking this button just deletes locally stored copies of **web pages** you've viewed. It doesn't delete your personal settings (called cookies) for viewing web pages.

4 Click OK to confirm the deletion of temporary **Internet** files.

5 Click OK to close the Internet Options dialog box.

Maintaining Your Disk

The Windows 98 Maintenance Wizard schedules maintenance tasks such as scanning your hard disk for errors, defragmenting the information on your hard disk, and running the Disk Cleanup utility (described earlier in this chapter). With the Maintenance Wizard, these activities happen automatically so you don't need to remember to initiate them. To use the Windows 98 Maintenance Wizard, follow these steps:

1 Click the Start button, point to Programs, point to Accessories, and point to System Tools.

2 Click Maintenance Wizard.

3 The first time you choose this command, the Maintenance Wizard asks you to set up a maintenance schedule, as shown in Figure 10-7.

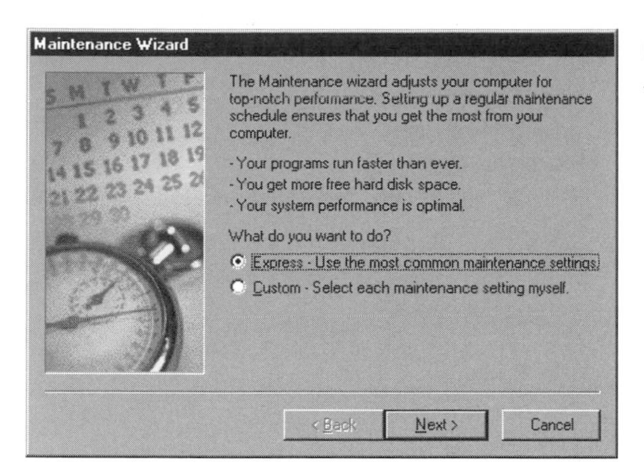

FIGURE 10-7

The first dialog box of the Maintenance Wizard.

4. If you want to run the standard maintenance programs that come with Windows 98 (ScanDisk, the Disk Defragmenter, and the Disk Cleanup tool), click the Express option button and click Next. If you want to add your own maintenance tasks, such as an antivirus program you purchased separately, click the Custom option button and click Next.
5. Choose a time of day during which your computer is usually running but you aren't working at it. Click Next.
6. Click Finish. The Maintenance Wizard scans your hard disk for errors, defragments your hard disk, and runs the Disk Cleanup utility automatically at the time you specified.

Scanning Your Hard Disk for Errors

If you have Windows 95, you don't have Maintenance Wizard. You do, however, have ScanDisk, which you can run on its own. The ScanDisk utility finds and repairs errors on your hard disk. If it can't repair an error it finds, it marks that part of the disk so Windows won't use it to store files. To run ScanDisk, follow these steps:

Notes

If you have Windows 98, you can also run ScanDisk independently if you need to. But if you schedule it to run regularly using the Maintenance Wizard, you'll probably never need to run it manually.

1. Click the Start button, point to Programs, and point to Accessories. If you see ScanDisk on the Accessories menu, click it. Otherwise point to System Tools to display the System Tools menu, and then click ScanDisk.
2. Click ScanDisk to display the ScanDisk **window**, as shown in Figure 10-8.

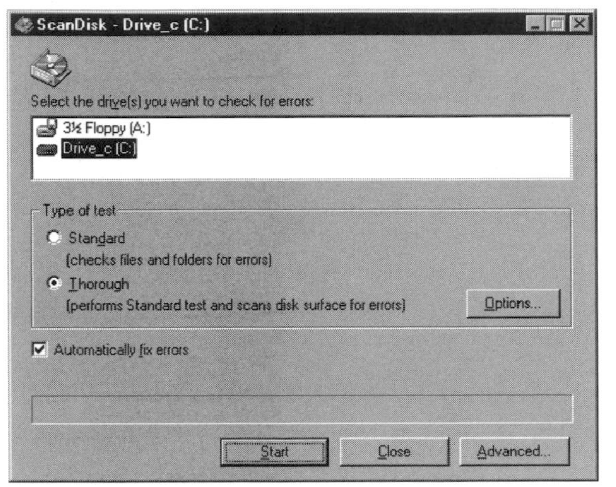

FIGURE 10-8

The ScanDisk window.

3. Select the hard drive you want to scan from the list box.

Although ScanDisk lets you scan disks other than hard disks, scanning removable storage disks (especially floppy disks) just isn't worth the effort. If a floppy disk or other removable disk has an error, you don't want to risk losing data you store on this disk—saving the cost of buying a new disk just isn't worth it. So salvage as much as you can from the old, damaged disk, throw the disk away, and use a new disk.

4. Click the Thorough option button.
5. Select the Automatically Fix Errors check box to tell ScanDisk to fix any error it finds.
6. Click Advanced.
7. Make sure the Always option is selected in the Display Summary area.
8. Make sure the Free option is selected in the Lost File Fragments area.
9. Click OK.
10. Click Start.

Defragmenting Your Hard Disk

If you have Windows 95, you also don't have Maintenance Wizard. But you might have the Disk Defragmenter, which you can run on its own. The Disk Defragmenter picks up the bits and pieces of files scattered throughout your hard disk and puts these fragments together. Reducing this fragmentation makes your computer run faster because Windows doesn't need to access several places on the disk every time you want to open a single file.

If you have Windows 98, you can also run the Disk Defragmenter independently if you need to. But if you schedule it to run regularly using the Maintenance Wizard, you'll probably never need to run it manually.

To defragment your hard disk using the Disk Defragmenter, follow these steps:

1. Save your work, and close all document files and programs you're working in.
2. Click the Start button, point to Programs, point to Accessories, and point to System Tools.
3. Click Disk Defragmenter.
4. Select the disk you want to defragment from the drop-down list box in the Select Drive dialog box, as shown in Figure 10-9, and click OK. The Disk Defragmenter begins defragmenting your disk.

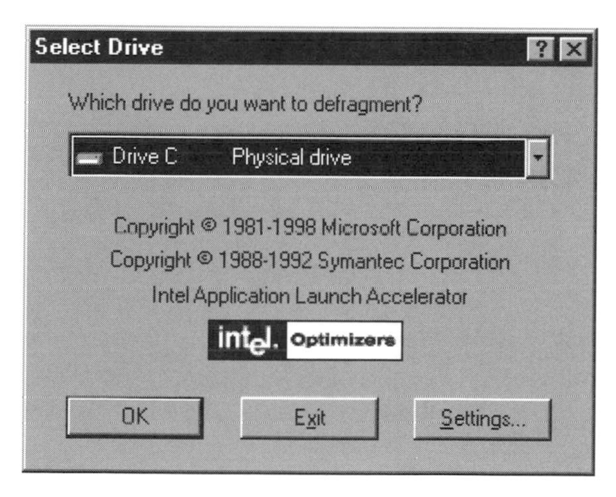

FIGURE 10-9

The Select Drive dialog box.

5 For fun, click Show Details to display a window showing the Disk Defragmenter's progress, as shown in Figure 10-10.

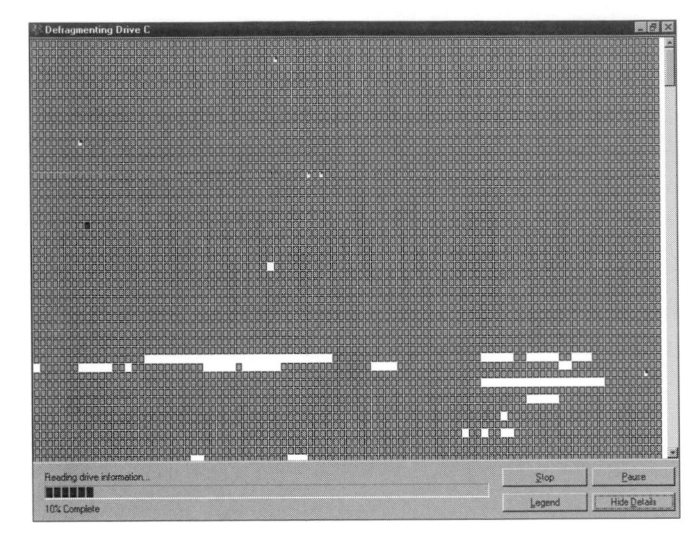

FIGURE 10-10

The Defragmenting Details window.

6 Click Legend to see what the colors of the boxes represent.

Updating Your Copy of Windows 98

If you're running Windows 98, you can use the Windows Update utility to make sure your copy of Windows stays up-to-date. To see if you have the latest copies of Windows files, follow these steps:

1 Click the Start button, and click Windows Update to start Internet Explorer and display the Microsoft Windows Update **home page**.

2 Click the Product Updates **hyperlink** from the list on the left.

3 Click Yes when Internet Explorer asks whether it can check your computer to see which files you already have. Internet Explorer displays a web page similar to the one shown in Figure 10-11.

FIGURE 10-11

The Microsoft Windows Update Products Updates web page.

4 Select the check boxes next to the components you want to upgrade or install.

5 Click the Download arrow button.

6 Click the Start Download arrow button.

Notes *If you made a mistake in your selection, click the Back toolbar button.*

---

7 Click the Device Drivers hyperlink from the list on the left to display the Microsoft Windows Update Wizard web page in its own separate window, as shown in Figure 10-12.

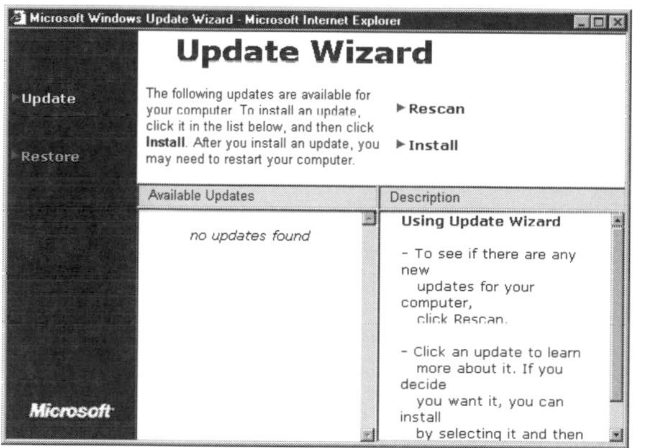

FIGURE 10-12

The Microsoft Windows Update Wizard window.

8 Click Yes when Internet Explorer asks whether it can see which versions of device **drivers** you have on your computer.

9 If the Update Wizard finds an available update, select it from the Available Updates list and click Install.

Converting Your Hard Disk to FAT32

Windows 98 comes with the Drive Converter **accessory** that converts your hard disk to **FAT32.** FAT32 is the table Windows creates to keep track of the location of files on your hard disk. With FAT32, Windows can use twice as many characters when describing a file's location, which means that it can create many more locations on larger drives. It also means that small files don't take up large blocks of space. This frees up space on your computer and makes your computer run faster.

Don't use the FAT32 converter if you have previously compressed your hard disk or if you think you might want to restore Windows 95.

The Drive Converter might take a few hours.

To convert your hard disk to FAT32, follow these steps:

1. **Back up** your files.
2. Click the Start button, point to Programs, point to Accessories, and point to System Tools.
3. Click Drive Converter (FAT32).
4. Click Next to begin.
5. Select the hard disk you want to convert from the drop-down list box, as shown in Figure 10-13, and click Next.

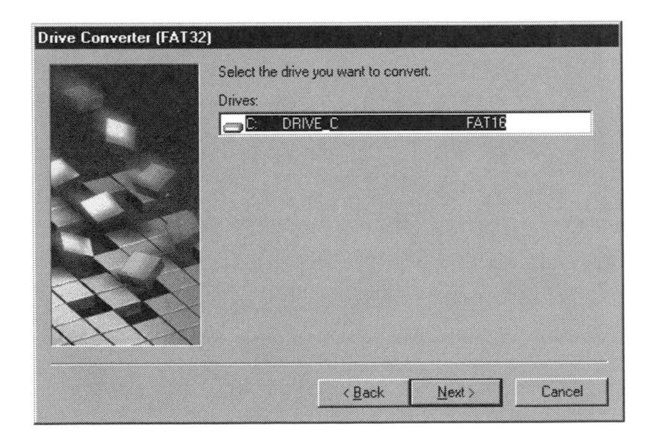

FIGURE 10-13

The Drive Converter.

6 Click OK to let the Drive Converter look for programs on your computer that might not work with FAT32. If it doesn't find any, click Next three times to restart your computer and begin the conversion.

Backing Up Your Data

Windows comes with a Backup accessory that you can use to back up your important files, or you can purchase one of a number of utilities to help guide you in the backup process. However, with a little bit of work, you can back up all the important files on your computer just using Windows Explorer. Here are some tips for backing up files:

- Create a folder on your hard disk for backup files and copy your important files to this folder, as shown in Figure 10-14.

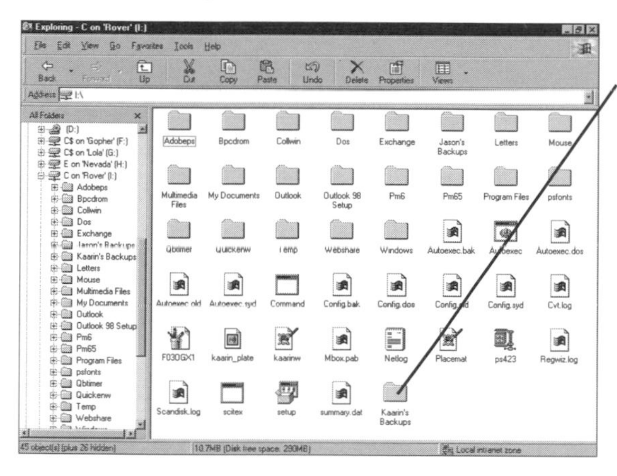

FIGURE 10-14

A folder for backed up files.

Chapter 4 describes how to create folders and copy files using Windows Explorer.

- Keep only one backup copy of each file on your hard disk. Otherwise, your hard disk soon becomes swamped with thousands of backup copies of files. These files not only take up space on your hard disk but they also make finding files a nightmare.

- If you back up your files to floppy disks, make sure you back them up to at least two disks. Floppy disks are notoriously unreliable.
- If a program provides a backup command, as shown in Figure 10-15, use it. Using the program's backup procedure ensures that you back up all the information you need. Make sure you back up to only one place on your hard disk, and then to at least one removable storage disk.

FIGURE 10-15

Using the Quicken program's Backup command.

- Don't back up all the contents of your hard disk. You probably only need to back up a few files.
- Don't back up program files. You should have all of these files on the floppy disks or CD-ROMs they came on. If something happens to a program file, you can reinstall the program from the original source. Backing up program files takes up a lot of unnecessary space and the backed up copies probably won't even work.
- Your My Documents folder probably contains most of the files you need to back up, as shown in Figure 10-16. When you create new document files, make an effort to save them to this folder, regardless of where the program wants you to save them. Remember that you can create **subfolders** within the My Documents folder for organizing the document files you store there.

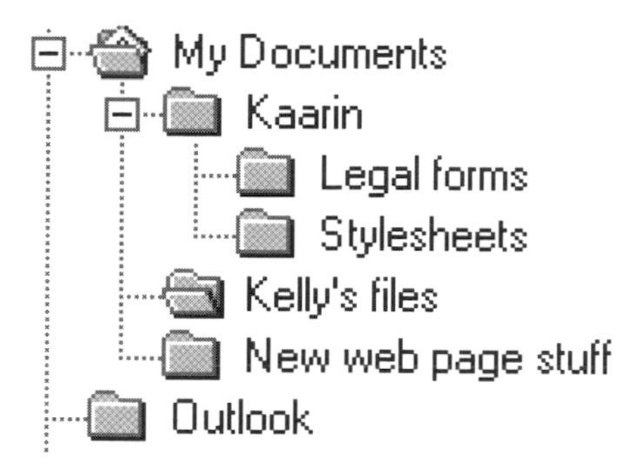

FIGURE 10-16

An organized My Documents folder ready for easy backup.

- Think about the programs you use and the files you work with in these programs. You're probably aware of the default locations where most of your programs save files. If not, check this out by creating a new document file in the program and seeing where the program wants to save the file. Use Windows Explorer to copy the files you've saved in this location to your backup locations.
- If you rely on **e-mail** to keep in touch with people, be sure to back up your messages, Address Book, and any other contact or appointment items you create with your e-mail program. Sometimes these items are difficult to find. You might want to search for files with the **file extension** .pab, .wab, or .pst. You might need to open your e-mail or **web browser** program and see whether you can find where it stores files. Or you might need to refer to the program's online help. If this process provides no clear answers, you can locate the program's folder on your hard disk using Windows Explorer and see which files it stores there. Look for files named or described as an Inbox or Address Book.
- After you've created a portable backup for your important files, store these disks in a different location.

Do-It-Yourself Troubleshooting

Even after taking only the best care of your PC, things are still bound to go wrong now and again. This section talks about steps you can take to determine what went wrong and then fix it.

My Computer Isn't Responding

When your computer doesn't do what you tell it to, one of three things might have happened: your computer is so busy working on something that it can't process your request, a program stalled, or Windows went belly up. To get your computer to respond again, follow these steps:

1. Does the mouse pointer move when you move the mouse? Does it look like an hourglass? Can you see a blinking light on the system unit or hear the hard drive to tell you that your computer's running? If so, your computer probably hasn't frozen—it's just working on something you told it to do. Wait a few minutes and see whether the hourglass goes away. If not, and you get tired of waiting, proceed to step 2.

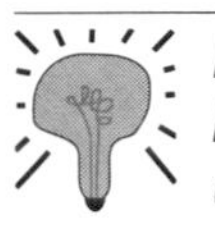

If the mouse pointer moves but the computer doesn't respond to the keyboard or vice versa, make sure that both the mouse or keyboard cable hasn't come loose from the back of the system unit.

If you haven't yet saved something important and the computer has stopped responding to the mouse but not the keyboard, use keyboard commands to save your work. You can often do this by pressing Ctrl+S.

2. If the hourglass doesn't go away or if your mouse pointer doesn't move at all when you move the mouse, the program you were working in has probably stalled. Press the Ctrl, Alt, and Delete keys (Ctrl+Alt+Delete) all at once to display the Close Program dialog box, as shown in Figure 10-17.

Close Program

Inbox - Outlook Express
Collage Capture <ORIGINAL.SET>
Exploring - Windows
Explorer
Internat
Realplay
Reminder
Findfast
Osa
Icqdetect
Systray

WARNING: Pressing CTRL+ALT+DEL again will restart your computer. You will lose unsaved information in all programs that are running.

End Task | Shut Down | Cancel

FIGURE 10-17

The Close Program dialog box.

3 The program you were working in is probably listed as Not Responding. Even if it isn't, select it, and click End Task.

4 Click End Task when Windows asks you if you want to force the program to close.

5 If closing the program doesn't solve the problem, shut down the computer. First, try to shut it down by choosing the Start menu's Shut Down command. If this doesn't work, click Shut Down in the Close Program dialog box.

6 If neither of these methods work, or if the Close Program dialog box doesn't even appear when you press Ctrl+Alt+Delete, try pressing this combination once or twice again to restart your computer.

7 If nothing happens when you press Ctrl+Alt+Delete a few times, push the Reset button on your system unit.

When your computer reboots, it might run ScanDisk to make sure that a disk error didn't cause the **crash**.

PCs don't like it when you restart them using the Reset button, so do this only after all other attempts at getting your computer to respond have failed.

I'm Getting Error Messages

If you get error messages, you could have a serious problem. Follow these steps:

1. Click the Ignore button if one is available.
2. Immediately save your work under a different name.
3. Close all open document files.
4. Quit any programs you have running.
5. Restart your computer by choosing the Start menu's Shut Down command, clicking the Restart option button, and clicking OK. If this doesn't work, try pressing Ctrl+Alt+Delete. Then click Shut Down to shut down the computer.

If the error messages you receive occur in the same situation, think about what you do just before you receive a message. Then refer to the section later in this chapter on accessing technical help resources. For example, if you always have the same program open when you receive error messages, the problem probably lies with the program, and you need to get help with the program. If the error doesn't seem to be program-related, but instead occurs during a Windows operation (such as when your **screen saver** comes on), your problem is probably Windows-related, and you need to get help with Windows.

*If you're using an Active Desktop, try turning off this feature. Right-click a blank area of the desktop, choose the shortcut menu's Active Desktop command, and then choose the Active Desktop submenu's View As Web Page command to clear the check box next to this command. Also turn off **channel** screen savers and choose a different screen saver.*

If you frequently receive error messages, or a blue screen of information, and there seems to be no rhyme nor reason to when this happens, or if errors prevent you from starting Windows, your problem is probably hardware-related.

1. Look at the back of your computer to make sure the fan is running. If it isn't, or if the outside of the system unit feels hot, have the fan looked at and replaced if necessary.
2. A piece of hardware inside the system unit might have come loose. Take your system unit in to have it looked at.

3. You might be low on **memory.** Have more memory installed in your computer. (Another indication of this problem is that your display sometimes looks funny after you've worked on the computer and haven't turned it off for a while.)

My Printer Won't Print

1. Make sure that the printer is plugged in, turned on, and that the cable is firmly connected to the back of the printer and to the system unit.
2. If you have more than one **port** on the back of the system unit that the printer cable's connector fits into, make sure the cable is plugged into the correct port. Usually, the printer port is labeled LPT1 or shows an icon of a printer. If this port doesn't work, try another port.
3. Make sure that the printer is online. "Online" just means that the printer is ready to accept print jobs. Your printer probably has an Online light and an Online button. If the online light isn't on, press the Online button.
4. Is your printer out of paper, or is it looking for paper in the wrong tray? Make sure that the trays have paper and are fully inserted. If one tray doesn't work, try using another tray.
5. Have you noticed that your printouts have gotten lighter or has your printer displayed messages that it needs new toner? Your printer is probably out of ink. Buy a new toner or ink cartridge for the printer, and install it according to the manufacturer's instructions.

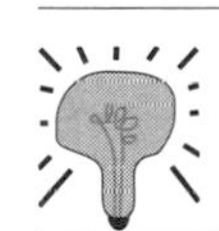

If only part of your printout is light, the toner might need to be redispersed. Carefully remove the toner cartridge from the printer and gently rock the cartridge from side to side.

6. Make sure you told the program to print to the correct printer. If you printed the document file by clicking the Print toolbar button, choose the File menu's Print command instead to verify the printer you're printing to.
7. Make sure that Windows knows about the printer. Click the Start button, and point to Settings. Then click Printers to display the Printers window, as shown in Figure 10-18. Does your printer show up in the Printers window? If not, you need to add it.

FIGURE 10-18

The Printers window lists all the printers you have installed.

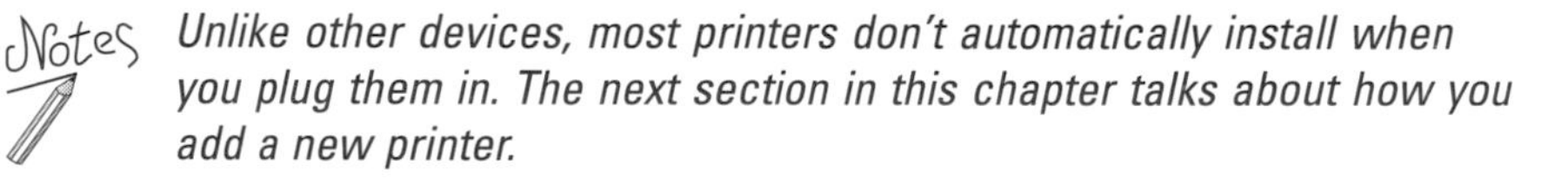

Unlike other devices, most printers don't automatically install when you plug them in. The next section in this chapter talks about how you add a new printer.

8 Try printing something else from a different printer to see whether the program's at fault. If the printer prints from another program, refer to technical support for printing from the program that wouldn't print.

9 Make sure that you didn't pause the printing. To do this, click the Start button, point to Settings, and then click Printers. Double-click the printer's icon in the Printers window to display the printer in its own window, as shown in Figure 10-19. See whether the window's title bar says "Paused." If it does, choose the Printer menu's Pause Printing command to clear the check box next to this command.

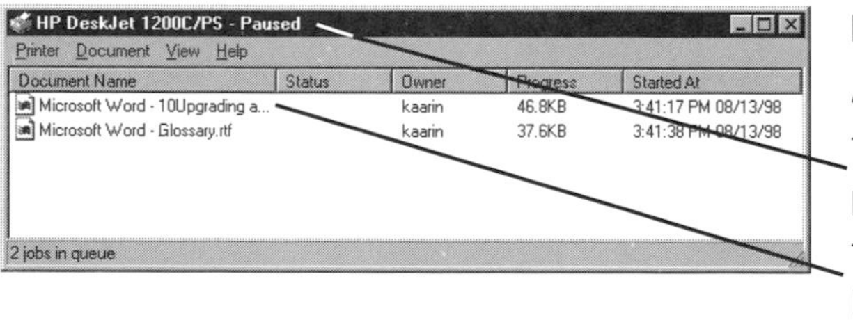

FIGURE 10-19

A window for a printer.

The printing on this printer has been paused.

These documents are in line to be printed on the printer.

10 Does your printer display error messages? Check your printer's user manual to see what they mean. Also make sure you have the latest driver for the printer. You can **download** printer drivers free from the **web sites** of most printer manufacturers.

11 If your printer constantly gets jammed or just spins its wheels, but can't pick up paper, try using a different thickness (or a heavier weight) of paper. The paper you're using might be too thin. If this doesn't work, your printer might need servicing.

Windows Won't Start

You probably accidentally changed or deleted a setting that Windows relied on. To start Windows so you can reverse your mistake, follow these steps:

1 Press the F8 key as your computer **boots.**

2 Select the option to start in safe mode.

3 Undo what you did before turning off the computer.

4 Restart the computer.

I Accidentally Deleted a File

If you accidentally delete a file, you can usually pull the file right back out of the Recycle Bin. To do this, follow these steps:

1 Double-click the Recycle Bin icon on the desktop to display the Recycle Bin window, as shown in Figure 10-20.

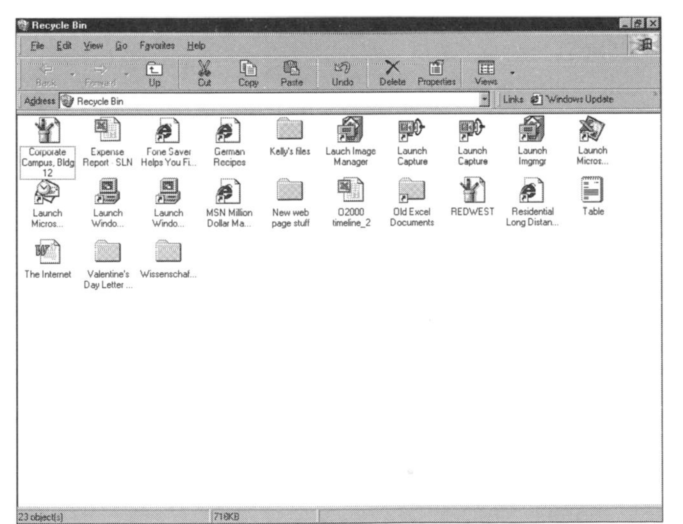

FIGURE 10-20

The Recycle Bin.

2 Right-click the file you accidentally deleted, and choose the shortcut menu's Restore command to return the file to its original location.

If you already emptied the Recycle Bin, you still have a slim chance of restoring the file you deleted, as long as you didn't delete the file too long ago. To restore such a file, you need to use a special utility for recovering deleted files. You can purchase one of these utilities from a ***software*** *store, or you can download a* ***shareware*** *program, such as RecoverNT, from the Internet.*

I Can't Connect to the Internet

1 If you don't hear any sounds coming from an external **modem**, verify that the modem is plugged in, turned on, and that the cables are firmly connected to the back of the modem and to the computer. If you don't hear any sounds from an internal or external modem, make sure you installed the modem. Click the Start button, point to Settings, and click **Control Panel.** Then double-click the Modems icon to display the Modems Properties dialog box, as shown in Figure 10-21. The Modems Properties dialog box lists the modems you have installed.

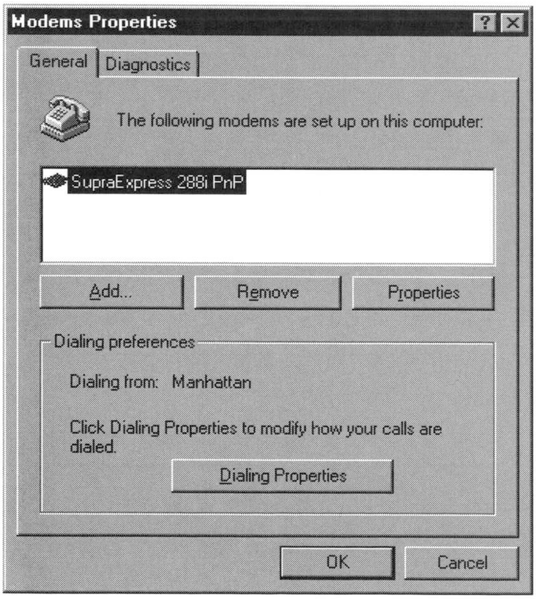

FIGURE 10-21

The Modems Properties dialog box.

2. Verify that the phone line is firmly connected to the back of the modem and into the wall jack. If your modem has two slots for a phone cord, see whether you can find labels on the slots. If you can find a label marked "line," use this slot for plugging the modem into the wall. If the slots aren't labeled, just give each one a try.
3. Verify that the phone line and phone cord work. Plug a regular telephone into the end of the phone line and see if you hear a dial tone and can dial out. If you can't, contact your telephone company to repair the line.
4. If you have a surge suppressor with phone line protection, check to see if the phone line protection has blown by plugging the modem line directly into the phone jack. If you can now call out, replace your surge suppressor—and be sure to get a new one with phone line protection.
5. If your modem makes all sorts of noise and doesn't connect, cancel the connection and try again. This happens frequently with modems and does not signal a problem.
6. If your modem doesn't finish dialing, or if you hear the operator's voice, make sure you've set up your dialing properties correctly. Click the Start button, point to Settings, and click Control Panel. Double-click the Modems icon, and click Dialing Properties to display the Dialing Properties dialog box, as shown in Figure 10-22. Verify that you entered the correct area code and that you disabled call waiting if you have this feature. If you need to dial a number to access an outside line (as is common in many office telephone systems), make sure you entered this number.

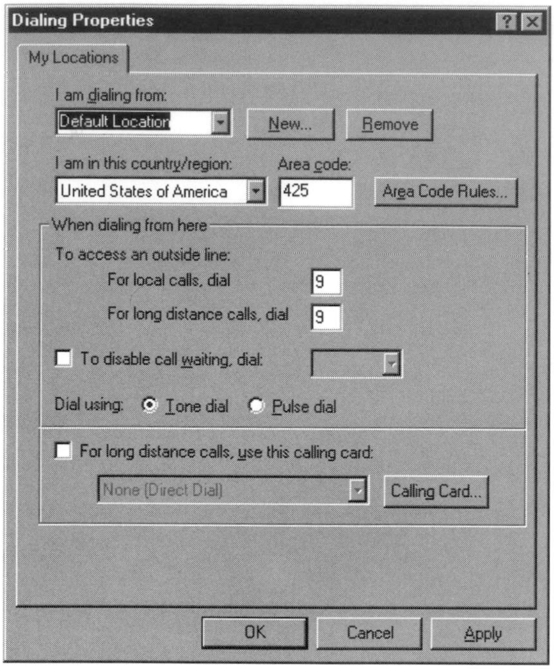

FIGURE 10-22

The Dialing Properties dialog box.

Notes — *By default, Windows assumes that all calls within your area code are not long distance, and all calls in other area codes are long distance. If this is not the case, click Area Code Rules.*

7 If your modem dials but can't establish a connection, the **server** you are dialing might be out of service. Try dialing a backup number, or wait a few minutes and dial again. Some **Internet service providers** (ISPs) might let you choose from a long list of numbers to dial. If the ones in your area don't work, try dialing a number in a different state.

8 If your modem establishes a connection but then disconnects, make sure that you entered your username and **password** correctly. Click the Start button, point to Programs, point to Accessories, point to Communications (if you have this option), and click Dial-Up Networking. Double-click the icon for the connection you're trying to make to display the Connect To dialog box, as shown in Figure 10-23. Make sure your username, password, and the telephone number you're trying to dial are correct.

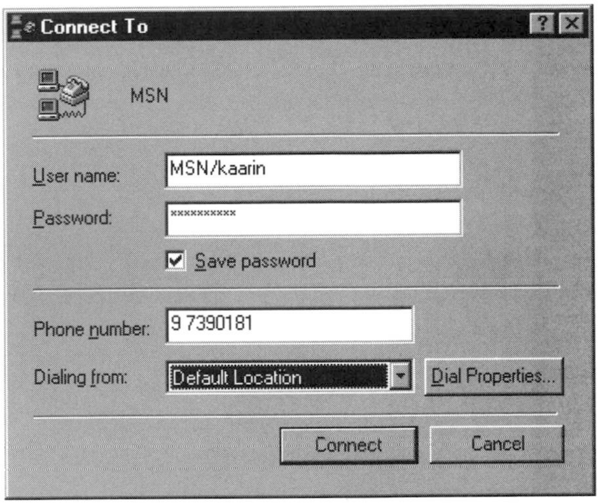

FIGURE 10-23

The Connect To dialog box.

9 If you're trying to connect to a mail or news server, make sure you entered the mail or news server correctly. Open Outlook Express, and choose the Tools menu's Accounts command. Click the Mail or News tab, depending on the type of connection you're trying to make. Select the account that isn't working, and click Properties to display the account's Properties dialog box, as shown in Figure 10-24. Use the tabs of the Properties dialog box to specify the account settings. If you need help with this, contact your ISP.

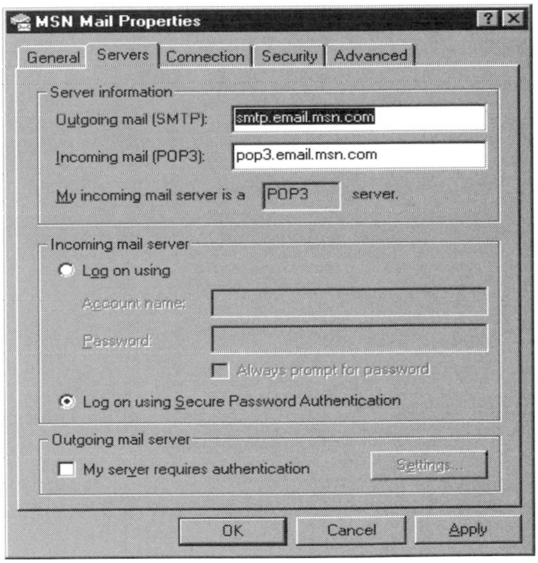

FIGURE 10-24

An e-mail account's Properties dialog box.

10. You can also use the Internet Connection Wizard to reset your account settings. Click the Start button, point to Programs, and point to Internet Explorer. Then click Connection Wizard. In the first Internet Connection Wizard dialog box, click the second option to reconfigure an existing account. Then go through the wizard to review or change the connection settings. You might need to refer to setup literature provided by your ISP or call your ISP when you verify or edit connection settings.
11. If you can connect to the Internet, but can't view the web page you want or download your e-mail, your server might be too busy. If your e-mail and web browsing have worked in the past, and you're sure you haven't changed any settings or deleted or installed new Internet software since then, your server is probably overloaded. Try connecting at a different time of day. Fewer people connect to the Internet in the morning than in the evening.

My Computer's Running Slowly

Most of the time, when a computer runs slowly, the culprit is a shortage of system resources. Maybe a program you have open in the background is performing an operation. Or maybe one of the programs you use doesn't free memory when you close it, for instance. (This is called a memory leak.) To speed up your slow computer, follow these steps:

1. Save your unsaved work, and close all document files and programs you're not using.
2. If this doesn't do the trick, restart your computer. This closes programs that never fully closed but continued to use your computer's resources.

Upgrading Your PC

This section talks about how to upgrade your computer by adding new hardware or software.

Adding Hardware

The trick to easily adding new hardware to your PC is a simple one: always buy Plug and Play hardware, regardless of how tempting a cheap piece of hardware is at a flea market. You don't have to buy hardware new, but make sure it's Plug and Play. If it is, it will say so on the box. Almost all hardware sold in computer stores over the last few years has been Plug and Play, so if you buy something new, or relatively new, you should have no problem.

The beauty of Plug and Play hardware is this: You don't need to go through any elaborate process to set it up on your PC. All you have to do is turn off and unplug the PC, install the hardware device, and then turn the PC back on again. When you do so, Windows displays a message box saying that it recognizes you added a new piece of hardware and asking whether you want to set up the hardware device. When you click Yes, Windows takes you through a wizard that asks for information about the piece of hardware—for instance, it might ask you to select the correct driver. Just follow the instructions that came with the hardware. You might need to insert a floppy disk or a CD-ROM to copy the correct driver to your hard disk.

Notes

If for some reason Windows doesn't recognize a new hardware device you plugged in, you can ask it to search for new hardware devices. To do this, close any open programs, click the Start button, point to Settings, and click Control Panel. Then double-click the Add New Hardware icon, and click Next.

If you're feeling adventurous, you can install internal hardware devices (like Zip drives and modems) yourself. Just be sure to unplug the computer first. And before you touch anything on the inside of the computer, touch an unpainted surface on the system unit's case to discharge static electricity you might be carrying. Then follow the hardware manufacturer's instructions, making sure to handle the hardware with care. If you're leery of installing internal hardware yourself, take your PC into a repair shop and have it installed. Some businesses will even install hardware for free if you purchase the hardware from them.

Advanced Plug and Play hardware devices that use **USB** ports are even easier to set up. You don't need to turn off your PC at all. Just plug in the device, and Windows recognizes it right away.

The only two non–Plug and Play pieces of hardware that you'll probably need to install are printers and memory. If you're comfortable installing internal hardware devices, you can install memory yourself (or have someone help you). But you can also take your computer into a repair shop to have memory installed. It's usually not too expensive for a desktop PC.

To install a printer, make sure the printer is connected to the computer, plugged in, and turned on, and then follow these steps:

1. Click the Start button, point to Settings, and point to Printers.
2. Double-click the Add Printer icon.
3. Click Next to start the Add Printer Wizard.
4. Click the Local Printer option button, as shown in Figure 10-25, and click Next.

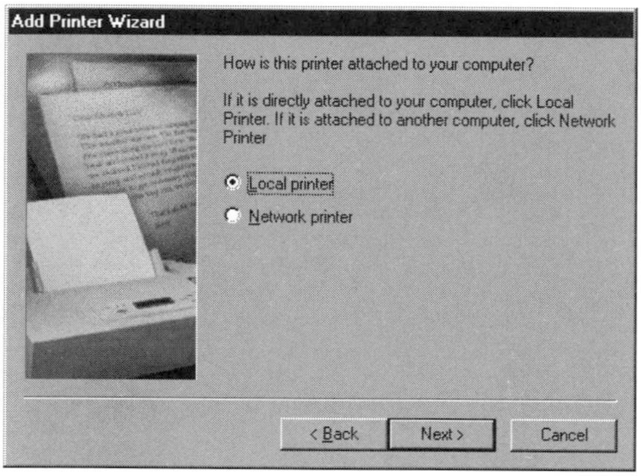

FIGURE 10-25

Adding a local printer.

If you're working on a ***network*** *and you want to use a printer that isn't attached to your computer but to another computer on the network, click the Network Printer option button.*

5. Select your printer manufacturer from the Manufacturers list and your printer model from the Printers list, as shown in Figure 10-26, and click Next.

FIGURE 10-26

Selecting your printer.

6 Select the port on your computer into which you plugged the printer from the Available Ports list, and click Next.

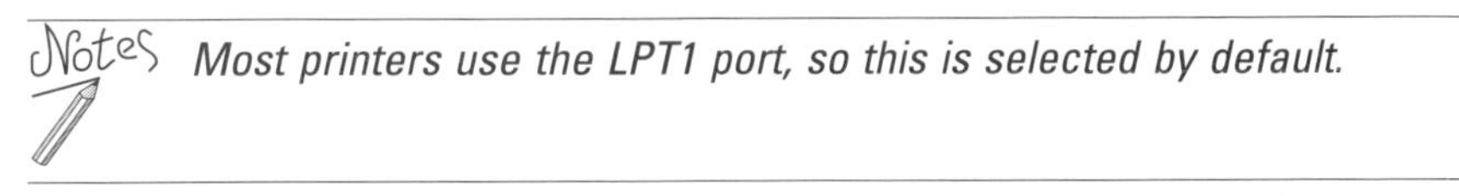

Most printers use the LPT1 port, so this is selected by default.

7 Accept the printer name or enter a new name for the printer in the Printer Name box.

8 If you want to use this printer by default for most of your printing, click the Yes option button. When you click the Print toolbar button in a program, the program will print to the default printer.

9 Click Next.

10 Click the Yes option button to print a test page, which verifies that you installed the printer correctly.

11 Click Finish.

Adding Software

Adding software to your computer is usually easy with Windows. Most of the time, all you need to do is insert the CD-ROM and Windows displays a message box asking whether you want to install what's on the CD-ROM. If you do, just click Yes and Windows starts a wizard to help you install the program. If this doesn't work, however, you can use the Add/Remove Programs Properties tool. To do this, follow these steps:

1. Click the Start button, and point to Settings.
2. Click Control Panel.
3. Double-click the Add/Remove Program icon to display the Add/Remove Programs Properties dialog box, as shown in Figure 10-27.

FIGURE 10-27

Adding software.

4. Insert the program's installation CD-ROM or the first installation floppy disk, and click Install.

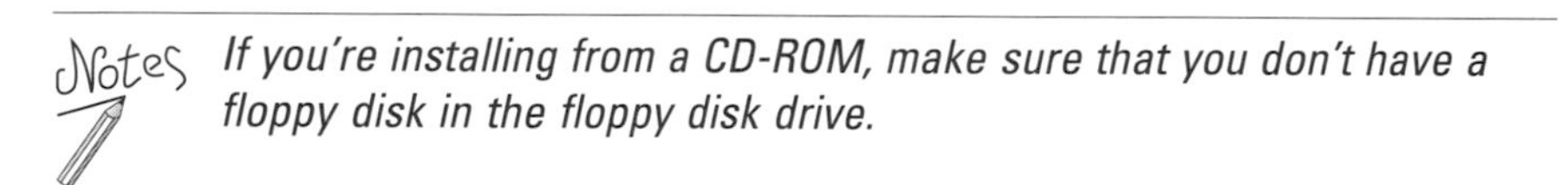

If you're installing from a CD-ROM, make sure that you don't have a floppy disk in the floppy disk drive.

5. Windows should find an installation program (usually named something like "setup") on the disk. If it does, click Finish. If it doesn't, click Browse and use the Browse dialog box to locate the setup program. When you find it, select it and click Open. Then click Finish. Windows starts the setup program for the software you're installing.
6. Follow the onscreen instructions of the software setup program.

Finding Technical Help

If after taking care of your PC and troubleshooting problems yourself, your PC's problems still aren't fixed, you need to turn to other sources of help.

The Help Information that Comes with Software

If a program's been giving you trouble, try using the Help information included in the program. You can usually access this information by choosing a command on the Help menu. For example, to access help in Microsoft Word, choose the Help menu's Contents And Index command to display the Help Topics: Microsoft Word dialog box, as shown in Figure 10-28.

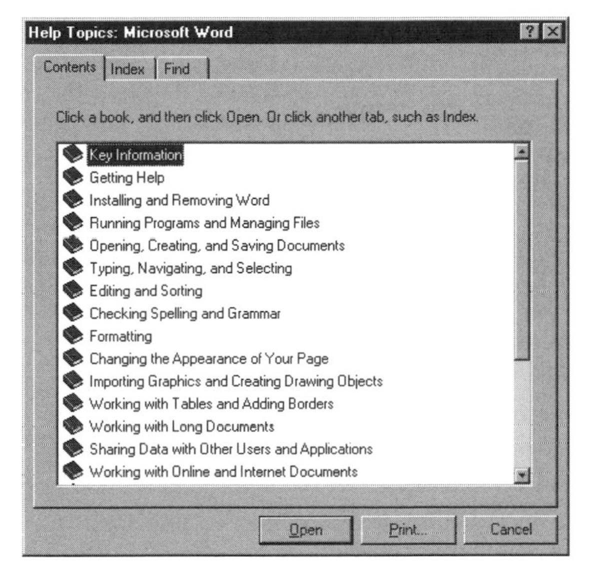

FIGURE 10-28

Help in Microsoft Word.

Notes *In other programs, you might choose a different command. For example, the command might be called Help Topics.*

If you're having trouble getting a Windows feature to work correctly, try using Windows Help. To do this, click the Start button and click Help.

Click the Contents tab to browse Windows Help much like you would look over the table of contents of a book. Figure 10-29 shows the Contents tab of the Windows Help window. To view the topics covered in a chapter, click the chapter's title. To view the articles covered in a topic, click the topic's title. To read an individual article, click the article's title.

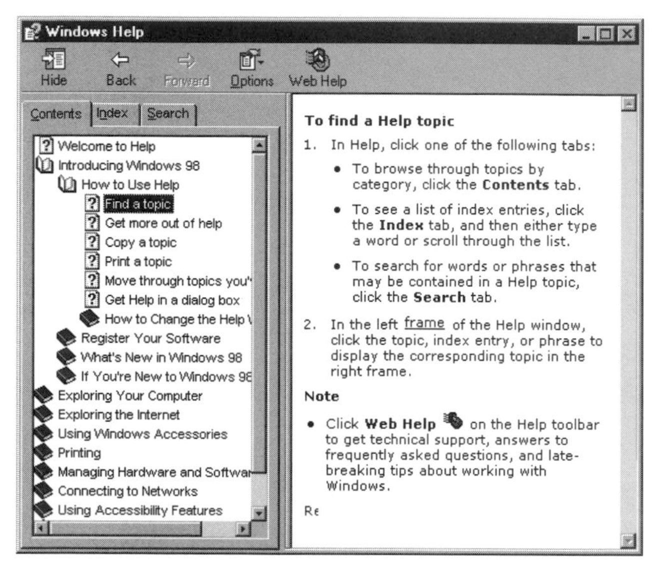

FIGURE 10-29

The Contents tab of the Windows Help window.

Click the Index tab, as shown in Figure 10-30, to search for articles by subject much like you would search an index of a book. Type the first few letters of a subject in the text box to turn to that area of the alphabetical list of subjects. Select a subject from the list, and click Display to view the article in the right pane of the Windows Help window. If more than one article exists on the subject, you might have to further select the one you want to read and click OK.

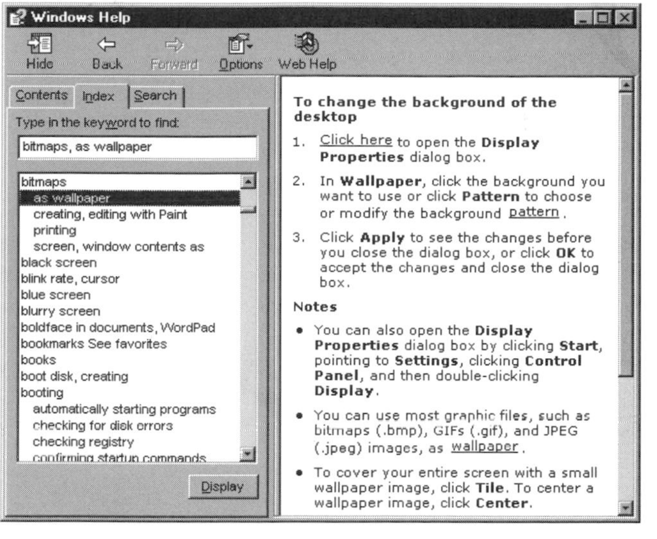

FIGURE 10-30

The Index tab of the Windows Help window.

Click the Search tab, as shown in Figure 10-31, to search the text of Help articles for the word or phrase you enter. Enter a word or phrase in the text box, and click List Topics. Then select the article you want to display, and click Display to display the text of the article in the right pane of the Windows Help window.

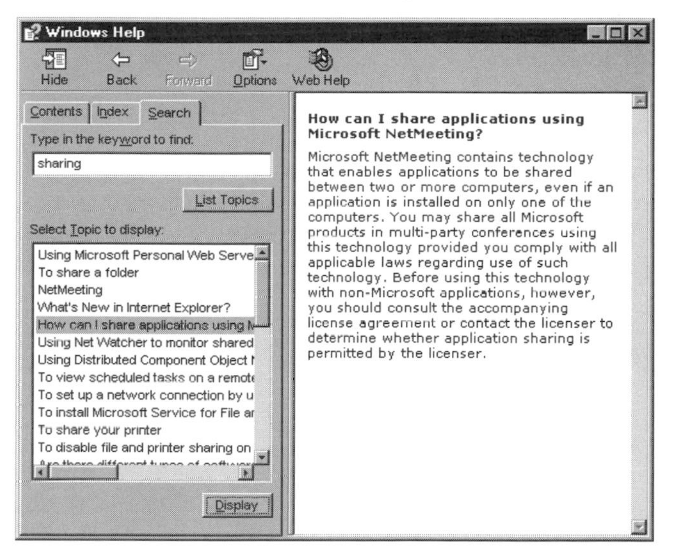

FIGURE 10-31

The Search tab of the Windows Help window.

Notes

In many programs, the Help window's Search tab is called Find.

The Windows troubleshooters are another great source of help in Windows. Windows includes troubleshooters on several topics. To access these troubleshooters, click the Troubleshooting chapter on the Contents tab and then click the Windows 98 (or Windows 95) Troubleshooters topic. To start a troubleshooter, select it and click Display. Windows then asks you questions, as shown in Figure 10-32. Based on your responses, Windows offers suggestions.

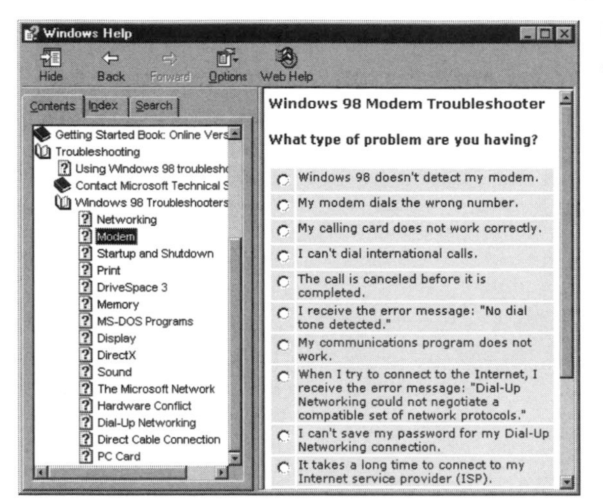

FIGURE 10-32

The Modem troubleshooter.

Technical Support on the Internet

Most computer hardware and software companies provide technical support on their web sites. Microsoft in particular provides a wealth of help information about Windows and Windows programs on the **World Wide Web.** Their technical support **database,** called the Knowledge Base, is an invaluable tool for finding solutions to problems. The Microsoft support staff even use this Internet database to find answers when people call in for support. To use the Knowledge Base yourself, follow these steps:

1. Open Internet Explorer or your web browser and go to the following address: http://support.microsoft.com. This displays the web page, as shown in Figure 10-33.

FIGURE 10-33

Searching Microsoft Support Online.

2 Select the software with which you're having a problem from the first drop-down list box.

3 Enter a keyword or phrase specifying the problem.

4 Click Find.

5 When Internet Explorer displays a web page listing articles including the word or words you entered, as shown in Figure 10-34, read the article summaries and see whether one relates to the problem you're having.

6 To display the full text of an article, click the article's title.

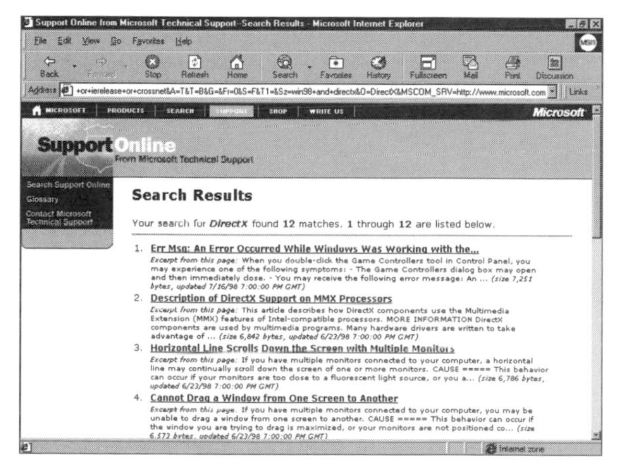

FIGURE 10-34

Knowledge Base articles.

Other Support Resources

If none of the help resources previously described were able to solve the problem, you need to ask for help. You do have a few options, and I suggest turning to the least expensive options first. Accordingly, you might take this plan of action:

1. If you have a friend or family member who loves computers and troubleshooting, tell that person about the problem and see whether he or she can help you. Many people pride themselves in their computer knowledge and derive a certain satisfaction out of conquering the unsolvable.
2. See whether the hardware or software comes with free technical support. Many hardware companies offer free technical support for a limited time after you purchase the product. If the problem even only tangentially relates to a free source of help, see whether the free source can help you before you pay for help from another source.
3. Along the same lines, most Internet service providers offer free support. So if you're having an Internet-related problem, your ISP is a good source to turn to. They are often well-acquainted with the wide array of hardware and software issues of their customers.
4. Take the problem to a computer service company in your area. A good company can fix most software and hardware problems for a reasonable fee and in a reasonable amount of time. Just make sure you get a quote first. For example, an initial inspection might cost around $30 or $40, and then the labor might be around $60 an hour, plus parts.
5. As a last resort, make a pay-per-incident call to the hardware or software manufacturer. And have your credit card ready—even a short call can quickly cost you a few hundred dollars.

GLOSSARY

Accelerator An accelerator, such as a graphics accelerator or a video accelerator, is a **hardware** device that speeds up or improves the performance of a feature on your **PC.**

Accessory Windows comes with some extra, miniature **programs** called accessories. One such accessory is the Calculator program, for example. Another is the Solitaire game program.

Adapter An adapter is a piece of **hardware** that you plug into your **PC**. Common adapters include **network** adapters and **ISDN** modems (which aren't really **modems**, but adapters).

AMD AMD is a company that makes **microprocessors.**

Applet An applet is a term used to describe a small **program**, or application.

Application Application is another word for **program.**

Backup To back up **files** on your computer means to make extra copies of the files for safekeeping. You can back up files by copying them to another location, or you can use one of a number of special backup **programs** designed to help you create backups.

Bay A bay is a slot inside your **system unit.** You can put **hardware** devices such as **disk** drives, tape drives, **CD-ROM** drives, and **Zip** drives into free bays.

BIOS The BIOS (an acronym for basic input/output system) is a set of instructions that tests your **hardware** and starts Windows when you turn on your **PC.** You can usually view the BIOS by pressing a special key when your PC is starting up.

Bit Bit stands for binary digit. A bit is the smallest unit of information a computer uses to express data. A bit is like the answer to a yes or no question—it can result in only one of two possible responses. Computers use either a 0 or a 1 to represent the response. A single bit alone isn't meaningful, but a string of bits can express a number, a letter, and other information. **Modem** speed is measured in kilobits per second (Kbps). A kilobit is 1,000 bits.

Bookmark Just as you might dog-ear an important page in a book, you can bookmark important **web pages** on the **Internet** so you can easily find them and quickly return to them. Internet Explorer and **Microsoft Windows** refer to bookmarked resources as Favorites.

Boot To boot your computer means to start it up. To reboot it means to restart it after it is already running.

Briefcase The Windows Briefcase is a tool you can use to transport **files** for travel. With the Briefcase, you can keep track of files and quickly compare and update files in different locations.

Browser; see Web browser

Bubble-jet A bubble-jet **printer** is a kind of printer that heats ink and then shoots the ink onto the paper.

Bug A bug is an error in a **program** or **operating system** that causes the program or operating system to malfunction in some way. Programs that have a lot of such errors are called buggy. To repair bugs, **software** manufacturers frequently offer free fixes (often called service releases or service packs) that you can install.

Byte A byte is an eight-character string of **bits.** Bytes represent individual characters, such as the letter "w," and occasionally other information. **Memory** and storage space are measured in bytes. For example, a **floppy disk** holds 1,440 kilobytes (or 1.44 megabytes) of information. (A kilobyte is a little more than 1,000 bytes; a megabyte is a little more than 1 million bytes.) Your PC's **hard disk** might hold anywhere from a few hundred megabytes to several gigabytes of information. (A gigabyte is a little more than 1 billion bytes.)

Cache The cache is the part of your PC's **memory** that holds the data you recently worked on in a **file.** Your **PC's** cache makes working with files much faster because your PC doesn't have to constantly retrieve information from a **disk** as you work with a file.

CD-ROM A CD-ROM is a compact disc (CD for short) that stores various types of information for use with a computer. Software **programs** often come on CD-ROM. In order to install a program from a **CD-ROM,** you need a **CD-ROM** drive.

Channel A channel is a special **web site** that you can subscribe to. Channel web sites are designed with a **downloading** schedule built into them, so when you subscribe, your **web browser** automatically retrieves their content based on this schedule. You can then read the channel content offline without connecting to the **Internet.**

Chat room A chat room is an area of the **Internet** where people meet and type back and forth to each other in real time (called chatting). As one person types, the words appear on the other person's screen and that person can type a response for the first person to see. To chat with others, you need a chat client such as mIRC, PIRCH, or Microsoft Comic Chat. (Chat is also often referred to as IRC for Internet Relay Chat.)

Chip A chip is a box of connected circuitry attached to a **circuit board.** Your **CPU** and other **microprocessors** are chips.

Circuit board A circuit board is a card (often green in color) on the inside of your **PC** made of a flat piece of insulating material with electrical components attached to it.

Click The process of pointing to an item and then pressing and releasing the left **mouse** button is called clicking the item.

Clipboard The Windows Clipboard stores whatever object (a block of text, a picture, or even an entire **folder)** you copy or cut so you can paste the object. The object remains on the Clipboard until you copy or cut another object.

Clock speed Clock speed refers to the speed of the **CPU** (expressed in megahertz or MHz).

Control Panel The Windows Control Panel contains several tools you use to customize your computing environment and view several settings.

CPU The central processing unit (CPU) is the main **microprocessor** in your computer. It executes almost all the instructions given by the **operating system** and software **programs.** For example, if you tell a **word processor** to check the spelling in a **document,** it's actually the CPU that compares the words in your document to the words in a spelling dictionary.

Crash When your operating system stops responding or otherwise becomes unusable, the computer is said to have crashed.

Cursor A cursor is the small arrow, hourglass, pointing hand, or other symbol that moves on your screen as you move the **mouse.** Cursors are also the blinking vertical bars or other indicators that mark where the next character will appear if you begin typing.

Cynx Cynx is a company that makes microprocessors.

Database A database is a type of **file** used for holding records.

Desktop The desktop is the Windows screen you see after you've started and, optionally, logged onto your computer.

Desktop publishing Desktop publishing just means using a **PC** to create **documents** for publishing. You can use a **word processor** and a **printer** to publish documents that have a basic layout design. To publish documents with more complicated layouts, people often use special desktop publishing **software** such as Adobe PageMaker, Quark, or Microsoft Publisher.

Dialog box A dialog box is a special kind of **window.** Unlike other windows, you can usually display only one dialog box at a time. To work in another window, you must first close the dialog box.

Disk Your computer uses disks to store information in **files. Hard disks** (also called hard drives), **floppy disks,** and **CD-ROMs** are all disk storage devices. Disks are called disks because they're most often round platters. If you see the word disk spelled disc (as in compact disc), it means that the disk is read and written to using **lasers.**

Disk drive; see Drive

Document The kind of **file** you create with a **word processor** is called a document. The term *document file* refers more generally to any type of file you create using a **program.** The **Start menu's** Documents **folder,** for instance, contains the list of document files you last worked on. And the term *document window* refers to the **window** in which a program displays a document file.

Domain In essence, a domain is a **network** of computers connected to the **Internet.** Domain names appear in Internet addresses, including **e-mail** addresses and **World Wide Web** addresses.

Double-click The process of pointing to an item and **clicking** the left **mouse** button twice in a row quickly is called double-clicking the item.

Download Downloading a **file** or **folder** means to retrieve a copy of the file or folder from the **Internet** or from a **network server.**

DPI DPI describes **printer** and screen **resolution.** DPI stands for dots per inch. The higher the DPI, the greater the resolution, because the **monitor** can display more dots per linear inch or the printer can print more dots per linear inch.

Drag To drag an object means to move the object using the **mouse.** You drag an object by pressing and holding the left mouse button, moving the mouse so the mouse pointer rests in the desired new location, and releasing the left mouse button.

Drive A drive is the hardware device that reads the contents from **disks** and writes information to disks. You insert removable disks (such as **floppy disks** and **CD-ROMs**) in their respective drives. Floppy disks typically fit in the A: drive and compact discs in the D: or E: drive. Your hard disk permanently resides in the drive that your **PC** probably labels as the C: drive.

Driver A driver is a **program** that helps a piece of **hardware** run. For example, in order for your **PC** to talk with your brand and model of **printer**, you need that printer's driver. Many drivers are built into Windows, but some come with the hardware.

DVD DVD stands for digital video disc. A digital video disc looks like a compact disc, but it can hold several times the amount of information. To use DVDs on your computer, you need a DVD **drive**, which looks just like a **CD-ROM** drive and can also read CDs.

E-mail An electronic message, usually in the form of text, that you send from one computer to another. The **Internet's** most popular feature is e-mail, by the way. To work with e-mail (and sometimes **newsgroups** as well), you use an e-mail client such as Eudora, Netscape Messenger, or Outlook Express.

Eudora; see E-mail

Expansion board An expansion board is a **circuit board** that fits inside your computer in what's known as an expansion slot on your PC's **motherboard.** Expansion boards can hold additional **memory**, video or sound cards, or internal **modems**.

FAT32 FAT stands for file allocation table. A file allocation table lists where information is stored on a **disk.** Windows 95 uses a 16-**bit** FAT (meaning that Windows has 16 places for describing a location on a disk), but Windows 98 uses a 32-bit FAT called FAT32. This allows Windows 98 to work with larger disks. It also frees up space on the **hard disk.**

File A file is what Windows stores on your **PC's** storage devices—devices such as **hard disks, floppy disks,** and sometimes CDs. There are two types of files: **document** files store the information you create with a program such as a word processor; **program** files contain the instructions your computer needs to do perform tasks.

File extension A file extension indicates a **file's** type, such as a **program** file you can run, a text file, or a certain type of image file. A file extension is the character sequence (usually three letters long) after the period in a file's name. Most of the time, **Windows Explorer** and the programs you run probably hide file extensions from you. But familiarizing yourself with the file extensions you use most can help you find lost files or determine which program was used to create a file.

Floppy disk A floppy disk is a small plastic **disk** that is used to store files. The most common type of floppy disk is the hard plastic, 3½-inch-square variety. Most floppy disks hold 1.44 megabytes of information. Although floppy disks can't hold very much information, they're still widely used and practical because they're inexpensive, small, and usable on virtually all **PCs.**

Font Font determines what the text you type looks like. Some fonts are rather plain, like the text you see in most books. Other fonts are loopy and flashy. Windows comes with many fonts that you can use with a **word processor** and other **programs.** Windows also allows you to customize the fonts it uses if you have vision disabilities or just want to spice up the look of your screen.

FTP FTP (file transfer protocol) is a set of instructions that lets you move **files** from one computer to another over the **Internet.**

Folder Windows uses folders to organize **files** on your **disks.** Most of the files that you create, for example, will probably be stored in a folder named My Documents.

Freeware Freeware is free **software**, often available over the **Internet.**

GUI GUI (pronounced like "gooey") stands for graphical user interface and refers to the colorful way an **operating system** like Windows looks and the user-friendly way you can communicate with the operating system. Before GUIs, people needed to carefully type special code words in order to tell their computers what to do. With a GUI, all you need to do is **click** buttons.

Hard disk A hard disk is the stack of hard, round platters inside a **PC** that stores most of the information your PC uses. Most PCs have one or two hard disks, usually given the **drive** labels C: and sometimes D:. Your **operating system** and **program** files are generally located on your hard disk. Hard disks differ from **floppy disks, Zip** disks, and other types of disks because hard disks tend to store much more information and are usually not removable.

Hardware Hardware is the physical gadgetry of your **PC.** Your **monitor, disk,** and **printer** are all hardware, for example.

Hertz Frequency is described in hertz, or cycles per second. Your PC's **microprocessor** speed is given in megahertz (MHz). Megahertz is 1 million hertz.

Home Page The term home page can refer to the **web page** that your **web browser** displays when you click its Home **toolbar** button. It can also refer to a web page you publish yourself or the main web page of a **web site.**

HTML HTML stands for hypertext markup language. Most **web pages** are HTML **documents.**

Hyperlink A hyperlink is a piece of text or an image that points to another resource (usually on the **Internet**), such as a **web page.**

Icon An icon is a little picture on your computer screen used to represent a feature or function. For example, the little picture on your **desktop** that looks like a wastepaper basket is the **Recycle Bin** icon.

Infrared An infrared **port** is a special type of port common on **laptop** computers. With infrared ports, two **PCs** can communicate without a cable connection. Infrared connections work like a remote control by sending an infrared signal.

Inkjet An inkjet **printer** is a type of printer that sprays ink as a mist onto paper.

Intel Intel is a company that makes **microprocessors**, such as the Pentium processor.

Internet The Internet is a global **network** of millions of single computers and smaller electronic networks. The Internet lets people across the world share information quickly and inexpensively, which is why the Internet is often referred to as the "information superhighway." A couple of the Internet's most popular services are electronic mail (**e-mail**) and the **World Wide Web.**

Internet Explorer; see Web browser

Internet service provider (ISP) An Internet service provider is a company that lets you connect your computer to their **network.** Because their network is part of the **Internet**, once you connect to this network, you're connected to the Internet and can use its resources.

I/O I/O stands for input/output. Each input and output device on your computer is assigned a unique I/O range, which serves as a channel through which it sends data to or receives data from the **CPU.** It's important that no two devices share the same I/O range, otherwise interference results.

IRC; see Chat room

IRQ Windows assigns all the **hardware** devices on your **PC** a unique interrupt request number, or IRQ. When a hardware device needs the **CPU's** attention because something has gone wrong, it uses the IRQ to tell the CPU to stop what it's doing and help with the problem. If two or more hardware devices share an IRQ, this is called an IRQ conflict and must be fixed.

ISDN ISDN is a fast digital connection to the **Internet.** With an ISDN **modem** (actually an **adapter**) and a special ISDN line from the phone company, you can send and receive information more than twice as fast as with a regular modem and phone line.

Joystick A joystick is an input device that often looks like a throttle with a few buttons and is most commonly used for playing computer games.

Keyboard A keyboard is an input device that holds rows of keys: letters, numbers, and other characters.

Laser Several computer **hardware** devices use lasers. **CD-ROM** and **DVD drives** use lasers to read data on discs. A laser **printer** uses lasers to draw images on a light-sensitive drum. The images on the drum attract toner, which is then transferred to the paper.

Logon You log on to a computer to identify yourself. To log on, you enter your username and **password.** Logging on to your **Internet service provider's** server computer is sometimes called logging in. To end a session after you're finished, you log off.

Lotus 1-2-3; see Spreadsheet

Macintosh The Apple Macintosh, or Mac for short, is a type of personal computer that uses its own **operating system** and often its own **hardware.** The Macintosh is very user-friendly—as a matter of fact, the Mac was the first popular personal computer to take advantage of **GUI** technology. Today Macs are extensively used for graphics and publishing and in education.

Megabyte; see Byte

Megahertz; see Hertz

Memory Your **PC's** memory is the space it has allocated for quickly storing and retrieving information. You can think of your PC's memory as its short-term memory. (Its long-term memory is the storage space on its **hard disk.**) Your PC uses memory to grab information from storage and to save information back to storage as you work at the computer. This means that if you **multitask** a lot, you place special demands on your PC's memory.

Menu Almost all **programs,** such as **Windows Explorer,** have menus. Near the top of a program **window** is a row of words. The first word in the row is often File, and the last is often Help. These words are the names of the menus. Menus hold a set of commands for working with related tasks. If you click the word File, for example, you open the File menu, which holds several commands for working with **files.**

Microprocessor A microprocessor is a piece of circuitry in a computer that performs some task. Your **PC's** main microprocessor (the one that does almost all the work) is called its **CPU.** But your PC might have other microprocessors carrying out functions on the sidelines, such as a special microprocessor for displaying graphics.

Microsoft Excel; see Spreadsheet

Microsoft Windows Microsoft Windows is an **operating system.** Windows uses a **GUI,** which makes it easy and fun to work with. Windows has been around for quite some time, so there have been several versions of it. The versions widely used today include Windows 3.x, Windows 95, Windows 98, and Windows NT.

Microsoft Word; see Word processor

Modem A modem connects your computer and sometimes your television to a telephone line so you can send or receive information. You can use a modem to connect to the **Internet** over a telephone line.

Monitor A monitor is that television-screen-like object that's connected to your computer.

Motherboard A motherboard is the **circuit board** that serves as the foundation of your **PC.** The motherboard connects the parts of your PC and has the **microprocessor** and **memory** attached to it. Your disk **drives** connect to your motherboard via cables. Your **keyboard, mouse,** and other external devices also plug into your motherboard from the back of your computer.

Mouse In Windows, you use a mouse to **click** and **drag** items. By clicking and dragging, you can often tell the **operating system** and **programs** what you want them to do.

MS-DOS MS-DOS (commonly referred to as "DOS," which rhymes with "floss") was the **operating system** used by most of the first **PCs.** To get a glimpse of MS-DOS, **click** the **Start button,** point to Programs, and click MS-DOS Prompt. Because MS-DOS doesn't have a **GUI,** to work efficiently with MS-DOS, you need to use a long list of codes to tell MS-DOS what to do.

Multimedia When a **program** or **document** (such as a presentation) is described as being multimedia, it means that it uses multiple media—sound, text, and pictures—for communicating information. **Web pages** are often multimedia documents, for example.

Multitask To multitask on your **PC** means to do more than one task at once. Windows lets you multitask. For example, while you are **downloading** a file from the **Internet** in one **program**, you can simultaneously write a letter using another program.

Netscape Messenger; see E-mail

Netscape Navigator; see Web browser

Network A network is a group of computers that are connected together so the computer users can share information and **hardware.**

Newsgroup A newsgroup is a collection of messages—typically text messages—that people post to a central server so other people can read them. Newsgroup messages closely resemble **e-mail** messages—in fact, you use the same basic process to create and post a newsgroup message as you do to create and send an e-mail message.

Online If you're working online (as opposed to working offline), it means that your **Internet** (or **network**) connection is open and ready for use.

Operating system An operating system is the **software** that manages your computer's **hardware**. For example, it's really the operating system that prints **files** on your **printer.** When you tell a **program** to print a letter, the program transmits a copy of the letter to the operating system, and it does the work of telling the printer how to print the letter.

Outlook Express; see E-mail

Password A password is a secret word or string of characters that you use to confirm your identity. When you **log on** to Windows, you might need to supply a name to identify yourself and a password to prove you're who you say you are.

Pathname The pathname to a **file** describes the file's location—on which **disk** and in which **folder** and possibly **subfolder** the file is located.

PC PC stands for personal computer. Most people use the term PC to refer to only personal computers that have **Intel**-compatible **microprocessors**, and not the **Macintosh.**

PCMCIA PCMCIA is a special kind of **port** common among laptops. PCMCIA ports accept devices that have PCMCIA cards (often just called PC Cards).

Pixel A pixel is the smallest square of light that makes up the elements you see on your screen. If you zoom in on an image on your screen, you can see that it is made up of thousands of such tiny squares.

Plug and Play Plug and Play refers to a type of **hardware** that does not require you to set up your **PC** for the hardware to run. With a Plug and Play device, after you plug in the device and turn on your computer, Windows recognizes the new device and sets it up for you.

Port A port is the name for the sockets on the back of your computer. For example, the socket into which you plug your **printer** is probably called the LPT1, or parallel, port.

Printer A printer is a **hardware** device you use to print files on paper. The printed file is often called a printout or hardcopy.

Program A program is a piece of **software** you use to do your work or have fun. Your **word processor,** if you have one, is a program. Other popular programs include **spreadsheet** programs, **web browsers,** and **e-mail** clients.

Quattro Pro; see Spreadsheet

RAM; see Memory

Read-only Read-only refers to a **file** that you can read or print, but cannot edit. It also refers to a storage device that you can read, but not write to, such as a **CD-ROM.** The "RO" in CD-ROM stands for read-only, because regular CD-ROM drives do not allow you to change the contents of the CD-ROM. To write on CDs, you need a CD-R drive, also called a CD burner.

Recycle Bin The Recycle Bin is a special **folder** that Windows uses to temporarily store the **files** you've deleted.

Resolution Resolution refers to the clarity and crispness of the objects you see either on your screen or printed on a piece of paper. The higher the resolution, the better the quality of the image. However, working with objects of a higher resolution also uses more **memory.**

Scanner A scanner is a **hardware** device used to create electronic copies of images or **documents.** For example, you might use a scanner to get a child's painting or a family photograph on your computer so you can e-mail it to others.

Screen saver A screen saver is a **program** that displays pictures on your screen when your PC has remained inactive for a set length of time. Windows comes with several screen savers, but you can also purchase screen savers or obtain screen savers over the **Internet.**

Scrollbar You use a scrollbar to move backward and forward or up and down when what's displayed on screen won't fit in the space it's allotted. Scrollbars typically run along the right and often the bottom sides of many **windows.** List boxes frequently use scrollbars to help you select items.

SCSI SCSI, pronounced "scuzzy," is a special interface used to connect **hardware** devices such as **hard disks** and **scanners.**

Search engine You use a search engine to find information on the **Internet**—such as a **web page**, a **newsgroup** article, a person's **e-mail** address, or a business's street address.

Server A server is a computer on a **network** that manages specific network resources or is in charge of network security. A server on the **Internet** is a computer that people log onto or visit in order to view **web pages** or download **e-mail** messages and files, among other things. For example, the computer that does the work of delivering the e-mail messages you send, and retrieving and storing the messages that people send you, is called a mail server. A news server holds **newsgroups** that you can browse and post messages to.

Shareware Shareware is **software** that you are encouraged to try out and distribute for free. But you must pay for it if you decide to keep it.

Shortcut icons Shortcut icons are clickable **icons** you can create and add to your desktop to start **programs** and to open files.

Software Software provides instructions to your PC. **Operating system** software, for example, tells your PC's **hardware** what to do. **Program** software (which people also sometimes call application software) performs tasks such as word processing, accounting, and **desktop publishing.**

Sound card A sound card is a piece of **hardware** that your **PC** uses to play sound.

Spreadsheet Spreadsheets are **files** that help you list, perform calculations on, and chart data. Popular spreadsheet programs include Lotus 1-2-3, Microsoft Excel, and Quattro Pro.

Start button The Start button, which appears on the left side of the Windows **Taskbar,** lets you start **programs.** You can also use it to stop Windows.

Subfolder A subfolder is a **folder** within another folder.

System unit The system unit is the main part of the PC containing the **motherboard,** the **CPU,** the **memory,** the **hard disk,** and other disk **drives** (such as a **floppy disk** drive and a **CD-ROM** drive).

Taskbar The Taskbar is the bar that usually appears at the bottom of the Windows **desktop.** The Taskbar provides the **Start button,** the Quick Launch buttons, and buttons for any programs you've started.

Toolbar Some programs display rows of clickable buttons beneath their **menu** bars, which you can use to issue commands to a **program.** These rows of clickable buttons are called toolbars.

URL URL stands for uniform resource locator. A URL is an address used to describe an **Internet** location.

USB USB stands for universal serial bus. If your PC has a USB **port,** you can use USB **hardware.** If you're running Windows 98, USB hardware is even easier to install than **Plug and Play** hardware because you don't even need to turn off your PC to install the hardware and have Windows recognize it and set it up.

User group A user group is a group of people who use the same **software** and meet to share experiences, advice, and other information relating to this software. User groups sometimes meet on the **Internet,** or they meet in person.

Utility A utility is a type of **program** that helps you maintain some aspect of your PC. Some common utilities include **antivirus** software, **backup** programs, programs that help prevent or restore data losses, and file compression programs.

Virus A computer virus is a **program** that a malicious person creates to impair the functioning of some part of your **PC**. Some viruses are designed to wipe the data off your **hard disk**, others to make a program run improperly. To protect your PC from viruses, use an antivirus program. You should also be careful and only **download** files from the **Internet** or share **floppy disks** with trustworthy sources. Some people refer to viruses as worms.

Web browser A web browser is a **program** that lets you view **web pages** on the **World Wide Web.** Popular web browsers include Microsoft Internet Explorer and Netscape Navigator.

Web page A web page is a **file** that a business or individual publishes to the **World Wide Web** for other people to see. Web pages commonly include **multimedia** elements—such as pictures, text, and even sound. They also almost always include **hyperlinks** connecting them to other web pages.

Web site A web site is a collection of **web pages** connected by **hyperlinks.** People and companies publish web sites on the **World Wide Web** when they have more information to share than will fit comfortably on one page. For example, a company's web site might include one web page listing their products and services, one listing employment opportunities, one with hyperlinks to the latest press releases, and so on.

Wildcard When you search for a **file**, a block of text, or even a resource on the **Internet**, you can often use wildcards to take the place of one or more other characters. The most common wildcard is the asterisk (*). For example, if I wanted to look for a file on my PC and I couldn't remember how I'd named it, only that it dealt with computers or computing, I might search for the file comput*. You can also use wildcards in Internet searches.

Window A window (little "w") is just a rectangle that Windows (big "W") and other **operating systems** use to display information.

Windows; see Microsoft Windows

Windows Explorer The Windows Explorer **program** on your computer lets you view and work with the contents of your **disks.**

Word processor The term word processor has two meanings. A word processor is a **program** that lets you create, save, and print text **documents** such as letters, school reports, and business documents. Some popular word processors include Corel WordPerfect, Lotus Word Pro, and Microsoft Word. A word processor is also a specialized computer (not a **PC**) that lets you type and edit documents.

World Wide Web The World Wide Web, or just Web for short, is a collection of **web pages** on the **Internet** that are connected by **hyperlinks.**

Zip The term zip has two different uses. To zip a **file** means to compress the file so it takes up less space. People often zip files when they share them over the **Internet** because zipped files take less time to send and **download.** The second use of the term Zip is a trademark for a type of **disk** and disk **drive** made by a company called Iomega. Many new **PCs** come with Iomega Zip drives.

INDEX

D

E

F

G

H

I

J

K

L

M

N

O

INDEX

P

INDEX

T

U

V

W

Y

Z

This book was prepared and submitted to Barnes & Noble Books in electronic form. The manuscript was written using Microsoft Word 97. Pages were composed using PageMaker 6.5 for Windows.

Interior Text Designer and Illustrator
Stefan Knorr

Writers
Kaarin Dolliver & Steve Nelson

Project Editor
Jeff Adell

Editor
Paula Thurman

Technical Editor
Steve Nelson

Reader
Jim Gallant

Typographer
Robert H. Brown

Proofreader
Paul Lagassé

Indexer
Julie Kawabata